本书上一版为"普通高等教育'十一五'国家级规划教材"

高等院校工业工程专业系列规划教材

工业工程专业英语
Professional English for Industrial Engineering

（第3版）

(3rd Edition)

王爱虎　编

北京理工大学出版社
BEIJING INSTITUTE OF TECHNOLOGY PRESS

内容简介

本书系统介绍了工业工程领域的概貌、发展历程和发展趋势，清晰地勾勒出工业工程的知识体系。全书共6篇（24章），分别是：对工业工程的认识、基础工业工程、现代工业工程、丰田制造模式、工业工程前沿和工业工程展望。编者对每篇文章中的主要专业词汇和晦涩难懂的句子进行了详细注释和解读，并结合文章内容和国内工业工程的管理实践提出了相关问题供读者思考。为方便读者查阅和使用，在书末还附有工业工程专业词汇汇总表。

本书既可以作为工业工程专业本科生的专业英语教材使用，也可以作为该领域专业硕士和博士研究生论文写作的参考用书。同时，也可以作为其他专业的学生和从业人员快速了解工业工程领域发展历程、内涵和趋势的专业参考书。

版权专有　侵权必究

图书在版编目（CIP）数据

工业工程专业英语/王爱虎编. —3版. —北京：北京理工大学出版社，2013.5（2020.4重印）
ISBN 978-7-5640-7709-9

Ⅰ.①工… Ⅱ.①王… Ⅲ.①工业工程-英语-高等学校-教材 Ⅳ.①H31

中国版本图书馆 CIP 数据核字（2013）第 106985 号

出版发行 /	北京理工大学出版社
社　　址 /	北京市海淀区中关村南大街5号
邮　　编 /	100081
电　　话 /	（010）68914775（办公室）　68944990（批销中心）　68911084（读者服务部）
网　　址 /	http：//www.bitpress.com.cn
经　　销 /	全国各地新华书店
印　　刷 /	北京虎彩文化传播有限公司
开　　本 /	787毫米×1092毫米　1/16
印　　张 /	20.5
字　　数 /	431千字
版　　次 /	2013年5月第3版　2020年4月第6次印刷
定　　价 /	56.00元

责任编辑 / 梁铜华
责任校对 / 周瑞红
责任印制 / 王美丽

图书出现印装质量问题，本社负责调换

第3版前言

时光飞逝！从《工业工程专业英语》于2004年6月推出第1版，到2006年9月推出第2版，再到2013年第3版的面世，9年时间转瞬即逝！

期间，经历了起始于2007年并波及全球的金融危机。从企业微观运作层面和政府宏观管理层面见证了我国企业和政府为应对危机而采取的各项举措。让编者欣慰的是在10余年的工业工程领域科研、教学和实践过程中，感受到企业家和政府官员对系统规划、流程优化，乃至仿真建模与分析等工业工程理论和方法的充分肯定、认可和运用，为工业工程在我国的发展提供了广阔的空间。

期间，见证了中国工业工程领域教育的长足进步。全国开展工业工程专业人才培养的高等院校从2002年的不足100所逐步发展到目前的150多所。其中，仅仅是具备工业工程领域工程硕士招生资格的院校数量就从2004年的58所增加到2012年的122所。可以说，过去的10年是工业工程领域本科、工学硕士、工程硕士和博士教育的高速发展期。

期间，感受到工业工程领域理论研究与实践应用的同步发展。一方面，在国内高校纷纷打造"研究型、国际化和高水平大学"的大背景下，工业工程理论研究得到高度重视，高水平学术论文和研究成果不断涌现；另一方面，面对日益成熟的国内市场和全球化的国际市场，中国的企业界对能够敏锐捕捉市场信息、适合产业特色和企业发展现状的行之有效的工业工程理论和方法提出了迫切的需求。如何在理论研究和实践应用间寻找到合理的平衡点，将研究成果转化为生产力，关系到国内工业工程领域的可持续发展。

期间，感受到工业工程领域科研、教学和实践带来的快乐。深刻体会到全日制学生在学习过程中可能感受到的彷徨和莺啼初试后的喜悦，在职学生将工业工程理论与自身的实践经验完美结合后的自信，企业家将工业工程理论和方法用于实践并在降低成本、提高效率和提升企业核心竞争力方面创造可喜业绩后的感叹。

然而，在此期间也感受到了工业工程从业人员在专业英语方面能力的不足。编者曾受邀为企业面试负责海外市场开拓和新产品导入的市场总监的应聘人员，遗憾的是，尽管每个应聘者都很优秀，但能够从专业的角度对企业的产品、成本、制造工艺、质量控制和售后服务等进行精确解读并能够用专业英语准确流利表达的人才则寥寥无几。这再次印证了编者在第2版前言中所下论断的准确性：

"国际竞争的加剧对工业工程专业人才的培养提出了更高的要求。未来的工业工程从业人员不仅需要掌握工业工程领域广博的专业知识，而且应该具备同来自世界不同国家和地区、具有不同教育和文化背景的同行用英语进行专业沟通和交流的能力。掌握大量的工业工程专业词汇无疑将对这种必要的沟通和交流起到巨大的促进作用。然而，目前国内关于工业工程专业的教材引进和编写正处于起步阶段，其中专业英语的教材尤为缺乏。这就是本教材的编写动机。"

有鉴于此，编写本书的目的有二：其一是为工业工程专业的学生（包括本科生、硕士生，乃至博士生）、老师和从业人员提供一本系统介绍工业工程专业概貌和专业词汇的学习材料，使其通过专业词汇的集中学习，提高专业英语阅读能力和专业沟通能力。其二是为其他专业的学生和从业人员提供一本快速了解工业工程领域发展历程、内涵和趋势并提升其沟通能力的专业英语教材。

本书有如下特点：
- 突出了对专业词汇的介绍，与普通英语的教学有很好的衔接；
- 内容基本上涵盖了工业工程的知识体系；
- 兼顾了对基础和现代工业工程的理论和方法的介绍；
- 在对工业工程基本概念、理论和方法进行介绍的同时，还重点对该领域最新发展动态做了解读；
- 突出了工业发达国家的学者和从业人员对工业工程发展过程中经验的总结、思考和对未来的展望；
- 大部分内容选自高水平国外刊物，有很强的前瞻性，有利于高年级本科生、研究生，乃至博士生的论文写作。

第 3 版主要在如下 3 个方面进行了补充和完善：
- 调整了全书的篇章结构：从第 2 版的 5 篇 21 章扩充至第 3 版的 6 篇 24 章。结构有所调整，内容有所充实。
- 在"第一篇 对工业工程的认识"中增加了"21 世纪工业工程面临的挑战"一章。从标题上看似乎更适合将其放到"第六篇 工业工程展望"中，但编者认为这篇文章的落脚点在于挑战背后揭示的工业工程领域人才培养机制和课程设置的调整，主题思想与第一篇中的其他两篇文章一脉相承。
- 增加了"第四篇 丰田制造模式"，其中补充了"丰田制造系统的工业工程解析"和"丰田公司全员秉承的实践思维"两篇文章。考虑到丰田制造模式在工业工程领域的影响力，这样的结构调整和内容完善应该是有其合理性的。

《工业工程专业英语》（第 3 版）的推出，首先感谢教材主要参考文献的作者。这些工业工程同行扎实的研究和系统的归纳，使我们领略到工业工程理论和方法精髓的同时，也感受到工业工程领域的研究应该具有的严谨和务实态度。其次，感谢美国纽约州立大学布法罗大学工业与系统工程系 Dr. Rakesh Nagi 和 Dr. Li Lin，北京交通大学查建中教授和鄂明成教授，暨南大学李从东教授和汤勇力教授，河北科技大学李军教授和徐瑞园教授，重庆大学易树平教授和内蒙古工业大学陈红霞教授等的支持。此外，感谢北京理工大学出版社对编者的垂爱和对教材编写所提供的支持和帮助。最后，感谢我的妻子王向莉女士在本书"一而再，再而三"的编写过程中所表现出的一贯理解、宽容和支持。

由于编者水平有限，书中难免有不妥和谬误之处，恳请读者批评和指正。

王爱虎
华南理工大学工商管理学院
bmawang@scut.edu.cn
2013 年 3 月 18 日

篇 目 简 介

第一篇　对工业工程的认识

1. Industrial Engineering Education for the 21st Century
   21 世纪的工业工程教育
   这篇文章详细介绍了处于世纪之交的美国工业工程专业的学者对美国几十年工业工程教育体系的总结和思考，包括教育质量如何控制、教学过程中理论和实践如何协调、教学方案如何整合、对工业工程作用的认识以及职业道德等。文章的最后对新世纪工业工程的教育予以了展望。

2. Real IE Value
   工业工程的真正价值
   随着社会的发展、技术的进步以及全球贸易环境的改善，工业工程的内涵和外延都在发生着相应变化。其结果是很难给工业工程下一个准确的定义。相应地，工业工程师的职责等也变得千差万别。这篇文章对工业工程的真正价值进行了深入思考。

3. Grand Challenges for Industrial Engineering in the 21st Century
   21 世纪工业工程面临的挑战
   介绍了美国国家工程学院识别出的 21 世纪工程领域面临的 14 项挑战，提炼了 21 世纪工业工程领域面临的 8 项挑战，对工业工程师在面对 8 项挑战的过程中可能起到的作用进行了细化，并从工业工程课程设置的角度提出了相关建议。

第二篇　基础工业工程

4. Operations Research
   运筹学
   在简单介绍了运筹学的发展历程的基础上，对已经取得的成就进行了总结并对未来的发展领域予以展望。

5. Work-Measured Labor Standards
   基于作业测量的劳动标准
   工作研究和作业测量是工业工程领域中最为传统的研究内容，而标准时间更是各种工业工程理论和方法得以正确应用所要依赖的基础。该文对基于 20 世纪 90 年代的标准时间测量方法进行了介绍。

6. Ergonomics
   人因学
   本文在对人因学的发展历史进行了简要介绍的基础上对基本的人因系统模型进行了详细阐述，并对未来的发展趋势予以了展望。

7. Next Generation Factory Layouts
   21世纪的工厂布局
   首先对传统的布局方法进行了系统介绍，然后对工业界的发展趋势进行了总结，并对新型工厂布局方法以及现代工厂布局研究面临的挑战予以了详细说明。

8. Operations Management
   运作管理
   对运作管理领域过去50年所取得的成就、面临的挑战以及未来的发展进行了系统阐述，是一篇发展回顾和综述性文章。

9. The Role of IE in Engineering Economics
   工业工程在工程经济学中的作用
   本文对全球经济环境下战略资本投资及其效果评价过程进行了总结，并对工业工程在投资评价过程中所扮演的角色和实现的功能进行了说明。

10. Systems Engineering and Engineering Management
    本文对系统工程和工程管理的概念、相互关系以及系统开发过程进行了概括和总结。

第三篇　现代工业工程

11. Concurrent Engineering
    并行工程
    对美国军方导弹指挥部系统开展并行工程工作的流程和方法进行了详细说明。

12. New Product Development
    新产品开发
    对新产品开发前期的市场调查、概念设计以及方案形成阶段应该如何有效开展工作进行了系统说明。

13. Computer Integrated Manufacturing
    计算机集成制造
    首先介绍了计算机集成制造的概念，然后对计算机辅助设计、计算机辅助工程、计算机辅助制造、网络和制造自动化等概念和内容进行了系统、全面的概括和总结。

14. The Evolution Simulation
    仿真的发展
    首先回顾了过去50余年间计算机科学、概率与数理统计和数学的发展对仿真领域的影响，其次对影响仿真发展的技术因素和组织因素进行了详细论述，最后对该领域的未来发展进行了展望。这是一篇概述性文章。

第四篇　丰田制造模式

15. Classification of JIT Techniques
    准时化技术的分类
    首先将与准时制造相关的技术分为纯工程性技术、与工人操作相关的技术和日式管理相关的技术3种类型，然后对各种类型的技术定义和内涵进行了系统阐述。

16. Industrial Engineering of the Toyota Production System
    丰田制造系统的工业工程解析
    在翔实文献研究的基础上,从管理学发展的历史角度解读了 TPS 与传统工业工程、质量管理、项目管理等领域,以及 Gilbreths, Taylor, Deming 等人管理思想的继承关系,并对 TPS 在管理理论上的贡献做了中肯的评价。

17. Toyota's Practical Thinking Shared Among Its Employees
    丰田公司全员秉承的实践思维
    根据实践中所用到的技能将工业工程领域划分为传统工业工程和现代工业工程两个阶段,之后运用潜在语义分析的方法对丰田制造模式与传统工业工程和现代工业工程间的关系进行了量化研究。结果发现,丰田制造模式的成功之处在于发动企业各层面的员工将传统的工业工程方法以持续快速改进的方式用于管理实践,强调全员参与以及从一线员工到企业高层管理理念的一致性,而不认可以单兵作战的方式对复杂的现代工业工程方法的应用。

第五篇　工业工程前沿

18. Total Quality Management
    全面质量管理
    同制造业如火如荼的全面质量管理运动相比,服务业的全面质量研究却不多见。基于此,作者提出全面质量服务的概念,并在系统、全面地综述了全面质量管理和全面质量服务文献的基础上,识别出全面质量管理的 12 个维度,并对这些维度给予了详细介绍。

19. Agile Manufacturing
    敏捷制造
    在综述了敏捷制造相关文献的基础上,对制造业敏捷性提出了新的看法,并对与敏捷制造相关的主要策略和技术进行了识别。

20. Theory of Constraints
    约束理论
    对约束理论的起源、关键概念和内容进行了系统综述,并在文章的最后对约束理论的研究方向进行了介绍。这是一篇综述性文章。

21. Experimental Economics and Supply Chain Management
    实验经济学与供应链管理
    以啤酒游戏为例,探讨了实验经济学方法在供应链管理中的应用。

第六篇　工业工程展望

22. The Evolution of Information Systems and Business Organization Structures
    信息系统与企业组织结构的衍变
    对比综述了信息系统和企业组织结构的演化过程,对期间的可能联系进行了推测。对信息技术与组织结构间的互动关系进行了深入研究,并对未来企业如何有机协调信息技术与组织结构的关系进行了分析。

23. The New IE: Information Technology and Business Process Redesign

   新工业工程：信息技术与业务流程再造

   进入 21 世纪的工业工程将何去何从，一直是人们非常关心的一个问题。这篇文章的作者认为，21 世纪的工业工程师应该将更多的注意力放在基于信息技术的企业流程再造上。若一个企业能很好地将信息技术和企业流程再造的理念应用于企业的管理实践，则这样的企业就具备了在新世纪获得成功的能力。

24. Post Industrial Engineering

   后工业工程

   这是由斯坦福大学管理科学与工程系的 Bailey 和 Barley 教授，基于对美国著名大学工业工程学科建设以及所开始课程的发展历程的深入分析，于 2005 年撰写的一篇详细介绍美国工业工程的起源、发展历程以及后工业工程为什么要回归作业研究的综述性文章。读史可以明鉴，相信文中的观点对正在蓬勃发展的我国工业工程学科的建设和完善有相当强的指导意义。

目 录
Contents

第一篇 对工业工程的认识

CHAPTER 1　Industrial Engineering Education for the 21st Century ········· 3
　1.1　Introduction ·········3
　1.2　Quality in IE education ·········4
　1.3　Theory and practice ·········4
　1.4　Curriculum integration ·········4
　1.5　Role of the IE ·········5
　1.6　Ethics in education ·········6
　1.7　Curriculum assessment ·········7
　1.8　Conclusions ·········7

CHAPTER 2　Real IE Value ·········9
　2.1　Introduction ·········9
　2.2　The name game ·········9
　2.3　Curriculum ·········11
　2.4　Other steps ·········12
　2.5　Expectations ·········13
　2.6　Future directions ·········14
　2.7　More challenges ·········15

CHAPTER 3　Grand Challenges for Industrial Engineering in the 21st Century ······ 19
　3.1　Background and introduction ·········19
　3.2　NAE grand challenges ·········20
　3.3　IIE council of fellows role for industrial engineering ·········21
　3.4　A research and contribution plan for industrial engineering ·········23
　3.5　Futurizing the IE curriculum ·········25
　3.6　Summary and conclusions ·········27

第二篇 基础工业工程

CHAPTER 4　Operations Research ·········33
　4.1　Brief history ·········33

4.2 Some OR accomplishments ··· 34
4.3 An outlook on a research agenda ··· 36

CHAPTER 5 Work-Measured Labor Standards ································ 42
5.1 Introduction ··· 42
5.2 Developing standard times ··· 43
5.3 Maintaining standard times ·· 45
5.4 Summary ·· 46

CHAPTER 6 Ergonomics ··· 49
6.1 The origin of ergonomics ··· 49
6.2 A system description of ergonomics ·· 51
6.3 The goal of safety ·· 54
6.4 The goal of productivity ·· 55
6.5 The trade-off between productivity and safety ···························· 55
6.6 The goal of operator satisfaction ·· 56
6.7 Conclusion ·· 56

CHAPTER 7 Research Challenges and Recent Progress in Next Generation Factory Layouts ·· 60
7.1 Introduction ··· 60
7.2 Emerging trends in industry ·· 62
7.3 Next generation factory layouts ··· 65
7.4 Research challenges ··· 67

CHAPTER 8 Operations Management ······································· 71
8.1 Celebration of history and accomplishments ······························ 71
8.2 The challenges of the 1970s and 1980s and the response ··············· 72
8.3 The department's history and current editorial mission ················· 75
8.4 The way forward ··· 78

CHAPTER 9 The Role of IE in Engineering Economics ··················· 83
9.1 Introduction ··· 83
9.2 Engineering economics ··· 84
9.3 Steps in the evaluation process ·· 86
9.4 Analytical problems encountered ··· 87
9.5 Tools of engineering economy ·· 88
9.6 The potential of IE for the firm ··· 91

CHAPTER 10 Systems Engineering and Engineering Management ········· 94
- 10.1 Nature of system development ········· 94
- 10.2 Systems engineering and engineering management ········· 96
- 10.3 Overlap, difference, and synergies ········· 98

第三篇 现代工业工程

CHAPTER 11 Concurrent Engineering ········· 103
- 11.1 Introduction ········· 103
- 11.2 The training philosophy ········· 103

CHAPTER 12 New Product Development ········· 110
- 12.1 Introduction ········· 110
- 12.2 What is the "Front End"? ········· 111
- 12.3 A well-engineered front-end process ········· 114
- 12.4 Balancing front-end explicitness and flexibility ········· 115
- 12.5 Diagnosing front-end activities ········· 115
- 12.6 Managing the transition ········· 116
- 12.7 Conclusion ········· 118

CHAPTER 13 Computer Integrated Manufacturing (CIM) ········· 121
- 13.1 Computer-aided design ········· 121
- 13.2 Computer-aided engineering ········· 122
- 13.3 Computer-aided manufacturing ········· 123
- 13.4 Networks ········· 125
- 13.5 Other key elements of factory automation ········· 126

CHAPTER 14 The Evolution of Simulation ········· 134
- 14.1 Introduction ········· 134
- 14.2 The early days ········· 135
- 14.3 Technical factors in simulation development ········· 136
- 14.4 Organizational factors ········· 145
- 14.5 Concluding summary ········· 147

第四篇 丰田制造模式

CHAPTER 15 Classification of JIT Techniques ········· 155
- 15.1 JIT's pure engineering elements ········· 155
- 15.2 Worker's operations/activities as JIT elements ········· 156
- 15.3 Japanese management-related elements of JIT ········· 156

- 15.4 Is the classification justifiable? ·· 157
- 15.5 Significance of the classification ·· 158
- 15.6 Lessons ·· 158
- 15.7 Summary ·· 161

CHAPTER 16　Industrial Engineering of the Toyota Production System ········ 163
- 16.1 Introduction ·· 163
- 16.2 Continuous material flow ·· 164
- 16.3 Holistic view of TPS ··· 166
- 16.4 Ancient rite of waste elimination ·· 167
- 16.5 Three pathways ·· 168
- 16.6 The Gilbreths' "four step" approach ·· 170
- 16.7 Origin of the MOI^2 process chart ··· 171
- 16.8 Contemporary industrial engineering ··· 172
- 16.9 Shigeo Shingo and the JMA ·· 174
- 16.10 Discussion ·· 175
- 16.11 Conclusions ·· 176

CHAPTER 17　Toyota's Practical Thinking Shared Among Its Employees ······· 179
- 17.1 Introduction ·· 179
- 17.2 Literature review ·· 180
- 17.3 Research approach ·· 187
- 17.4 Conclusions ·· 187

第五篇　工业工程前沿

CHAPTER 18　Total Quality Management ·· 193
- 18.1 Introduction ·· 193
- 18.2 The research problem ·· 195
- 18.3 The critical dimensions of TQS ·· 195
- 18.4 Summary ·· 201

CHAPTER 19　Agile Manufacturing ·· 204
- 19.1 Introduction ·· 204
- 19.2 Agile manufacturing — definitions ·· 205
- 19.3 Agile manufacturing strategies and technologies ····························· 209
- 19.4 A framework for the development of agile manufacturing ·················· 209
- 19.5 Summary and conclusions ··· 210

CHAPTER 20 Theory of Constraints ········213
- 20.1 Introduction ········213
- 20.2 Historical background and basic concepts of TOC ········213
- 20.3 Issues and research opportunities ········217

CHAPTER 21 Experimental Economics and Supply Chain Management ········222
- 21.1 Introduction ········222
- 21.2 Why do we need an experiment? ········224
- 21.3 The beer distribution game ········225
- 21.4 Behavioral causes of the bullwhip effect ········227
- 21.5 Methods for reducing the bullwhip effect ········228
- 21.6 Conclusions and lessons for managers ········232

第六篇　工业工程展望

CHAPTER 22 The Evolution of Information Systems and Business Organization Structures ········239
- 22.1 Introduction ········239
- 22.2 Early developments ········239
- 22.3 Computers in business ········240
- 22.4 Growth of information systems and business organizations ········241
- 22.5 Integrating computer architectures and organizational structures ········244
- 22.6 The impact of computers on organizations ········246
- 22.7 Phases of the computerization in organizations ········247
- 22.8 Linkages between computers and organizational structures ········248
- 22.9 Implications for emerging and future organizations ········249
- 22.10 Internet, stand-alone computers and small businesses ········250

CHAPTER 23 The New IE: Information Technology and Business Process Redesign ········254
- 23.1 Introduction ········254
- 23.2 IT in business process redesign ········254
- 23.3 Redesigning business processes with IT: five steps ········256
- 23.4 Defining process types ········260
- 23.5 Management issues in IT-enabled redesign ········262
- 23.6 Summary ········265

CHAPTER 24 Post Industrial Engineering ········268
- 24.1 Introduction ········268
- 24.2 Methods ········270

24.3	The history of work studies in IE	272
24.4	The changing nature of work	283
24.5	Bringing work back into IE	285

Summary of Professional Vocabularies and Expressions ········ 291

Bibliography ········ 311

第一篇

对工业工程的认识

CHAPTER 1

Industrial Engineering Education for the 21st Century[①]

1.1 Introduction

The 21st century is just a few years away. Strategic planners all over the world are using the year 2000 as the focal point for future business activities. Are we all ready for that time? Is industrial engineering education ready for that time? As the industrial world prepares to meet the technological challenges of the 21st century, there is a need to focus on the people who will take it there. People will be the most important component of the "man-machine-material" systems competing in the next century. IEs should play a crucial role in preparing organizations for the 21st century through their roles as change initiators and facilitators. Improvements are needed in IE undergraduate education if that role is to be successfully carried out.

Undergraduate education is the foundation for professional practice. Undergraduate programs are the basis for entry into graduate schools and other professional fields. To facilitate this transition, urgent improvements are needed in education strategies. Several educators have recognized that the way engineering is practiced has changed dramatically over the years and an upgrade is needed in engineering education. Educators, employers and practitioners are calling for a better integration of science with the concepts of design and practice throughout the engineering curriculum. Such integration should be a key component of any education reform in preparation for the 21st century.

The hurried attempts to improve education are being made in many areas. We now have terms like "total quality management for academia," "just-in-time education," and "continuous education improvement." Unfortunately, many of these represent the mere rhetorics that are not backed by practical implementation models. IE should take the lead in reforming its own curriculum so that it can help to develop the practical implementation

---

[①] 这篇文章完成于1994年,作者在世纪之交即将来临之际,对工业工程教育的质量、理论研究与实践探索的平衡、培养体系的设计、工业工程的道德伦理教育等主题展开了全方位思考,并对21世纪工业工程教育的发展给予了展望。

models that can be used by other disciplines. Many educators and administrators are searching for ways to transform improvement rhetorics and slogans into action. The models developed by IEs can provide the answers.

1.2 Quality in IE education

Incorporating quality concepts into education is a goal that should be pursued at national, state, local and institution levels. The existing models of total quality management (TQM) and continuous process improvement (CPI) can be adopted for curriculum improvement. However, because of the unique nature of academia, re-definition of TQM will be necessary so that the approach will be compatible with the academic process. For example, in industry, the idea of zero defects makes sense. But in academia, we cannot proclaim zero defects in our graduates since their success on the job cannot be guaranteed. Nonetheless, the basic concepts of improving product quality are applicable to improving any education process. Clynes, while reflecting on the discussions he participated in at a National Research Council colloquium on engineering education, said, "Teaching quality, like a company's customer service, can never be too good and always needs attention for improvement." This is true. A careful review of IE curriculum will reveal areas for improvement. This will help avoid the stale curricula that may not meet the current needs of the society.

1.3 Theory and practice

Teaching determines the crux of research while research determines the crux of teaching. Integration of teaching and research is required for effective professional practice. The need to incorporate some aspect of practice into engineering education has been addressed widely in the literature. Pritsker recommends that professors must combine research interests with teaching responsibilities. The declining state of university education was described by Samuelson with respect to waste, lax academic standards and mediocre teaching and scholarship. These specific problems have been cited in the literature:

(1) Increasing undergraduate attrition despite falling academic standards at many schools. Decreasing teaching loads in favor of increasing dedication to research;

(2) Migration of full professors from undergraduate teaching in favor of graduate teaching and research;

(3) Watered down contents of undergraduate courses in the attempt to achieve retention goals; and

(4) Decreasing relevance of undergraduate courses to real-world practice.

1.4 Curriculum integration

Curriculum integration (interdisciplinary approach) should be used to address the problems cited above. Curriculum integration should be a priority in reforming education programs. Students must understand the way the world around them works and be capable of becoming responsible contributors to the society. Interdisciplinary education offers a more holistic approach to achieving this goal. Interdisciplinary course and curriculum improvement should link separate but related subjects to provide students with comprehensive skills so that they can adapt to the changing world. One form of interdisciplinary integration involves the projects in which students from more than one academic department participate in joint industrial projects. This facilitates the sharing of views from different angles.

1.5 Role of the IE

Enhanced IE education will prepare students to lead efforts to integrate entities in manufacturing and service organizations of the 21st century. The IE profession, as a whole, faces an important challenge in educating future IEs for this leadership role. The current IE curriculum provides good exposure to its many unique facets. Individual courses at both undergraduate and graduate levels in many institutions are comprehensive. Yet there are some fundamental deficiencies as discussed below.

The academic curriculum rarely emphasizes the fundamental philosophy of IE itself. That philosophy is a holistic approach to the design, development and implementation of the integrated systems of men, machines and materials. Students go through courses in operations research, manufacturing, human factors and so on without understanding the interrelationships between these areas and the synergistic impact this integrated approach has on man-machine systems.

IE is quickly losing its identity as a value-adding profession. The basic cause of this problem is that many IE graduates can't resolve the question of the identity related to the following questions:

(1) What separates an IE from other engineers?
(2) What contribution does the profession make to an organization?

The root of this identity problem lies in the structured and isolated approach of various IE courses. This results in the specialization that is too narrow. For example, graduates today tend to associate more with focused professional societies rather than the general IE. This is a disturbing drift that may destroy the identity of IE as we now know it.

There is a big difference between academic and industrial approaches to performance evaluation. The academic community evaluates its members by the number of publications and research grants. By contrast, industry measures performance in terms of real contributions to organizational goals. This has had a detrimental effect on the learning interaction that faculty and students must share for students to graduate with professional loyalty, technical competence and capability of integrating theoretical concepts and industrial practice effectively.

In the attempt to prepare students for graduate level education, the academic curriculum often has a strong mathematical orientation. Though a required approach, it develops a very structured approach to problem solving among students. Consequently, students expect all problems to have well-defined inputs, processing modules and outputs. Thus, when faced with the complex, ill-defined, and unstructured problems that are common in the real world, many new graduates perform poorly. Chisman points out that the bulk of teaching should be done for undergraduate students since over 85 percent of them go into industry, not into graduate schools. Unfortunately, the attempt to improve the curriculum is often tilted in favor of research-oriented education, thereby depriving the majority of the students of the skills they need to survive in the business world.

Many young graduates mistakenly perceive their expected roles as being part of the management personnel, having little or no direct association with shop-floor activities. Such views impede hands-on experience and prevent the identification of root causes of industrial problems. Consequently, this leads to the development of the solutions that are short-term, unrealistic, and/or inadequate. The growing reliance of simulation models that cannot be practically validated in real-world settings is one obvious symptom of this problem.

Like many other engineering curricula, IE is growing within an isolated shell. Students do not realize the importance of developing the solutions beneficial to a system rather than for individual components. Many new graduates take a long time to become productive in developing the solutions that require multidisciplinary approaches.

1.6 Ethics in education

Professional morality and responsibility should be introduced early to IE students. The lessons on ethics should be incorporated into curriculum improvement approaches. IE graduates should be familiar with the engineering code of ethics so that they can uphold and advance the integrity, honor and dignity of their professions by:

(1) Using their knowledge and skill for the enhancement of human welfare;
(2) Being honest, loyal, and impartial in serving the public, their employers and clients;
(3) Striving to increase the competence and prestige of their professions; and
(4) Supporting the professional and technical societies of their disciplines.

Some points to consider when developing curriculum improvement approaches are:

(1) Education should not just be a matter of taking courses, getting grades and moving on. Lifelong lessons should be a basic component of every education process. These lessons can only be achieved through a system view of education. The politics of practice should be explained to students so that they are not shocked and frustrated when they go from the classroom to the boardroom.

(2) Universities face a variety of real-world multi-disciplinary problems that are often

similar to industrial operation problems. These problems could be used as test cases for solution approaches. IE students could form consulting teams and develop effective solutions to such problems.

(3) Schools should increase their interaction with local industries when such industries are available. This will facilitate more realistic and relevant joint projects for students and industry professionals.

(4) The versatility of IEs in interacting with other groups in the industrial environment can be further enhanced by encouraging students to take more cross-disciplinary courses in disciplines such as mechanical engineering, computer science, business, etc.

(5) Students must keep in mind that the computer is just a tool and not the solution approach. For example, a word processor is a clerical tool that cannot compose a report by itself without the creative writing ability of the user. Likewise, a spreadsheet is an analytical tool that cannot perform accurate calculations without accurate inputs.

1.7 Curriculum assessment

Performance measures and benchmarks are needed for assessing the effectiveness of IE education. The effectiveness of curriculum can be measured in terms of the outgoing quality of students. This can be tracked by conducting the surveys of employers to determine the relative performance of graduates.

The primary responsibility of a curriculum improvement team is to ensure proper forward and backward flow of information and knowledge between the academic institution and industry. The percentage of students passing the engineer-in-training (EIT) exam can also be used as a performance measure. The percentage of the students going on to graduate programs and staying on to graduate will also be a valuable measure of performance. Entrance questionnaires and exit questionnaires can also be used to judge students' perception of the improved curriculum.

1.8 Conclusions

Significant changes are occurring in the world. These changes can come in terms of technological, economic, social and political developments. To adapt to these changes and still be productive contributors to the society, IE students must be prepared to be more versatile than their predecessors. This preparation requires significant changes in the contents and delivery of IE education. Educators and administrators institute plans immediately for reforming IE education in preparation for the landmark expectations of the 21st century. The efforts to improve IE education now will eventually lead to the development of the leadership roles that other disciplines can emulate. This is a kind of worthwhile service to the whole society that IE educators and professionals should not overlook.

Professional Vocabularies and Expressions

Industrial Engineering	工业工程
Total Quality Management	全面质量管理
Continuous Improvement	持续改进
Human Factors	人因学，功效学
Man-Machine Systems	人机系统
Shop-Floor Activities	车间活动
Simulation Model	仿真模型
Code of Ethics	道德标准，职业准则
Performance Measure	绩效测量
Benchmark	标杆

Discussion Questions:

1. Browse through the Internet and find the IE curriculum of three universities, in which you are interested the most, at the undergraduate and graduate levels respectively. What features do they have and how are they different from the curriculum of your university?
2. How is the IE education quality guaranteed in your university?
3. Search either the Internet or your library to find the evaluation metrics of the IE education at the undergraduate and graduate levels separately in China. What are your comments?

编者注：

  目前我国有 150 余所高校已经开始了工业工程专业的学士、工学硕士、工程硕士，乃至博士的教育和培养。考虑到我国将成为 21 世纪的全球制造中心，市场对具有高水平工业工程素质的复合型人才将有较大的需求。有理由相信，工业工程专业的教育将成为我国继 MBA 教育后的又一个亮点。然而，我国工业工程专业的教育体系还处在逐步建设和健全之中。培养方案的设计、实验室的建设、核心课程的确定和开发、教学环节的把握、论文研究的指导、教材的编写和师资队伍的建设等都是亟待解决的主要问题。这篇短文对美国教育界积累的将近一个世纪的工业工程专业办学经验进行了深入分析，并就 21 世纪工业工程教学体系的建设予以了展望。相信文中的观点能够对正处于启蒙阶段的我国工业工程教育体系的建立起到指导和借鉴作用。

Chapter 2

Real IE Value

2.1 Introduction

Industrial engineers are great at solving problems. Ironically enough, there is still one age-old problem they are unable to solve — identity. And the problem is not getting any easier to solve. In fact, "identity" is just one of the several challenges currently facing the IE profession.

Today's competitive global economy and tighter corporate budgets are forcing IEs to deal with the issues that were barely mentioned a decade ago. Companies are flattening corporate structures; IE departments are being eliminated or renamed; and universities and colleges are under even greater pressure to provide industry with the graduates who are better trained to handle a much wider variety of job responsibilities.

On the other hand, today's IE has at his or her disposal more technology and tools than what the IE of 30 years ago could have ever imagined. New technologies have improved accuracy and speed and generally have increased the IE's ability to cover a more diverse set of interests.

In addition, the IE now has a greater opportunity to concentrate on any one of a broad variety of areas that many companies now recognize as individual departments — including simulation, operations research, ergonomics, material handling and logistics.

2.2 The name game

What problems could possibly throw a shadow on such a bright array of opportunities? For starters, as new opportunities have developed for the IE, new questions have formed about what types of jobs the industrial engineer is qualified to perform.

At one time, it was easier to define what an IE did. "Industrial engineering was simple in those days when we dealt with methods, work standards and work simplification," says Carlos Cherubin, director of engineering for The Limited Co. "But there has to be some way to get past the old industrial engineering definition."

Even today, in many companies, IEs are still performing the traditional type of work that makes up what is now considered classical IE. "The big change is that the commercialization of a lot of these areas has turned them into 'niche thrusts,'" says John Powers, director of the Management Services Department at Eastman Kodak Co. While IEs have always been very adaptable to these "thrusts" as a skill set, he says, they are now competing for the headlines.

Says Jerry Zollenberg, director of IE for United Parcel Service, "If a person loses sight of the total job and starts looking at the individual pieces, it comes out a little hairy." For example, Zollenberg says that he has an operation research (OR) group of 40 to 50 individuals who are working on the cutting edge of computer technology. At one time these people were designated as IEs. But Zollenberg says that even though they are not called IEs, the job they are doing is certainly IE-oriented and could be IE, depending on how you set up the organization.

Like it or not, the trend today is specialization, and companies are following suit. Tough economic times are forcing many companies to redefine corporate structures, with a primary goal of flattening their organization in an attempt to cut costs and speed the decision-making process. In the case of the IE department, that trend has moved departmental names from the generic "IE" to specific functions or areas that are being performed. Former IE departments have been decentralized or renamed and are now described using such terms as Quality Improvement Engineering, Management Services or Engineering Services, just to name a few.

"What I see is the companies getting away from the IE name and trying to have the names that are more descriptive of the broader set of skills," says Powers.

For many, including Rebecca Ray, IE manager at Glaxo Inc., it is a step in the right direction. Her department will soon carry the title Performance Improvement Engineering. "IE is probably the only engineering profession that insists on wearing its degree on its departmental door," she says. "We have focused too much on maintaining our degree, instead of identifying our function within our company."

Dr. Vinod Sahney, corporate vice president at Henry Ford Health Systems agrees. "One of our biggest difficulties is we equate industrial engineering with an IE department," he says. "I have never seen a mechanical engineering department, but yet they are hired and get a wide-range of jobs."

Tony Vieth, IE manager at Boeing Georgia Inc., believes that the individual persons, depending on how they are trained, can bring the right skills to the right job and they do not need to be in a department called industrial engineering. He also thinks IEs have gotten hung up on that over the years. On the other hand, the decentralized type of environment appears more threatening to others. "If we assume that decentralization will continue to the point of transferring IE responsibilities to others, as seen in the Volvo organization, we will see a profound impact upon the profession, namely unemployment," predicts Donald Barnes of Barnes Management Training Services.

But, a centralized IE department does not guarantee employment for the industrial engineer. Many large companies have "IE" departments where only a handful of industrial engineers can be found. An example is Boeing. Boeing has some very large IE departments, but often less than two or three people within the department have IE degrees. According to Vieth, it is because some of the functions within the department are so diverse.

The problems associated with renaming IE departments to describe their particular function may have more to do with appearance than with the actual job being performed. While IEs actually perform many of the specialized jobs, little credit is given to IE principles used in the approach. In fact, it often turns out that many of the individual functions and skills used by IEs are viewed by management as industrial engineering. As a result, the individuals who can master one of those skills are mistakenly referred to by management as "industrial engineers."

Yet, those who understand the real value of industrial engineering still realize that the degreed IE brings to the job a unique way of thinking.

"There are things you can teach non-degreed people that are basic repetitive tasks," says Vieth. "But what you can't teach is how to take what you see, translate it, and recognize there is a problem, and then come up with a solution to that problem."

Erin Wallace, director of IE at Walt Disney World Co., would not hire anyone who was not a degreed IE. "I insist on it," she says. "When you've got a group of people who are distinctly IEs, they carry with them what we like to refer to as distinct competencies. Those distinct competencies for an IE at Walt Disney World include their ability to do quantitative analysis. You need an IE degree to be able to do that type of work."

Wallace says that when someone hires IE technology-type majors, they do not get some of the rudimentary problem solving skills acquired from taking engineering courses.

2.3 Curriculum

Since there is a favorable consensus about the technical qualifications of degreed IEs, universities and colleges must be doing all industry believes, which is necessary to prepare today's IE students. Appearances may be deceiving.

In fact, even though ABET accredits many IE and IET programs in the United States, there remains much variance and flexibility among the programs. Evidence of this fact can be found in a recent Australian study undertaken by the Industrial Engineering/Management (IE/M) group of the School of Mechanical and Manufacturing Engineering Swinburne Institute of Technology (SIT).

The school initiated a set of promotional activities to rejuvenate the industrial engineering name and status. One of the school's goals was to help convince managers and the government to reconsider the role of industrial engineering.

In preparation for the events, the IE/M group surveyed more than 150 U.S. universities with accredited IE programs at the undergraduate and graduate levels. Of those universities that answered, 37 were randomly drawn for analysis.

The main purpose was to analyze the quantity and quality of the IE subjects. According to Shayan and Hamadani at SIT, the most important point is that the coverage of IE is not yet standardized.

2.4 Other steps

Two key projects currently working toward helping academia improve the overall IE curriculum include the Southeastern University and College Coalition for Engineering Education (SUCCEED) sponsored by the National Science Foundation (NSF), and IIE's joint effort between the Council on Industrial Engineering (CIE) and the Council of Industrial Engineering Academic Department Heads (CIEADH).

SUCCEED, which is aimed at all engineering disciplines, is an engineering education coalition established by NSF in March 1992. The coalition has proposed a new curriculum model, CURRICULUM 2 1, as a mechanism to focus its efforts on specific goals such as restructuring the engineering curriculum and improving the quality and quantity of graduates.

The second project, between CIE and CIEADH, has been ongoing since the fall of 1990. Specifically, CIE (corporate-level directors whose span of control includes IE functions) meets with CIEADH (98 academic department heads from universities and colleges) at scheduled times during the year to better define what industry needs from academia. IIE acts as a facilitator between the two groups to help inform academia. The ultimate goal of these meetings is the development of a clearly defined set of output characteristics that will help academia design an improved undergraduate IE curriculum.

This is not to say that these organizations are attempting to standardize the IE curriculum, rather, they are trying to provide basic guidelines. The question of whether the IE curriculum should be standardized throughout every university is not an issue. The leaders in industry and academia readily agree that there is no possible way for every curriculum at every college to be identical.

"I don't think you can require every IE curriculum to be cookie cutter of each other," says Glaxo's Ray.

What appears to be a problem is the perceived gap between what type of students academia is providing and the type of students industry seeks. Most industry leaders acknowledge that the majority of universities and colleges should provide, and do provide, the students who are technically competent. To expect that IE students be highly knowledgeable about every possible aspect of industrial engineering upon graduation may be unrealistic, says Zollenberg. Students are required to take a broad range of IE courses to help them understand the principles of IE and provide a solid academic foundation. A graduate student can then go on to specialize in a particular area if he or she desires to do so.

Zollenberg insists that it is impossible to expect students to learn everything they need to know about the jobs they will encounter. "I'm not sure anybody coming out is going to learn all of the required skills in four years of school. I don't think it's fair to the universities and I don't think it's fair to the kids," he says.

2.5 Expectations

What industry leaders do expect, however, is the students who have the ability to operate in the environment in which they are placed. These areas where there appears to be a deficiency include interpersonal skills, knowledge of computers, nontechnical/business skills, quality management skills, and an appreciation for the plant floor. Depending upon what industry the new graduate is placed, the need for certain skills will vary.

Wallace, who works for a service-oriented company (Walt Disney World), thinks today's students are well-trained in most areas, with the exception of computer skills. She says she still sees a lot of students who come out of school without very good computer skills. "Nowadays, that should be a prerequisite."

In the manufacturing sector, Jack Broadway, director of corporate IE for Reynolds Metals, believes today's students are probably better educated than in the past, but they have some misconceptions about the types of jobs they will perform. "A lot of (students) coming out today want to sit behind a computer and they think that is their job. Well, a computer is just another tool. It's just something you use to do the job and then you go on and do something else," he says. He suggests that on-the job training while in school may be one of the best ways to prepare students.

On the healthcare side, Sahney (Henry Ford Health Systems) thinks that in general terms, schools are providing properly trained students, but they often are not given the opportunity to become well-rounded in other areas. Because what he says is the profession's "roots of accreditation," the curriculum is too tightly controlled. He does not think individual institutions have enough variety. In other words, he says, the electives are very limited by the time all of the required courses are finished. This problem is often exhibited as a lack of writing and presentation skills in many of the new graduates.

Most IEs eventually must sell their ideas and plans to management, which often requires above-average communication skills. For many IE graduates, this is a tough challenge. Russell Cartmill, IE director at The Coca-Cola Co., says he is frequently confronted with the hiring recent graduates who lack basic communication skills. He says Coca-Cola ends up having to teach people things once they get in the areas of public speaking and report writing, "some of the basic things that you really need to have in industry in order to make a good presentation."

One way schools are combating this problem, which is also a problem with students in other engineering disciplines, is semester-long undergraduate and graduate-level courses directed at familiarizing engineering students from all disciplines with the non-technical aspects of engineering. These courses focus on the topics such as financial management, project management, business planning and business development.

Other schools have even gone as far as offering graduate degrees that are a combination of an IE degree and business degree in an attempt to target students seeking manufacturing engineering jobs.

But Vieth is not sure that the business route is the best path for the industrial engineering curriculum to follow. "I think if we lose track of the technical knowledge, we're just going to look like a high-priced business graduate," he says.

Another option IE departments at universities and colleges might consider is specializing in a particular function of IE (i. e. operation research, material handling, ergonomics, human factors, etc.), and marketing their program accordingly. For example, says Cherubin, if a college student wants to be an IE and has a particular interest in material handling, that student should be able to choose certain schools whose charter is very specific. In addition to helping the student, he says, it provides an important service to a potential employer. "Don't put students out in the work environment and, at that point, let them start defining their career," says Cherubin.

Vieth has similar views. "Maybe the IEs that our universities train today should be trained to be part of a specific department," he says.

Ray thinks that the problem might not be what is taught, but the way it is taught. IE classes and departments at universities are structured in a way that teaches students to work alone, she says.

Students model themselves after the people they admire, Ray states. "While students are in college, they are looking at their professors. If they see their professors operating autonomously — on their own island — and not interrelating across other disciplines, the IE is going to come out of that program thinking they don't need anybody's help to solve a problem," she says.

She says it takes her up to 18 months to put a newly hired graduate through "boot camp" to make them realize that they have to work as a member of a team to facilitate the flow of information within her organization.

2.6 Future directions

With all of these challenges facing the IE profession, there may be some who doubt the IEs' future. But if the individual IE will assume the role as a change implementor — not a change follower — broad opportunities are on the horizon.

Some see a renewed interest in traditional IE functions, specifically, in cost estimation and analysis. E. Franklin Livingston, senior industrial engineer at Weber USA Inc., a manufacturer of carburetors and fuel injectors, cites a recent request from General Motor's vice president of world-wide purchasing, J. Ignacio Lopez de Amortua, as proof. "He is expecting drastic cost reductions from suppliers over the next five years," says Livingston.

Livingston points out that Chrysler and Ford will probably follow suit and make similar demands on their suppliers. If that is true, Livingston foresees in the next 10 years that probably more emphasis will be placed on conventional industrial engineering. "But I don't think it will ever go back to the way it was 25 years ago," Livingston says.

Others see the IE heading in the direction of large processes and systems. Process thinking has become widespread in recent years, due largely to the quality movement. The industrial engineers seeking to expand their opportunities and improve the quality of operations are now looking at the entire process, rather than just a particular task or business function.

Two areas that may be of special importance to IEs in the coming years include information technology (IT) and business process redesign/reengineering (BPR). As IT continues to evolve, technological advancements will have a big impact on how companies (IEs) look at business processes of the next decade. Working together, IT and BPR has the potential to create a new type of industrial engineering, changing the way the discipline is practiced and the skills necessary to practice it.

This whole area of business process re-engineering offers a great opportunity that many IEs have been unwilling to explore. As a result, managers have been reluctant to look to the IE to carry the banner, Powers says. "If we've got a problem, it's of our own doing and our own unwillingness to take the lead in a lot of these major improvement activities," he states.

One area where IEs have not been so reluctant to get involved is the system integration arena. If the system integration function continues to develop at its current rate, this particular role — that of system integrator — will most likely get so sophisticated that it will requite someone with technical knowledge who can look at the bigger picture. "This is a function for which industrial engineers are uniquely trained," says Thomas Hodgson, with the Design and Manufacturing Division at NSF.

As a result, many of the traditional IE functions could be handled by IE technology individuals, while degreed IEs would serve in the consultant role. In this scenario, IEs could have the responsibility of training others, who would then apply it.

However, many of those opportunities in system integration are already opening up and if IEs do not step up to the current challenge of system integration, others may step in and take that function from the IE, says Hodgson.

"We need to grow in our understanding of the other engineering disciplines so as to better do our job. We need to grow in our capability to make use of the rapidly improving computational capabilities that are available," he says.

2.7 More challenges

Whatever the future holds, the biggest threat to IE may be what people do not know about the profession. In an economy where every company is cutting costs and looking for ways to trim excess "fat," one might think CEOs and managers would be snatching up every available IE. Instead, many corporate executives and human resource managers are turning to other disciplines to fill jobs ideally suited for IEs. "It's really quite silly, since IEs are the people who save you money," says Wallace.

Why is this happening? Because IEs need to do a better job of showing management all of their abilities and talents. While TQM and business process reengineering may pose big challenges, the IE's broad, fundamental background has provided them with the training and education found in no other profession. Sadly, the specialized tasks that companies are asking individuals from other disciplines to perform are the tasks that IEs have always been trained to perform! It is time for IEs to market those abilities accordingly.

"We have not done a good job of demonstrating and selling ourselves in a way that we truly get recognized for what our mission and our capabilities and our supposed demonstrative performance really are," says Powers.

IEs must take the proactive approach and position themselves as the leaders of the changes occurring in all sectors of industry. In fact, IEs must create the changes. Says Zollenberg, "I think we have to step up to the front and take a leadership role, rather than just sit back and wait for somebody to ask us to do a study."

And what about the identity problem? Rudy Herrmann, president of Rotary Lift, sums it up well when he says, "The 'name game' goes away if we can learn how to be effective functional professionals, and be respected and understand all of our contributions."

The key is "we." If every industrial engineer, in industry and academia, will work together to tackle these challenges and make other companies and individuals aware of the IE's many talents, the age-old identity problem just might be on the brink of fading away.

 Professional Vocabularies and Expressions

industrial engineering (IE)	工业工程
industrial engineer	工业工程师
simulation	仿真
operations research	运筹学
quality improvement engineering	质量改善工程
management services	管理服务
engineering services	工程服务
performance improvement engineering	绩效改善工程
ergonomics	人因学，功效学
material handling	物料搬运
logistics	物流

financial management	金融/财务管理
project management	项目管理
business planning and development	商业规划与开发
information technology (IT)	信息技术
business process redesign/reengineering (BPR)	业务流程再设计/再造
human resource management	人力资源管理
quality movement	质量运动

Notes

1. On the other hand, today's IE has at his or her disposal more technology and tools than what the IE of 30 years ago could have ever imagined.

可翻译为：另一方面，现在的工业工程师可以使用许多 30 年前的同行想都不可能想到的技术和工具。

2. If a person loses sight of the total job and starts looking at the individual pieces, it comes out a little hairy.

可翻译为：如果一个人不能对整项工作做全面把握，而是将注意力放在个别的方面，则结果将不会令人满意。

3. The problems associated with renaming IE departments to describe their particular function may have more to do with appearance than with the actual job being performed.

可翻译为：将工业工程部重新命名，以明确描述其具体职能，期间所出现的问题与其说与实际完成的工作有关，倒不如说与问题的表象有关。

4. In fact, even though ABET accredits many IE and IET programs in the United States, there remains much variance and flexibility among the programs.

ABET 是工程与技术鉴定委员会(The Accreditation Board for Engineering and Technology) 的简写。该委员会是美国用来检查和评价各工程类大学全部课程的官方机构。ABET 的鉴定目的是向公众和工程类毕业生的雇主保证学校的课程满足了规定的最低标准。

该句可翻译为：实际上，尽管工程与技术鉴定委员会鉴定了美国的许多工业工程和工业工程与技术项目，但这些项目之间仍然存在很大的区别和灵活性。

5. Two key projects currently working toward … and the Council of Industrial Engineering Academic Department Heads (CIEADH).

该句中提到了如下几个机构：

（1）美国东南地区大学和学院工程教育联合会(SUCCEED)：1992 年美国自然科学基金委员会资助东南地区的 8 所工程类学院而成立的教育联合会，旨在提高工程类本科的教育水平。详见 http://www.succeed.ufl.edu。

(2) 自然科学基金委员会 (National Science Foundation)。

(3) 工业工程师学会 (Institute of Industrial Engineers, IIE): 是世界上最大的专门支持工业工程领域和个人从事质量和生产率改善活动的非营利性行业协会，成立于1948年，现有会员15 000余人，在全球范围内有280个分会。文中提到的工业工程理事会(Council on Industrial Engineering, CIE)和工业工程系主任理事会(Council of Industrial Engineering Academic Department Heads, CIEADH)为工业工程师学会的下属机构。详见 http://www.iienet.org。

6. But if the individual IE will assume the role as a change implementor — not a change follower — broad opportunities are on the horizon.

可翻译为：然而，如果每个工业工程师都承担起变化的实施者，而不是变化的追随者的角色，则广泛的机会就会出现。

7. If we've got a problem, it's of our own doing and our own unwillingness to take the lead in a lot of these major improvement activities.

可翻译为：如果我们遇到了问题，这些问题也是由于我们自己的所作所为和不愿意在一些重大的改进活动中承担领导角色所造成的。

Discussion Questions:

1. What is your own definition of Industrial Engineering?
2. In your opinion, what are the features of IE that distinguish it from other engineering disciplines? What is the relationship between IE and management?
3. What do you think is the true value of IE?
4. In Chinese human resource market, what kinds of positions are most suitable for the people with IE background? What kind of companies prefer to hire IE graduates?

CHAPTER 3

Grand Challenges for Industrial Engineering in the 21st Century

3.1 Background and introduction

Demographic and economic trends along with recent scientific developments present grand challenges and opportunities for industrial engineering. In response to the National Academy of Engineering's list of Grand Challenges for the 21st century, the IIE Council of Fellows produced a list of Grand Challenges for IE. This list provides significant opportunities for the future of industrial engineering but also implies necessary changes in IE education to ensure our role in critical future engineering practice and research. In this paper, we review the grand research challenges for the IE profession and their implications for IE curriculum. A vision is offered for how the IE profession can impact the 21st century to the same degree that its development of mass production, quality engineering, ergonomics, and other technologies impacted the last 100 years. Recommendations are provided for changes in the IE curriculum involving new science, technology, modeling tools, application areas, and social/cultural knowledge that will be necessary to meet IE's challenges.

In considering the obstacles facing IE in its effort to establish visibility and maintain applicability, it is insightful to examine the program for the Summit on the Grand Challenges in Engineering being held the first week of March, 2009 at Duke University. The grand challenges tend to revolve around large system problems and we view ourselves as the engineers of "integrated systems." Yet of the nineteen invited speakers and panelists, covering engineering, physical and biological sciences, innovation and engineering education, none would be primarily considered to be an industrial engineer. Indeed, the closest affiliation is one participant with an M. S. degree in Management Science and Engineering. In the recent bestseller *The World Is Flat*, Friedman describes at length the challenges and advances we consider to be integral to IE, yet the term "industrial engineer" does not appear. Thus, along with asking ourselves how industrial engineers will contribute to the future as we have to the past, to ensure a sustainable and relevant future for ourselves, we must also ask why it is that despite our contributions, our visibility is limited at best. If we are so instrumental in obtaining results, why are we not better recognized? Along with determining our technical role in the coming century, how will we exhibit leadership and gain public acknowledgement to the point that young students without familial connections to IE will still aspire to join the profession?

3.2 NAE grand challenges

In 2006, the National Academy of Engineering tasked a committee to define the Grand Challenges of Engineering for the 21st Century. Chaired by William J. Perry, former Secretary of Defense and current faculty member in the School of Engineering at Stanford University, the committee sought input from a broad spectrum of the general public and knowledgeable professionals. In early 2008, the panel released its findings listing the following Grand Challenges:

(1) Make solar energy economical — Solar accounts for less than 1% of the energy today, but there is a significant potential to increase its usage. More efficient capture and conversion systems along with more economical means of production and deployment are needed.

(2) Provide energy from fusion — The challenge is to develop fusion technology that is scalable and provides an environmentally benign alternative.

(3) Develop carbon sequestration methods — Methods are needed to capture and store excess CO_2.

(4) Manage the nitrogen cycle — To aid in meeting global needs, better fertilization techniques are needed along with methods to capture and recycle nitrogen.

(5) Provide access to clean water — Greater access to clean water was a key driver of increased life expectancies. Growing populations and climate change will make it more difficult to make sufficient water available to all to continue enhancing the quality of life globally.

(6) Restore and improve urban infrastructure — Better and more sustainable system designs and materials are needed for transportation, water, waste, power and other urban infrastructure as well as urban services such as health care, public safety and emergency management.

(7) Advance health informatics — The future will permit individualized health care. The result will be better everyday care and prevention of bio attacks and pandemics.

(8) Engineer better medicines — More direct and less invasive delivery methods to the targeted areas, personalized drugs, and body diagnostics/sensing/ monitoring will improve the quality and length of lifespans.

(9) Reverse engineer the brain — Neuroscience and engineering must come together to truly understand the brain. Rehabilitation for instance could be significantly improved.

(10) Prevent nuclear terror — Society needs protection from increasing risks and the

proliferation of nuclear devices.

(11) Secure cyberspace — A reliable, expanded infrastructure is needed with the bandwidth to support rapidly growing demand for new uses and broader access.

(12) Enhance virtual reality — The future world may be virtual to reduce energy consumption and congestion. Training, treatment, communication, and entertainment will be revolutionized through virtual reality.

(13) Advance personalized learning — Learning speeds, styles, and content should be personalized and evolve with the individual's needs and life stage.

(14) Engineer the tools of scientific discovery — Science and engineering must blend to better explain nature and exploit that knowledge for better tools for accelerating the rate of discovery and depth of understanding of individual aspects of the world and their interrelationships. Better tools (smaller, cheaper, more reliable and accurate, and more easily deployable) are needed for modeling and allocation as well as monitoring, measuring, and detecting.

While not all fourteen of the NAE Grand Challenges fall within the traditional scope of IE, it is obvious that several could be led by IEs. Health informatics and cyberspace security, for instance, rely heavily on the statistical modeling tools we own and virtually all the challenges require the leaders with expertise in system modeling.

3.3 IIE council of fellows role for industrial engineering

In May 2007, the IIE Council of Fellows convened to discuss the Grand Challenges for industrial engineering in the 21st century with an emphasis on the role of and relevance to IE. Eight primary challenges were identified and follow-up subcommittees drafted position statements for the challenges. The challenges and a brief overview of the Council's comments are provided below:

(1) Reengineering Healthcare Delivery: An Integrated Approach — Life expectancy in the US increased 30 years over the past century yet the current system is inefficient and many individuals lack access to these advances. Rapid advances in biological and information science afford major opportunities for improving health care technologies and systems. There is a need to move towards the advanced diagnostics and individualized treatment protocols supported by new information systems, drug therapies, and rehabilitation robotics.

(2) Creating a Technology Oriented Society — Throughout human history, during the rise of civilizations, many of the brightest and most energetic focused on innovation and creation of wealth. As societies matured and living standards improved, there was less urgency for technological advancement and foci wandered. Ultimately, dominance and prosperity declined. Particularly in a democracy, it is essential that the best and brightest be prepared to make intelligent allocation decisions and strive to expand their intellectual and economic horizons. This becomes very challenging in a world of rapidly expanding largess

and technical complexity. Instilling a devotion to science and engineering as a means to self-fulfillment among the brightest youth when they are surrounded by other media messages and options is a daunting task. Educational opportunities and high expectations must lead this effort.

(3) Engineering a Sustainable Society — Population growth rates and climate change forecasts present a new scale of challenges for urban systems and our human condition. Engineering built systems that are sustainable under these conditions require novel, multidisciplinary modeling and innovative infrastructure paradigms that serve the needs of all members of society and our natural world.

(4) Developing Better Decision Making Tools in a Dynamic World — As problems become global in scope and highly dynamic, new modeling and decision tools are needed that can integrate broader perspectives and factors — technological, organizational, and physiological — to preserve the environment, enhance the global quality of daily life, and increase security. These models must account for the externalities impacted by decisions. We must learn what data to collect, how to fuse disparate, heterogeneous data sources with different time and scope scales, and make implementable and sustainable decisions. The new tools must facilitate construction, validation, and exercising of complex system models.

(5) Mitigating and Responding to Disaster — Natural and man-made disasters are increasing in scale and frequency as the climate changes, population increases, and the world becomes more intertwined. Improved techniques are needed for planning and allocating available resources to eliminate or reduce risks and mitigate consequences using knowledge in a proactive as well as reactive manner.

(6) Point-of-Use Manufacture — The mass production of the past century is giving way to expectations for mass customization in the new century. Unfortunately, previous technologies are neither sufficiently flexible nor efficient to meet future expectations. Solid free-form fabrication is creating the opportunity to produce highly complex parts and anticipated research developments in nano and mega technologies will create new opportunities for manufacturing unique products in real-time at the desired location for the individual customer. From houses to furniture, hip joints to jewelry, the future of manufacturing will be distributed and individualized.

(7) Infrastructure Construction — Construction is still performed today in an inefficient manner much as it has been for centuries with inadequate planning, excessive material and effort waste, and high variability in schedule and product quality. New methods and information-driven automated procedures and processors are needed to satisfy the infrastructure needs of the future at an affordable cost.

(8) Safe, Available and Affordable Food and Water — Food, water and sanitation are essential for humanity to survive and prosper. Currently, much of the world struggles with hunger while many other areas fight obesity. Political, environmental, economic, and

technical issues must be integrated into an adaptable, systemic solution that integrates efficient distribution methods, traceability, and resource allocation decisions.

While the NAE list is broader, it is noteworthy and exciting that a clear overlap, indeed in many cases, almost a one-to-one matching exists from the IE Fellows to the NAE list. This clearly demonstrates a significant need and role for IE for the foreseeable future.

3.4 A research and contribution plan for industrial engineering

Making and delivering products that delight customers. More technical and lengthy definitions of Industrial Engineering exist, but essentially, that's been our role. Among the key IE subdisciplines, manufacturing designs and executes the tooling and processing plans to produce products. Production logistics plans and executes the acquisition of materials, flows them through the production process, and delivers them to customers. Quality (and reliability) ensures the repeatable condition and functioning of the product. Ergonomics ensures the safety and comfort of those making the product and those using it. Engineering economics decides the selection and allocation of resources to most economically accomplish production plans. And at some higher level, an unnamed group of enterprise engineers ensures the whole system fits together in a sustainable manner. While written from our primary historical focus of providing tangible products, this description can be easily adapted to match the role of industrial engineering in industrial and government services such as finance and health care. Going forward we have critical roles to play both in the evolving manufacturing enterprise and in broader societal planning.

Consider first the future manufacturing enterprise (including associated function such as logistics). Competitive and contradictory thrusts are visible for the future. Potential developments in rapid, point-of-use, manufacturing technologies will support sustainability efforts by reducing waste and excess energy consumed in transport. Can you envision a home "replicator" which receives the packets of powered materials through the urban pipeline, downloads the process instructions and operating intelligence for the replicator and resultant product, allows some customization on your home terminal and then produces your new shoes, jewelry, or furniture? Could a "disintegrator" then dissolve your used products back into their constituent materials to start the reverse logistics process? As long term research moves us towards that far-off future, global enterprises will look for ways to use economies of scale and risk management opportunities to grow and dominate markets. Enterprise information systems for coordinating operations and guiding financial planning will proliferate. The research need is for the better models and better ways of exercising those models to guide decision making. Several dimensions of increased sophistication are required, as is evidenced by our continuing struggles with inter-cultural issues and poor investment decisions. Not only must decisions be made based on the stochastic analysis of multiple scenarios, we need better methods for identifying the range of possible scenarios. Real-time risk management must be integrated with stochastic decision making to quickly act and mitigate unintended and undesirable consequences from external events. How do we know what to do, deliver the data in a timely fashion, and educate/train the decision makers to take the right actions are all research questions deserving exploration. Current enterprise planning systems are time-consuming and costly to implement, unintelligible to the user, and too inflexible to be of use in highly dynamic environments. How do we simplify and modularize while ensuring flexibility and validity? And, in addition to building better models for operational decisions, there is a need to improve strategic planning. Such planning is currently dominated by qualitative approaches. The quantitative models that incorporate all relevant concerns and scenarios are needed that also integrate the impact of optimal operational decisions into those models. As the recent economic situation illustrates, at this point we do not even have competent financial analysis models for operational decisions. Yet these are just one component of the comprehensive enterprise resource planning model.

IEs have an opportunity and responsibility to help society meet the challenges of accommodating a large population with growing economic aspirations while reducing harm to the planet. The issues such as designing affordable and maintainable systems for supplying clear water to all fall naturally into the realm of IE methods. Civil engineers may develop the technological options and manage deployment, but IEs are best prepared to determine which options to implement and assist in determining how to implement in concert with other plans. At a different scale, data mining and network models will be important for reverse engineering the brain and improving medical treatment protocols. In recent years, industrial engineers have used operation research tools to determine the optimal use of medical technology (radiation treatment) and the allocation of organs for transplant. Numerous opportunities exist for human rehabilitation and enhancement through integrating information and mechanical technologies. IEs, with their understanding of mechanics, physiology, and psychology should be able to engineer these products. This would appear to be a wide open field for future development. At the next scale up in health care, industrial engineers have the ideal toolset for operating health care clinics and improving the operational efficiency of the existing system. But beyond that, the entire health care system in the U.S. needs an overhaul to simultaneously reduce cost while improving access and outcomes. Health care policy is clearly not something IEs can do alone, but they need to be part of the team that will overhaul health policy. Clear, complete, and comprehensive system models will be a prerequisite for moving towards a solution that makes sense from a performance perspective as the political pressures will be overwhelming in this activity. Homeland security is a prime opportunity for the integration of incomplete, contradictory, and heterogeneous information into critical decision models. Combining information and decision technologies for preventing terrorism and expanding logistics models for emergency management are both areas ripe for IE modeling.

3.5 Futurizing the IE curriculum

As a discipline, industrial engineers' broad technical and social understanding along with our expertise in modeling complex systems with interacting components positions us well to be at the forefront of solving the new challenges. Nonetheless, with a historical focus on industrial problems and physics based engineering science, the preparation of the next generation of industrial engineers must update if we are to play a leading or even meaningful role in meeting these new challenges. In addition to incorporating the new educational techniques and personalized learning tools, the following innovations in IE curriculum would help to better prepare IEs for the 21st century grand challenges. The underlying premise is that the IE must be able to bring unique value to the team, value beyond what other educated individuals can provide with the smart devices that will be on everyone's desk. A broad system perspective with expertise in certain modeling disciplines represents the opportunity for industrial engineers. As such, IE education must provide:

(1) Greater Emphasis on Global Cultures — Whether involved in supply chain issues for global networks or pursuing new challenges in engineering social service systems, industrial engineers in the future will interact with and need to accommodate a more diverse set of colleagues and clients. Understanding differences and how to work effectively across diverse environments will require both academic and experiential knowledge. As English has virtually become the default language of business, foreign language acquisition has become less important. Understanding the cultures, customs, communication styles and thought processes of the various global population centers with rapidly expanding economies has become more important.

(2) Ability to Serve on and Lead Multidisciplinary, Multicultural, Politically Pressured Teams — Multidisciplinary here means not only various engineering disciplines but engineering, natural and social scientists, and cultural anthropologists. Conflict resolution, consensus building, and the ability to synthesise and interpret perspectives are key skills that can be learned.

(3) Dynamic, Nonlinear, Large Scale Modeling — The systems of the modern world are broader in scope and more complex than the enterprise systems that have been the domain of industrial engineers. The rapid change in technology, increased competition, and more highly stressed systems create the need for rapid modeling with greater detail and fidelity. High level discrete-event simulation and linear programming models will be important but not sufficient. For IEs to have value, they must have modeling tools beyond those at the disposal to everyone on their desktop. Better information will come from detailed, nonlinear models that can be built, validated and maintained efficiently.

(4) Understanding of Human Behavior and Preferences — The physiology used in human factors/ergonomics is necessary but not sufficient. IEs must understand the human at

the cell, individual, and community level.

(5) Risk Management — The tendency for the increased uncertainty and dynamic behavior in social and industrial systems is likely to continue and even accelerate in the future. IEs must be able to make decisions and manage risks in such environments. Students should be well schooled in statistical sciences, risk management tools and risk mitigation strategies.

(6) Broader Science Knowledge — Chemistry and Physics must be augmented with Biology and Ecology.

(7) Enterprise Perspective and Beyond — Scientific reductionism moved our understanding forward in the 20th century. Now we must truly consider the entire system as an entity with a consciousness beyond that of its parts and must optimize at the system level to ensure the components work towards a common goal. With large scale systems modeling capability, IEs will bring a unique, value-adding perspective to teams.

(9) Sophisticated Information Technology — The IE will add value by being able to engineer the entire decision problem solving process: problem recognition, definition, defining data requirements, sensor network design and data acquisition, compiling information, and analyzing alternatives. Integration of sensing and measurement technologies with dynamic decision making will be important. IEs do not need to be able to write new operating systems but they should be the best at manipulating data and information and able to design and manage large software systems.

(10) Mindset of Major Socio-technological Problem Solving — Industrial engineers must truly receive the well-rounded education we have tended to profess but not necessarily implement. Cognitive psychology and mathematical modeling will not be options to choose from, but rather basic requirements to enable the IE to provide value. Beyond the individual and the workstation, IEs must be able to consider the whole human at work, play, and home to create integrated devices and experiences that will find markets in an increasingly technologically capable and customer-driven economy.

(11) Exposure to Varied Application Areas — IE can no longer afford to be identified primarily with manufacturing and its associated service functions. Certainly manufacturing, supply chains and logistics will remain key areas for industrial engineers, but the perspective now must include new manufacturing scales such as nanotechnologies and rapid manufacturing technologies. At a higher level, supply chains must include the global issues of cultural differences, 24/7 communication, and the economic and risk management aspects of global corporations and partnerships. Beyond that, IEs should understand the opportunities and issues unique to many service industries, particularly health care. The health care industry has important problems and system design issues in diagnostics and treatment at the medical level, and organizational design and resource allocation at the system level.

3.6 Summary and conclusions

Industrial engineering has been a success. IEs were clearly a major, and arguably the dominant factor responsible for enhancing the quality of life of everyday citizens over the past 100 years. The tools we developed were essential for turning knowledge of physics and the human into functioning systems that could efficiently provide high quality goods to a broad spectrum of society at an affordable price. Working with other engineers and business, the economic engine of the developed world moved into high gear. Now we must take those skills and expand them to conquer the artificial service systems that permeate the modern economy. It seems clear that our relevance and growth demand that we take leadership in meeting one or more of the grand challenges. Health care delivery and global distribution of food/water/medicine are natural issues for us to tackle given our background and expertise. Beyond that, we must team with new generations of scientists and politicians as well as engineers and business leaders to design integrated, robust and flexible systems that can sustainably co-exist with the natural environment.

Thus, we have a call to action. Will IE fade as ubiquitous computing, desktop tools, and the decline of manufacturing eliminate our value and home? Will we continue to be the "make it better engineers" playing a valuable role in the drivers of the new economy but still in the background? Or, will we truly expand our preparation and aspirations to take leadership in transforming the world? I believe we have the natural mindset and technical skills that qualify us as much as any other discipline to succeed. What remains to be seen is whether we have the vision, aspiration, and energy.

 Professional Vocabularies and Expressions

mass production	大规模制造
quality engineering	质量工程
solar energy	太阳能
fusion technology	聚变技术
environmentally benign	环境友好
carbon sequestration	碳固存
nitrogen cycle	氮循环
urban infrastructure	城市基础设施
health informatics	卫生信息学
cyberspace security	信息空间安全
virtual reality	虚拟现实
rehabilitation robotics	康复机器人

technology oriented society	技术导向型社会
point-of-use manufacture	使用点制造
mass customization	大规模定制
nano technology	纳米技术
mega technology	巨型技术
civil engineer	土木工程师
organs transplant	器官移植
homeland security	国土安全
heterogeneous information	异构信息
cultural anthropologist	文化人类学家
conflict resolution	冲突解决
human factors	人因工程
cognitive psychology	认知心理学

Notes

1. Thus, along with asking ourselves how industrial engineers will contribute to the future as we have to the past, to ensure a sustainable and relevant future for ourselves, we must also ask why it is that despite our contributions, our visibility is limited at best.

因此，在思考工业工程如何像过去那样服务于未来的同时，必须思考为什么功勋卓著的工业工程仅仅获得社会的有限认可。

2. Going forward we have critical roles to play both in the evolving manufacturing enterprise and in broader societal planning.

展望未来，工业工程将会在不断发展的制造领域和更广泛的社会规划领域起到至关重要的作用。

3. Nonetheless, with a historical focus on industrial problems and physics based engineering science, the preparation of the next generation of industrial engineers must update if we are to play a leading or even meaningful role in meeting these new challenges.

然而，鉴于（现有的工业工程课程）历来关注于工业问题（的解决）以及基于物理学的工程科学（知识的普及），面向21世纪的工业工程领域相关课程的设置必须要更新，以确保本领域的专业人才能够在解决这些挑战的过程中起到领导或有价值的作用。

4. Industrial engineers must truly receive the well-rounded education we have tended to profess but not necessarily implement.

（21世纪的）工业工程师必须真正领会我们这里试图专业化的、面面俱到的教育思想，而并不一定（懂得）具体实现（的细节）①。

Discussion Questions:

1. How many of the grand challenges mentioned in the text can also be applied to Chinese industrial engineers?
2. Try to come up with your own list of grand challenges for Chinese industrial engineering in the 21st century.
3. How well are you prepared for the above self-summarized grand challenges?

编者注：

本文是亚利桑那州立大学工业、系统与运作工程系 Askin 教授 2009 年发表在工业工程研究会议上的一篇论文。作者首先介绍了美国国家工程学院识别出的 21 世纪工程领域面临的 14 项挑战。之后，提炼了 21 世纪工业工程领域面临的 8 项挑战，进而对工业工程师在面对 8 项挑战的过程中可能起到的作用进行了细化。最后，从工业工程课程设置的角度提出了相关建议。

在一定程度上，文中提及的使用点制造正在以 3D 打印和 4D 打印的方式逐步变为现实，可能在传统制造领域引领一场根本性变革；太阳能的利用、核聚变和炭固化等技术的发展，对面临能源短缺和环境压力的我国需求同样迫切；中国人口老龄化问题的解决在很大程度上有赖于个性化医疗服务体系的建立和完善。相信文中提及的各项挑战也能够引起我国工业工程同行共鸣，更希望能够针对我国自身经济发展面临的挑战系统优化和调整各层面的工业工程培养体系，为社会输送有全球竞争力的专业人才。

---

① 编者注：对比美国和日本关于工业工程的发展展望，可以发现一个非常有趣的现象。美国倾向于以大系统为研究对象，系统集成各领域最先进的技术和知识，因而强调工业工程师要具备系统化的思维；而日本则更多地关注较为局部的问题，倡导以小规模的快速持续改进提升系统的效率，不片面追求现代化技术的应用，而是强调现场的改善和全员参与。这个观察启发我们：每个国家和地区的工业工程都应该有"自己的味道"，关于工业工程发展的取向没有对错之分，只要是密切结合所在国家和地区的社会、经济、产业和企业等发展实践的，就具备了发展的基础和条件，就有其合理性。希望国内同行能够共同打造"中国特色"的工业工程！

第二篇

基础工业工程

CHAPTER 4

Operations Research

4.1 Brief history

Operations research is a relatively young discipline, being organized as a separate professional field of study only since the end of World War II. The Operational Research Society of the United Kingdom (ORS), the Operations Research Society of America (ORSA), and the Institute of Management Sciences (TIMS) were founded in 1948, 1952, and 1953, respectively. However, the methods and practices of operations research were being applied just prior to the war by British scientists working for the Air Ministry. In fact, two of these scientists are credited with first coining the phrase "operational research."

The earliest application of operations research involved improving the early warning system of the RAF's Fighter Command. This system was quickly put to the test during the Battle of Britain. Throughout the remainder of the war, the methods of operations research were used by all the branches of the British Military to improve the results of their operations. As might be expected, the armed forces of the United States began to apply similar techniques soon after the Pearl Harbor.

After WWII, the use of operations research continued in the military and was greatly expanded. In addition, the businesses on both sides of the Atlantic began to apply operations research to a broad range of management problems, such as accident prevention, production planning, inventory control, and personnel planning.

The first formal university courses and curricula also began to be developed during the immediate postwar period. MIT, Case Institute of Technology (now Case Western Reserve University), and the University of Pennsylvania were among the first universities to offer formal degree programs in the United States in the early fifties. It is interesting to note that similar academic programs did not develop in the United Kingdom until later, although lectures and courses were offered at a few universities.

University programs in operations research in the United States and Canada are located in a wide variety of colleges, schools, and departments, reflecting the field's highly interdisciplinary nature. Programs are found in departments of mathematical sciences, decision sciences, statistics, industrial engineering, computer science, management science, engineering management, mechanical engineering, and operations research. These departments are located in the schools or colleges of engineering, business, management, industrial engineering, and applied science.

Operations research, as defined by the Operations Research Society of America, "is concerned with scientifically deciding how to best design and operate man-machine systems, usually under the conditions requiring the allocation of scarce resources." The importance to the field is the development, testing, and use of models to predict various outcomes under differing conditions or to optimize the outcome for a given condition. This gives decision makers the ability either to choose the "best" outcome or to enhance the likelihood of a given set of desired outcomes. The application of quantitative methods is also very important.

4.2 Some OR accomplishments

Some important breakthroughs of the 1970s and 1980s are highlighted below, with descriptions of how they have been employed and the resulting economic impact.

(1) Integrative OR Systems — In 1983 and 1984, Citgo Petroleum Corporation, the nation's largest independent refining and marketing company, with 1985 sales in excess of $4 billion, invested in a unique set of comprehensive and integrative systems that combine such OR disciplines as mathematical programming, forecasting, and expert systems, with statistics and organizational theory. Citgo applied the OR systems to such operations as crude and product acquisition, refining, supply and distribution, strategic and operational market planning, accounts receivable and payable, inventory control, and setting individual performance objectives, and now credits these OR systems with turning a 1984 operating loss that exceeded $50 million into a 1985 operating profit in excess of $70 million.

(2) Network Flow Problems — The 1970s were marked by a number of breakthroughs in the modeling and solution of network flow problems. The initial developments created specialized primal simplex algorithms for the problems of transportation and transshipment. Later, algorithms were developed for generalized networks and linear programs with large embedded networks. These algorithms demonstrated unprecedented efficiency, having speeds that ranged from 10 to 200 times faster on network problems than the best general purpose linear programming systems — efficiencies entirely above and beyond any afforded by changes in computer hardware or compilers.

It is now possible to solve huge network flow problems routinely, and as a result, important new applications are emerging. Companies such as Agrico, Ciba-Geigy, W. R. Grace, International Paper, Kelly-Springfield, Owens-Corning Fiberglass, Quaker Oats, and R. G. Sloan have successfully coupled their data gathering systems with network flow models to improve the cost effectiveness and service effectiveness of logistics decisions. For instance, Agrico reported a decrease in net working capital requirements of 13% and 5-year savings of

$43 million, Kelly-Springfield reported savings of over $8 million annually, and Cahil May Roberts credits OR with a 20% reduction in delivery and transportation costs.

(3) The Hypercube Queueing Model — A computer implemented, multiserver queueing model resulting from National Science Foundation supported research is now routinely used for deploying heterogeneous servers in cities in both hemispheres. The hypercube model is the basis for emergency services deployment in New York, San Diego, Sacramento, Dallas, Portland (Oregon), Caracas, and Rotterdam. Typical reported productivity improvements are on the order of 10%-15%.

(4) Lagrangian Relaxation — Lagrange multipliers, used to relax complicating constraints in hard combinatorial optimization problems, facilitate the use of polynomial algorithms for computing bounds. In the last decade, this approach has grown from a successful theory to a proven tool that is the backbone of a number of large-scale applications. Used to schedule the distribution of industrial gases at Air Products and Chemicals, Inc., this technique has been credited with saving 6%-10% of the operating costs, amounting to annual benefits of about $2 million for the company.

(5) Network Queueing Models — The networks of queues can represent the situations such as the flow of messages through a communication network, jobs through a computer system, or products through work centers in a factory. A typical application may have hundreds of customer types and work centers. Traditionally, realistic queueing models have proven intractable, even for one work center: However, recent technical breakthroughs in the analysis of such networks involve the creative use of approximations to solve large networks. IBM used this approach to analyze and justify a major factory of the future, thereby gaining a competitive edge of several months in bringing a new product to the market.

(6) Mathematical Programming Models — Enormous progress has been made by using large-scale mathematical programming models to route raw materials, components, and finished goods optimally among production plants and warehouses. One such technical achievement is the use of approximation methods to analyze models with nonconvex cost curves representing the economies of scale that typically arise in trucking operations, an approach General Motors used in more than 40 plants to achieve a 26% logistics cost savings, for an annual saving of $2.9 million.

(7) Simulation Modeling — With the development of numerous interactive simulation languages, simulation continues to be an important tool. Simulation models were recently used to describe the water distribution system in the Netherlands. These models were part of a broad analysis focused on building new facilities and changing operating rules to improve water supply, as well as on the adjustment of prices and regulations to reduce demands. The analysis is credited with saving hundreds of millions of dollars in capital expenditures and reducing agricultural damage by about $15 million per year. The Dutch government adopted

the methodology and uses it in train water resource planners from many nations.

(8) Stochastic Network Analysis — Headway has been made in incorporating stochastic effects into mathematical programming models. A stochastic network analysis was used by North American Van Lines to dispatch thousands of trucks daily from customer origins to customer destinations. This analysis reduced the cost of their operations by an estimated $2.5 million annually.

(9) Inventory Control — Progress continues in the control of inventories, a domain of important application since the earliest days of OR. For example, a model controls the inventories of blood at blood banks in Long Island, schedules blood deliveries according to the statistical estimates of the needs of each bank, and uses actual requirements to adjust deliveries. It forecasts short-term shortages and surpluses to control the movement of the blood from adjoining regions. As a result, the reductions of blood wastage of 80% and of delivery costs by 64% have been realized.

(10) Markov Decision Processes — Our ability to analyze large-scale constrained Markov decision processes is continually expanding. This approach was used to develop optimal maintenance policies for each mile of the 7,400 mile network of highways in Arizona. The model integrates management policy decisions, budgetary policies, environmental factors, and engineering decisions. During the first year of implementation the model saved $14 million, almost one-third of Arizona's highway preservation budget. The forecast for future annual savings is about $25 million.

(11) Stochastic Service Systems — Using the Defense Communications Engineering Center's queueing based circuit switch integration and analysis model, the Defense Communications Agency saved $150 million over the past 10 years by a yearly reconfiguration of the CONUS AUTOVON network, a Department of Defense telephone network in the United States which handles military communications and has a precedence and preemption capability.

4.3   An outlook on a research agenda

Operations research is a rich field possessing deep intellectual content. It has many varied subfields and numerous applications in engineering, physical sciences, economics, management, and social sciences. A dynamic field, it has successfully renewed itself through new lines of inquiry and application. No brief assessment of a research agenda could do the field justice.

What follows highlights five major OR areas. They are not meant to be all inclusive — many areas are not covered. Two are theoretical (optimization and stochastic processes), one is applied (manufacturing and logistics), one has major elements of both theory and practice (the OR/AI interface), and one studies underlying processes (operational and modeling science).

(1) Optimization — Optimizing — determining how to get an objective function or performance index to its maximum within the limits of available resources and technology — is a fundamental goal of decision making and, moreover, an important tool in engineering design. For more than three decades, research in optimization — a considerable fraction of which has been funded by the STOR program of NSF — has been active and fruitful, with payoffs accumulating through a multitude of applications.

Linear programming is widely used throughout the world. Optimization also involves techniques for solving large-scale, discrete, nonlinear, multiobjective, and global problems. Some recent advances in the field have such great potential that they have been cited prominently in popular publications, including the *New York Times* and the *Wall Street Journal*. Moreover, optimization is in a new stage of proliferation because its techniques are now accessible to microcomputers. Since optimization has achieved a degree of maturity, it is natural to take a hard look at what can be expected from further research.

In the more mature areas such as linear programming and unconstrained optimization, and in those of intermediate maturity such as integer and constrained convex optimization, emphasis will be placed on rapid, large-scale computation. This will be driven both by the need to solve large problems in manufacturing and logistics, and by the opportunities created in new computer technologies such as parallel processing. Research in such newer and lesser understood areas as global, multicriteria, and qualitative optimization, will necessarily deal with basic issues.

(2) Stochastic Processes — We live in a world in which we have limited knowledge and an inability to predict the future with certainty. A telecommunications network may suddenly be flooded by calls; a vital machine in a manufacturing plant may fail unexpectedly; a firefighting service may be called into action without warning. The study of stochastic processes provides us with a systematic way to model, design and control service systems characterized by such uncertainty. Operations research will continue to provide an observational framework for such studies through fundamental research into the foundations of probabilistic phenomena.

Flexible manufacturing systems (FMS) and computer/communication networks exemplify the complex systems that fall into a class called discrete event stochastic systems (DESS). The efficient design and operation of these systems is extremely important to economic competitiveness, yet system behavior is not completely understood. The present methods of the analysis and design of DESS focus on their behavior in the steady state, a conceptualization that requires performance measures to be made "in the long run" or "averaged over time." Yet, most systems exhibit dynamic behavior on their way to (or sometimes even during) the steady state that may produce a deviation in performance from that computed by steady state analysis. The design and control of such systems (for example, multiechelon spare parts inventories, integrated manufacturing cells, or computer/

communication nets) involving explicit consideration of the cost or impact of transient behavior, are now a real possibility.

Similarly, most current analyses presume time stationary of input parameters (arrival rates, processing time, movements, linkages) when, in fact, the actual parameters often vary with time, perhaps with some degree of regularity or even control. The errors introduced into existing design and analysis models by "average" or "typical" parameter values need to be addressed and the resultant understanding utilized. Some relatively new methodology already incorporates time varying system parameters; more must be developed.

There are two major problems in modeling and analyzing stochastic service systems: design and control. System design is concerned with finding the answers to the strategic questions of resource allocation, such as how many machine maintenance repair stations should be built in a manufacturing facility, or what the capacity of data links incorporated into a telecommunications system should be. System control deals with day-to-day operations or tactics; for example, when to activate additional repair crews, or when to temporarily prevent new messages from entering a system.

(3) The OR/AI Interface — The primary objective shared by OR and artificial intelligence (AI) is to provide the methods and procedures that support effective problem solving and decision making. The two disciplines approach this common objective in fundamentally different but complementary ways: AI problem solving techniques tend to be inferential and to rely on expert knowledge and heuristics; OR uses algorithmic, mathematically based approaches. Artificial intelligence emphasizes the qualitative aspects of problems; OR emphasizes the quantitative. The careful integration of these two approaches to problem solving shows significant promise for improving the capability and, notably, the acceptability of problem solving systems.

(4) Operational Science and Modeling Science — Most current research in OR focuses on the development and improvement of its technological methodologies for passing from a formalized model of the phenomena and preferences arising in some problem of design or decision, to a "solution" of a problem using the model (a recommended design or operating policy, for example). This natural focus has scored notable successes, and remains rich in intellectual promise. But the narrowing of emphasis from problem solving to model utilization has limited the development of two equally fundamental research areas underlying problem solving.

One of these is operational science, which may be defined as the systematic study — empirical and analytical — of the major generic processes, such as routing or maintenance, arising in OR. Whereas other branches of engineering may turn to well established sciences for basic data and theory, OR must often develop on its own much of the descriptive and predictive "science" of the phenomena it treats.

The other area is modeling science, the application of OR methodology, to the identification of fundamental principles and concepts for guiding the construction, use, and evaluation of OR models. The process of model building — considering the parameters such as resources available and time pressures — is a fertile area for further research.

While the enhancement of OR model utilization technology must continue, it needs to be reinforced and balanced through intensive research into both operational science and modeling science.

(5) Manufacturing and Logistics — The design, evaluation, and control of production and distribution systems have been, and will continue to be, the vital focuses of OR. The scope of research here includes all activities by which labor, raw materials, and capital are mobilized to bring goods to market. While this discussion focuses on physical production, the provision of services involves the similar issues of resource allocation and management.

To compete effectively in the markets of today and tomorrow, the entire production and distribution stages of the product realization process must act in concert, so as ultimately to deliver the right products at the right prices to the right places at the right times. Failure to do so predictably results in waste: excess inventory, poor quality, poor customer service, and unnecessary cost. The globalization of markets and the compression of product life cycles have only increased the urgency of this issue. The powerful impact of coordination has become widely recognized in recent years because of the success of the just-in-time (JIT) system, first used in Japanese companies, and now in several firms in the United States. This approach only works in certain settings, however; for example, supply and production lead-times must be regular and predictable. The attempts to impose the JIT system on inappropriate settings have resulted in spectacular and well publicized failures. The best features of the method must be adapted to designs for realistic, integrated approaches to coordination.

Professional Vocabularies and Expressions

operations research	运筹学
mathematical programming	数学规划
forecasting	预测
expert system	专家系统
statistics	统计学
organizational theory	组织理论
simplex algorithm	单纯形（算）法
transportation problem	运输问题
network problem	网络问题

linear programming	线性规划
hypercube queueing model	超立方排队模型
Lagrangian relaxation	拉格朗日松弛法
Lagrange multiplier	拉格朗日乘数
combinatorial optimization problem	组合优化问题
polynomial algorithm	多项式算法
constraint	约束
bound	界限
network queueing model	网络排队模型
nonconvex	非凸的
simulation modeling	仿真建模
stochastic network analysis	随机网络分析
Markov decision process	马尔可夫决策过程
stochastic service system	随机服务系统
objective function	目标函数，目标方程
discrete optimization	离散优化
nonlinear optimization	非线性优化
multiobjective optimization	多目标优化
unconstrained optimization	无约束优化
integer optimization	整数优化
flexible manufacturing system (FMS)	柔性制造系统
discrete event stochastic system (DESS).	离散事件随机系统
artificial intelligence (AI)	人工智能

Notes

Operations research, as defined by the Operations Research Society of America, "is concerned with scientifically deciding how to best design and operate man-machine systems, usually under the conditions requiring the allocation of scarce resources."

美国运筹学学会将运筹学定义为：在需要对紧缺资源进行分配的前提下决定如何最好地设计和运作人–机系统的决策科学。

Discussion Questions:

1. From the standpoint of nowaday IE students, OR might be too abstract to grasp. Many of them may argue that there is a gap between OR and industrial reality. Survey OR related literature and see how OR forerunners had developed OR methods to solve

real world problems during the wartime. Further elaborate on the contingency factors of the situation mentioned above.
2. Based on your own experience or simply by surveying the literature or companies, explain how OR can help manufacturing or logistics enterprises to gain competitive advantages in the 21st century?

CHAPTER 5

Work-Measured Labor Standards

5.1 Introduction

Work-measured labor standards have been around for about a century, and they will continue to be around for the foreseeable future. They are useful tools applicable to many areas of business. Perhaps the only thing wrong with these tools is their lack of a buzz word or catchy acronym. Maybe they should be called WMLS to keep up with the times.

For many years, work-measured labor standards were recognized as being very helpful in identifying remedies for those companies ailing from productivity problems. Dr. W. Edwards Deming was one of the first persons to down-grade labor standards. Point 11b of his famous 14 points states: "Eliminate numerical quotas for the work force."

Using labor standards to determine workers' pay has generally proven to be demoralizing and adversarial — and ineffective in the long run. Workers end up achieving 150-200 percent of the old standards, or perhaps they simply loaf around once the standard is met. Stock holders are unhappy; management is unhappy; and workers end up losing respect for management. It's a demoralizing situation for everyone. Labor standards are not really useful for whipping workers into being productive. Dr. Deming's point makes sense.

But have you ever had to cost out a product or service, or cost estimate a proposed new product or service? Have you ever had to schedule a job and give a customer an estimated delivery date, and then organize workers to produce the product? Have you done any simulation? What did you use to determine the labor times? Was it just magic? Of course not. You used some form of standard times, even if they were only quick estimates on a napkin over lunch.

If you're a manufacturer, chances are you have a bill-of-materials (BOM) system to determine standard parts cost. Do you also have an equivalent bill-of-labor system to determine standard labor costs?

Basically, you need to formalize your labor times, and your labor costs. If your standard labor times are realistic, your costing is more accurate, and your delivery times are also more accurate. The complaint "I can't afford to set standard times" should be followed by the question — "Can you afford not to?"

Let's be realistic about it. There is no such thing as an "accurate" labor standard time. Human workers come in at least a billion models with varying physical, mental, and emotional specifications and work under varying environmental conditions. This variety makes "average" or standard times extremely difficult to determine. Standard times are standard times only because all parties involved agree they are standard times. This is an important point.

The key is to quickly and economically develop and maintain the standard times that are as close to real life as possible.

5.2 Developing standard times

Five techniques are commonly used to develop standard times: motion analysis, time study, activity sampling, historical data, and estimates.

Motion analysis — This technique involves dividing a task into its component motions, then looking up the motion times on a chart or data card of a pre-determined motion times system (PMTS). PMTSs currently in use include Methods Time Measurement (MTM), Maynard Operation Sequence Technique (MOST), Modular Arrangement of Predetermined Time Standards (MODAPTS), Master Standard Data (MSD), Motion Standard Times (MST), and Work Factor.

Motion analysis is applicable to short-cycle, highly-repetitive tasks. Most PMTSs have been computerized by one or more vendors. Computerization ranges from rapid code validation and automatic calculation, to question and answer scenarios, to interactive expert systems. Choosing a PMTS is basically a matter of finding one you like, then selecting the computer implementation that is appropriate and affordable. Computerized PMTSs are typically part of larger, often expensive, standards management software. Applying a PMTS can be time-consuming, whether it's computerized or not. However, a PMTS forces you to look at the method you use to accomplish a particular job, which promotes methods improvement. But, remember, a PMTS is best for shortcycle, highly-repetitive tasks.

Time study — The most widely used tool to develop standard times is still time study. Time study reflects what is happening in your job or project. It is also easy to learn and use. Now, the PC has made the summarization of time study data a matter of seconds instead of hours.

A computerized study is taken on an electronic hand-held data collector by assigning a code number to each element. Element codes are entered into the data collector as they occur. A time key is pressed at the end of each element, at the breakpoints. The data become a series of code, time, code, time, etc. Rating or leveling factors are also entered into the data collector. The data are then sent to the PC for almost instant summarization. Statistical error figures and graphical histograms can quickly point out any highly variable elements, possibly indicating a bad method.

The real key in computerized time study is actually the data collector, not the software. For example, many firms have used spreadsheet software for summarization. However, taking the study by stopwatch and typing the values into the spreadsheet save little if any time. But it does invite entry errors. It's far better to use a data collector or hand-held computer — even a laptop computer — for conducting the study. This applies no matter what software you use for summarization.

Activity sampling — An often overlooked tool is activity sampling, usually called work sampling by North American IEs. In this technique, a group of workers are observed at random times and their individual activities noted each tour. After a week or two, the average time spent on each activity can be calculated, and statistically justified. The average time per piece can then be determined.

Activity sampling can quickly establish standard times on highly variable or long-duration tasks. The key to fast and easy activity sampling is an electronic data collector and PC software. Subject or activity codes are entered into the data collector. The data are then sent to the PC on a daily basis. This allows for almost instant summarization at any time during the course of a study. Activity sampling can also uncover bottlenecks and determine reasonable allowances.

Historical data — This really is not a tool as much as it is a good shop practice. Keep accurate job records. If you have an electronic joblock system, historical times from past jobs offer an excellent source for standard times. As methods change, the standard times gradually change, using a moving average approach. This can be especially beneficial on long tasks that might change from job to job as methods improve.

Estimates — A well-reasoned estimate is what makes a standard a good standard, especially for seldom-performed, highly variable tasks. Be sure to get estimates from at least three people who do the task. Then average them, and discuss the average with all three individuals. Put it in your computerized standards system.

Let's quickly review the techniques, and put them into perspective according to the tasks for which they apply:

(1) Motion analysis: very short, repetitive tasks;

(2) Time study: short, repetitive and variable tasks;

(3) Activity sampling: longer, variable tasks;

(4) Historical data: long, repetitive and variable tasks;

(5) Estimates: seldom performed, variable tasks.

The main point is this: Use the tool that develops the standard time consistent with the type of task involved. Use a computer program if a large amount of data are involved, such as time study and activity sampling data.

5.3 Maintaining standard times

Far too many U.S. companies have developed — or had a consultant develop — standard times and then stopped there. One of the biggest problems in American industry is "creeping methods changes." Methods improve, but acceptable standard times are not updated to reflect the newer standards. It is as important to update your standard times as it is to develop them in the first place.

How can you do that economically? A computer can help a great deal. Although you can use spreadsheet and database software, programs are available specifically for maintaining standard times. The programs typically store measured times, and then use them to develop and maintain worker and product standards. Such programs feature several "levels" of standard times, but they can usually be characterized as having three major levels: elements, operations and routers.

Elements — Individual work-measured times are often referred to as standard elements or standard data. Some companies maintain standard data in ring binders, but most don't even bother cataloging individual work-measured time elements. A PC-based system encourages standard data development and application because it simplifies the process and eliminates extra paperwork. Most software programs offer integrated motion-level standard data in the form of the integrated PMTS. But your time study, activity sampling, historical data, and estimate elements are also legitimate standard data elements. Such elements can be cataloged in a computerized standards system for rapid application to worker standards. This is much faster than looking them up in a ring binder.

Operations — Worker standards are often referred to as operation or process standards, and are typically paper systems just begging for computerization. The operations or process level is the core level in any PC-based standard system, and it often offers side benefits such as manufacturing line balancing. Frequencies, allowances, internal elements, setup elements, workplace layouts, assembly sketches, operator instructions, and other worker-oriented aspects are also handled at this level.

Routers — Product standards are usually called routers or routings, and then summarize setup and run times from several operations. Costing and scheduling are accomplished at this level. Routers are typically computerized as parts of an MRP II or other mainframe costing system. However, routers can also be part of a PC-based standards system, offering automatic updates as operation times change.

Like any standards system, a computerized standard system won't help — and can be counter-productive — if it is not kept up-to-date. If you expect to continue to produce accurate labor costs and cost estimates, and meet promised delivery dates, keep your labor standards current. Actual time spent updating isn't burdensome, especially when your standards are computerized.

Most computerized standard systems feature an integrated PMTS to help the user develop standards. But don't let that be your primary purpose for "buying into" computerized standards. Maintaining your standards comes first. Look upon an integrated PMTS as a bonus, but just for those highly-repetitive short-cycle tasks. The primary purpose of a computerized standard system should be to manage standards, not create them.

5.4 Summary

Since practically everyone is already using standard times in one form or another, using work measurement to develop these times is simply an improvement on what you are already doing. (You're using times from some source, even if they are simply educated guesses.) Computerization not only speeds development, but also fosters the maintenance of standards. The following 6 points will help clarify some points regarding standard times:

(1) Standard times are necessary for costing and cost-estimating, and for scheduling and manpower allocation.

(2) a. A standard time is not a standard time unless all parties involved agree it is a standard time.

b. Never use the word "accurate" when discussing standard times.

(3) The more realistic your standard times, the more realistic your costing and scheduling.

(4) Use the fastest, easiest work measurement technique that is consistent with the task being measured: motion analysis, time study, activity sampling, historical data, or estimates.

(5) a. Constantly check to be sure the method being used is the same as the standard-time method.

b. Change a standard time as more data becomes available for the task (such as historical data).

c. Change a standard time whenever the method changes.

(6) Use a computer.

Professional Vocabularies and Expressions

work-measured labor standards	作业测量的劳动力标准
motion analysis	动作分析
time study	时间研究
activity/work sampling	活动/工作抽样
historical data	历史数据
estimate	估算
pre-determined motion times system (PMTS)	预定动作时间系统

methods time measurement (MTM)	方法时间测量法
Maynard operation sequence technique (MOST)	梅纳德操作排序技术
modular arrangement	模块化安排法
pre-determined time standards (PTS)	预定时间标准法
master standard data (MSD)	主时间数据法
motion standard times (MST)	动作标准时间法
work factor	工作要素法
interactive expert system	交互式专家系统
data collector	数据收集器
rating or leveling factor	评比因子
histogram	直方图
moving average approach	移动平均法
manufacturing line balancing	生产线平衡

 Notes

1. Perhaps the only thing wrong with these tools is their lack of a buzz word or catchy acronym.

也许这些工具的唯一缺点是它们没有一个能够反映其内涵的响亮的词组或引入的字母缩写。

2. Human workers come in at least a billion models with varying physical, mental, and emotional specifications and work under varying environmental conditions.

由于物理、精神和感情等方面以及工作环境的不断变化，工人至少可以被分为十亿种不同的类型。

3. Standard times are standard times only because all parties involved agree they are standard times.

标准时间之所以是标准的，仅仅是因为相关的所有部门都承认其是标准时间。

4. Like any standard system, a computerized standard system won't help — and can be counter-productive — if it is not kept up-to-date.

同其他的任何标准系统一样，如果不能做到与时俱进，计算机化的标准系统将起不到相应的作用并且可能会降低生产率。

Discussion Questions:

1. "Standard times are standard times only because all parties involved agree they are standard times." How to understand this statement?
2. In manufacturing sector, what is the current situation of the standard times

development in Chinese enterprises, especially private, small and medium-sized enterprises (SMEs)? Under what circumstances do you think the SMEs might resort to IE to cultivate their competitive competencies?

3. Is it necessary for service companies to establish standard times? Why? And how can traditional IE methods and techniques do to help with this regard?

CHAPTER 6

Ergonomics

6.1 The origin of ergonomics

Ergonomics is the scientific discipline that is concerned with the interaction between humans and artifacts and the design of the systems where people participate. It deals with the design of the systems that people use at work and leisure, the tools that are used to perform tasks, and the procedures and practices that organize human activity. The purpose of the design activities is to match systems, jobs, products and environments to the physical and mental abilities and limitations of people. A complementary way to make a system function is to train and educate the operator or the user of the system. Ideally, however, systems should be designed so that they are intuitive to use and do not require special training or education.

The word ergonomics comes from the Greek ergo (work) and homos (rules, law). It was first used by Wojciech Jastrzebowski in a Polish newspaper in 1857. One may argue that ergonomics is nothing new. Hand tools, for example, have been used since the beginning of mankind, and ergonomics was always a concern. Tools concentrate and deliver power, and aid the human in the tasks such as cutting, smashing, scraping and piercing. Various hand tools have been developed since the Stone Age, and the interest in ergonomic design can be traced back in history.

Ramazzini, in the eighteenth century, published a book, *The Diseases of Workers*, where he documented links between many occupational hazards and the type of work performed. He described, for example, the development of cumulative trauma disorder and believed that these events were caused by repetitive motions of the hand, by constrained body posture, and by excessive mental stress.

LaMettrie's controversial book *L'homme Machine* was published in 1748, at the beginning of the Industrial Revolution. Two things can be learned from LaMettrie's writings. First, the comparison of human capabilities and machine capabilities was already a sensitive issue in the eighteenth century. Second, by considering how machines operate, one can also learn much about human behavior. Both issues are still debated in ergonomics today. For example, the comparison of robots and humans has made us understand how industrial tasks should be designed to better fit humans.

Rosenbrock pointed out that during the Industrial Revolution there were efforts to apply the concepts of a "human centered design" to the tools such as the spinning-jenny and the spinning-mule. The concern was to allocate interesting tasks to the human operator, but to let the machine do repetitive tasks.

At the beginning of the twentieth century, Frederick Taylor introduced the "scientific" study of work. This was followed by Frank and Lillian Gilbreth who developed the time-and-motion study and the concept of dividing ordinary jobs into several small micro-elements called "therbligs." Today there are sometimes objections to Taylorism, which has been seen as a tool for exploiting workers. Nonetheless, these methods are useful for measuring and predicting work activities. Time-and-motion study is a valuable tool if used for the right purpose!

Industrial psychology in the beginning of the twentieth century emphasized how one could select, classify and train operators who were suitable to perform the task. The research on accident proneness is typical of this era. Accident proneness implies that there are certain individuals with enduring personality characteristics, who incur a majority of accidents. If one can understand how these individuals differ from "normal" people, one can exclude them from the activities where they incur accidents. This approach, which dominated research for about 20 years, was not fruitful, since accident proneness and many personality features are not stable features, but change with age and experience. In current ergonomics there is a reality that human error is mostly caused by poor design, and the emphasis is to design the environments and artifacts that are safe for all users.

In Europe, ergonomics started with industrial applications in the 1950s, and used information from work physiology, biomechanics and anthropometry for the design of workstations and industrial processes. The focus was on the well-being of workers and manufacturing productivity. In the USA, human factors engineering, human factors and engineering psychology developed from military problems, and had their origin in experimental psychology and systems engineering. The purpose was to enhance systems' performance. Today these two traditions have fused. It is indicative that the Human Factors Society in the USA recently changed its name to the Human Factors and Ergonomics Society.

Since the 1950s ergonomics and human factors have proliferated in Asia, Africa, Latin America and Australia. In many industrially developing countries (IDCs), ergonomic problems have manifested themselves, and have become more obvious in the era of rapid industrialization. The transformation from a rural agrarian to an urban, industrialized life has come at a cost, and workers are "paying" in terms of a tremendous increase in industrial injuries and in terms of worker stress. Many of these problems remain hidden, because the official statistics that can illuminate the true state of affairs are not usually available. Industrialization has come about too quickly, and many societies have difficulties in coping with the changes in infrastructure.

In the transition to the new industrial world IDCs are bypassing several stages of development and are immediately immersed in the computerized global environment. What took the western world 200 years, may be accomplished in 20 years. Associated with this development is a new ergonomics problem that deals with the globalization of communication, integration of resources and global management. This problem is shared by the IDCs and the Western countries. The "Asian tigers" are well positioned to take the lead in this area, but at the present time they lack some of the necessary infrastructure in terms of experience and trained personnel. There is tremendous economic potential in designing usable systems for global communication and customized markets. Technology transfer from the Western world is important, but must be concerned not only with the adaptation and use of machines but also with the entire infrastructure of training local users to develop independent capabilities so that they can act freely on the global market. The ergonomists who understand these problems will have a significant role to play.

6.2 A system description of ergonomics

The purpose of this section is to describe the evolving science of ergonomics in a systematic context. Most ergonomics problems are well described by a system approach. In Figure 6-1, an environment-operator-machine system is considered. The operator (or user) is the central focus in ergonomics and should be described in an organizational context, which is the purpose of Figure 6-1. The figure illustrates only the most important operator concepts. In reality, human perception, information processing, and response are much more complex with many feedback loops and variables that are not detailed in Figure 6-1.

In scientific studies, a classification of independent and dependent variables is often used to analyze a problem. Since ergonomics studies the effect of environmental and machine design features on the operator, the dependent variables are associated with the operator sub-system. These are detailed in Figure 6-1, and include the measures of negative and positive outcome and satisfaction. The independent variables are associated with design parameters of the environment and the machine (such as alternative task allocation, different controls and displays).

The operator perceives the environment — mainly through the visual and auditory senses, then considers the information, makes a decision and finally produces a control response. Perception is guided by the operator's attention. From the millions of bits of information available, the operator is forced to choose the information most relevant to the task. Some attentional processes are automatic and subconscious (pre-attentive) and are executed instantaneously. Some processes become automatic with training, while some are deliberate and slow strategies that provide more time for the analysis of the situation.

52 CHAPTER 6

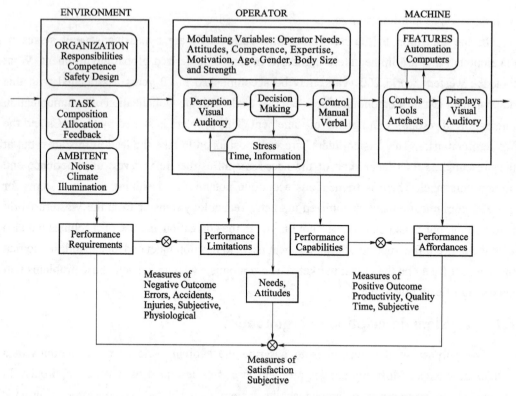

Figure 6-1 Ergonomics systems' model for the measurement of safety, productivity and satisfaction

For new or unusual tasks decision-making can be time consuming. The operator will have to interpret the information, the alternatives for action, and to what extent those actions are relevant to achieve the goals of the task. For routine tasks, decisions are more or less automatic and much quicker to accomplish. In this context researchers question whether "decision making" is an appropriate term. "Situated action" may be more appropriate to describe the automaticity in response.

The purpose of the operator's response is to convey information through either manual response, such as the control of a machine (e.g. a computer) or a tool (e.g. a hammer) or an artifact (e.g. a football) or verbal response such as computer voice control of a machine or verbal message to a co-worker.

There are several modulating variables that affect task performance, including: operator needs, attitudes, competence, expertise, motivation, age, gender, body size and strength. These are idiosyncratic variables and they are different for different individuals. For example, an experienced, competent operator will perceive a task differently than a novice operator. She/He will focus on the details of importance, filter irrelevant information and "chunk" the information into larger milts so that it is possible to make faster and more efficient decisions. Body size is an example of another modulating variable, and the purpose of anthropometry is to design the physical workspace to fit operators with different body sizes.

Stress is an important variable that affects perception, decision-making and response selection. High psychological stress levels are normal when the time to perform a task is limited or when there is too much information to process. Under such conditions the bandwidth of attention may narrow, and operators develop "tunnel vision." Thus the probability of operator error increases.

In general, high stress levels lead to increased physiological arousal and can be monitored by using various physiological measures (e.g. heart rate, EEG, blink rate, and excretion of catecholamines).

The sub-system environment is used to conceptualize the task as well as the context in which it is performed. It could be a steel-worker monitoring an oven. Here the organization of work determines the task allocation; some tasks may be allocated to fellow workers, or supervisors, or computers. Task-allocation is a central problem in ergonomics: How can one best allocate work tasks among machines and operators so as to realize both company goals and individual goals? Task allocation affects how information is communicated between employees and computers, and it also affects systems performance.

The operator receives various forms of feedback from his/her actions. There may be feedback from task performance, from co-workers, from management and so forth. To enhance task performance, communication, and job satisfaction, such feedback must be informative. This means that individuals must receive feedback on how well or poorly they are doing, as well as feedback through communication.

The ambient environment describes the influence of environmental variables on the operator. For example, a steel-worker is exposed to high levels of noise and heat. This increases physiological arousal and stress, thereby affecting task performance, safety and satisfaction.

The importance of the organizational environment has been increasingly emphasized during the last few years. This movement in ergonomics is referred to as "macroergonomics." Ergonomics is undertaken in an organizational context, which deeply affects the appropriateness of alternative design measures. Company policies with respect to communication patterns, decentralization of responsibilities, and task allocation have an impact on ergonomics design. One should first decide who should do what and how people should communicate. Following this analysis, individual tasks, machines, displays and controls can be designed.

Macroergonomics is a much neglected area, and until recently there had not been much research. One exception is the socio-technical research developed in the UK in the 1950s (e.g. the Tavistock group). It may be because the human factors research in the military setting was so dominating in the USA that the importance of organizational context was deemphasized.

For the purpose of completeness of description it is noted that organizational considerations are important in the work context, but are less important for the design of leisure systems and consumer products. These are typically used by the individuals who do not have to consider collaboration and task delegation.

The machine sub-system is broadly conceptualized in Figure 6-1. The term "machine" is in a sense misleading, since it symbolizes any artifact. The "machine" could be a computer, a VCR, or a football. The term "controls" denotes machine controls that are used by the operator. Note that machine control may be taken over by automation and computers through the allocation and delegation of tasks to autonomous processes.

As a result of machine control, there is a changing state that is "displayed" — It can be seen or heard; a pocket calculator will show the results of a calculation, the melting iron in a steel plant will change temperature and color, a computer will produce a sound, and the toaster will "pop" the bread. All of these are the examples of displays. They convey visual or auditory information, and they can be designed to optimize systems, performance.

It is important to note that the system in Figure 6-1 has feedback. Machine information is fed back to the environment sub-system and becomes integrated with the task. Ergonomics is concerned with dynamic systems. It is necessary to go around the loop and incorporate the effect of feedback. Ergonomics is in this matter different from other disciplines. In experimental psychology, for example, there is no requirement for study of dynamic systems.

The system in Figure 6-1 will be used to discuss three major system goals in ergonomics: safety, productivity, and operator satisfaction.

6.3 The goal of safety

Ergonomics is rarely a goal by itself. Safety, operator (user) satisfaction and productivity are common goals. Ergonomics is rather a design methodology that is used to arrive at safety, productivity and satisfaction.

The safety status of a system can be assessed by comparing the performance requirements of the environment with the performance limitations of the operator (Figure 6-1). A task will impose a demand for operator attention, and this demand varies over time. For example, a car driver must sometimes look constantly at the traffic and at other times the traffic situation is less demanding. At the same time the operator attention varies over time. A sleepy driver has a low level of attention, while a driver of a racing car has a high level of attention. If the task demands are greater than the available attention, there is an increased risk of accidents or errors. Hence it is important to understand how the limitations imposed by operator perception, decision-making and control action can be taken into consideration in design, so as to create the systems with low and stable performance requirements.

Injuries and accidents are relatively rare in the workplace. Rather than awaiting the accidents to happen it may be necessary to predict safety problems by analyzing other indicators (or dependent variables) such as operator errors, subjective assessments and physiological response variables. These measures are indicated in Figure 6-1 under the heading of "Measures of negative outcome."

In the case where the system must be redesigned to make it safer, there may be several different options, including:

(1) The allocation of tasks between workers and machines/computers. Workers may be moved from a hazardous area and automation could take over the job.

(2) Work processes and workstations can be redesigned to optimize worker posture, comfort and convenience.

(3) The exposure to ambient parameters including illumination, noise and heat stress can be reduced.

(4) Organizational factors such as allocation of responsibility and autonomy as well as policies for communication can be changed.

(5) Design features of a machine can be improved, including changes of controls and displays.

These and other options for redesign can be derived from Figure 6-1.

6.4 The goal of productivity

As mentioned, system design has three goals: safety, productivity and operator satisfaction. Their relative importance varies depending on the system. In a nuclear power plant, the safety and production of electricity are two self-evident goals, and together they determine the design of the plant.

To enhance system performance one can design a system that improves performance affordances. This means that through efficient design of the system the operator can excel in exercising his/her skills. Such system design makes it possible to perceive quickly, make fast decisions, and exercise efficient controls.

To improve system performance an ergonomist could, for example, design system affordances so that they enhance important skill parameters: The handling of machine controls becomes intuitive (e.g. through control-response compatibility), and the interpretation of displays becomes instantaneous (e.g. through the use of ecological displays).

In Figure 6-1 several measures of positive outcome are indicated. One can measure productivity, quality, time to perform a task, and one can ask the operator how well the system works (subjective assessments). These measures are the common dependent variables used to measure the productivity of a system.

6.5 The trade-off between productivity and safety

Ergonomics improvements may focus on reducing operator errors as well as increasing the efficiency or speed of operation. It may, however, be difficult to simultaneously improve both safety and productivity. In general, the greater the speed (of vehicles, production machinery, etc.), the less will be the time available for the operator to react. A shorter time for operator reaction will compromise safety but increase productivity. Operators have a choice between the increased speed and increased accuracy, which is referred to as speed-accuracy trade-off or SATO. Industrial managers often encourage employees to increase both speed and accuracy (productivity and quality). This is contrary to the concept of SATO and hence difficult or impossible to achieve.

In industrial production systems it will, however, be possible to improve safety and quality of production at the same time. A reduction of operator errors will typically lead to improved safety as well as improved production quality. An emphasis on the quality of production may therefore be more appropriate and more effective than the traditional approach in industry to stress on the quantity of production.

6.6 The goal of operator satisfaction

Operator satisfaction is conceived in a broad sense: from workers' satisfaction to users' satisfaction. Various aspects of dissatisfaction such as job dissatisfaction or consumer dissatisfaction are also considered. The main point in Figure 6-1 is that (dis)satisfaction may be predicted by comparing operator needs and attitudes with the performance requirements of the environment and the performance affordances of the machine.

Satisfaction and dissatisfaction are mediated through operators' needs and attitudes. Since needs and attitudes are different among different individuals, some users can be satisfied with a system while others are dissatisfied. Needs and attitudes vary substantially between countries and cultures. What are considered workers' rights in Sweden (e.g. to have a window in your office) are less important in other countries. In Sweden, a lack of window would cause great dissatisfaction, since office workers have "acquired" a need, but the workers in the USA may not think twice about this.

For safety and productivity, it was noted above that there is a trade-off: improved safety leads to lower speed of production and vice versa. For job satisfaction or dissatisfaction there does not seem to be any similar trade-offs. One would think that a satisfied worker would produce more and a dissatisfied worker would produce less. One would also think that a satisfied worker would be safer and a dissatisfied worker not so safe. However, extensive research on these issues has not been able to demonstrate that there is a connection.

6.7 Conclusion

Owing to the diffusion of computer technology and complex machinery new interests have emerged in ergonomics. Cognitive ergonomics, usability studies, human reliability, and human-computer interaction are current top priorities. Organizational design and the study of industrial change processes and continuous improvements are also important. Biomechanics and work physiology are less dominating than they were in the past, except that there is a renewed interest in biomechanics due to musculoskeletal disorders.

It is interesting to note that this trend is valid not only for industrialized countries but also for industrially developing countries. Since the beginning of the history of ergonomics around 1950, society and technology have developed tremendously. Brian Shackel characterized the development as follows:

1950s — military ergonomics

1960s — industrial ergonomics

1970s — consumer products ergonomics

1980s — human-computer interaction and software ergonomics

1990s — cognitive ergonomics and organizational ergonomics

The interest in the 2000s will be on global communication. This type of ergonomics is driven by the global market and its main purpose is to enhance global trade and interaction. It is facilitated by Internet communication, and it makes it feasible to start virtual organizations.

There is also an ergonomics interest in dealing with global environmental and social problems, such as the pollution of big cities, crime, the trend of unemployment, and so forth. Moray (1991) suggested that ergonomics methodology could be used for solving these types of problems, since they are based on the behavior of the individual and may be solved by giving forceful feedback to the individual.

Ergonomics is a science of design. The design methodology as illustrated in the system approach in Figure 6-1, is well suited to solving problems outside the traditional sphere of interest. Ergonomics will continue to evolve and professional ergonomists must extend their knowledge to deal with a rapidly changing scenario. This will require increasing interaction with other disciplines to solve the problems of an interdisciplinary nature. There is also a need for communication and collaboration between ergonomists in proposing ergonomics design measures. Activities in research and development may be based on local information, but the design solution may be supported by many ergonomists working in synergy around the world.

Clearly the profession is driven by design requirements from users, markets, industries, organizations and governments. Ergonomics must be able to quickly respond to the changing needs of society.

Professional Vocabularies and Expressions

ergonomics	功效学，人因学
occupational hazards	职业危险
human centered design	面向人类的设计
time-and-motion study	时间和动作研究
industrial psychology	工业心理学

accident proneness	事故倾向性
work physiology	工作生理学
biomechanics	生物力学
anthropometry	人体测量学
human factors engineering	人因工程
engineering psychology	工程心理学
experimental psychology	实验心理学
systems engineering	系统工程
human perception	人类感知
information processing	信息处理
response	响应，反应
feedback loop	反馈回路
independent variable	独立变量
dependent variable	非独立变量
visual sense	视觉
auditory sense	听觉
manual response	手动响应
verbal response	语音响应
idiosyncratic variable	（人类的）特征变量
physiological arousal	生理干扰
macroergonomics	宏观功效学
speed-accuracy trade-off (SATO)	速度和精度的平衡
cognitive ergonomics	认知功效学
usability study	使用性研究
human reliability	人类可靠性
human-computer interaction	人机交互
musculoskeletal disorder	肌骨失调，肌骨紊乱

Notes

1. Accident proneness implies that there are certain individuals with enduring personality characteristics, who incur a majority of accidents.

事故倾向性指具有某类特性的个体导致主要事故的发生。

2. The transformation from a rural agrarian to an urban, industrialized life has come at a cost, and workers are "paying" in terms of a tremendous increase in industrial injuries and in terms of worker stress.

从以田园式为主的农业经济向以城市化为主的工业经济的转变付出了一定的代价，这些代价是工人以显著增加的工业伤害和工作压力的形式付出的。

3. Technology transfer from the Western world is important, but must be concerned not only with the adaptation and use of machines but also with the entire infrastructure of training local users to develop independent capabilities so that they can act freely on the global market.

尽管从西方引进技术很重要，但技术转让的过程不仅要考虑如何使本土使用者适应和使用机器，而且还要考虑如何建设能够培训这些本土使用者的独立能力，以便其能够在全球化的市场中运用自如的整个基础设施。

4. Ergonomics is rather a design methodology that is used to arrive at safety, productivity and satisfaction.

应该说功效学是一种用来实现系统安全性、生产率和操纵者满意度的设计方法。

Discussion Questions:

1. Summarize the past, current situation and the future of ergonomics in China.
2. Human computer interaction (HCI) has become one of the major components of modern ergonomics with the advent and prosper of computer and IT technologies. Write an essay that briefly introduces the concept and development track of HCI.

CHAPTER 7

Research Challenges and Recent Progress in Next Generation Factory Layouts

7.1 Introduction

There is an emerging consensus that existing layout configurations do not meet the needs of multiproduct enterprises and there is a need for a new generation of factory layouts that are more flexible, modular, and easy to reconfigure. With increased flexibility, modularity, and reconfigurability, factories could avoid redesigning their layouts each time their production requirements changed. Creating new layouts can be expensive and disruptive, especially when factories must shut down. Because the factories that operate in volatile environments or introduce new products regularly cannot afford frequent disruptions, plant managers often prefer to live with the inefficiencies of existing layouts rather than suffer through costly redesign, which may quickly become obsolete.

Conventional layouts, such as product, process, and cellular layouts, do not meet these needs. They are typically designed for a specific product mix and production volume that are assumed to continue for a sufficiently long period (usually, three to five years). The evaluation criterion used in most layout design procedures — long-term material-handling efficiency — fails to capture the priorities of the flexible factory (For example, scope is more important than scale, responsiveness is more important than cost, and reconfigurability is more important than efficiency). Consequently, layout performance deteriorates as product volumes, mix, or routings fluctuate. A static measure of material-handling efficiency also fails to capture the impact of layout configuration on the aspects of operational performance, such as work-in-process accumulation, queue times at processing departments, and throughput rates. Consequently, the layouts that improve material handling often cause inefficiencies elsewhere in the form of long lead times or large in-process inventories.

When product variety is high or production volumes are small, a functional layout, with all resources of the same type in one location, is often thought to provide the greatest flexibility (Figure 7-1). However, a functional layout is notorious for its material-handling inefficiency and scheduling complexity, which can lead to long lead times, large work-in-process inventories, and inefficient material handling. While grouping resources based on function provides some economies of scale and simplicity in allocating workloads, it makes the layout susceptible to manufacturing inefficiencies when there are changes in product mix or routings. Such changes often require costly redesign of the plant layout or the material-handling system.

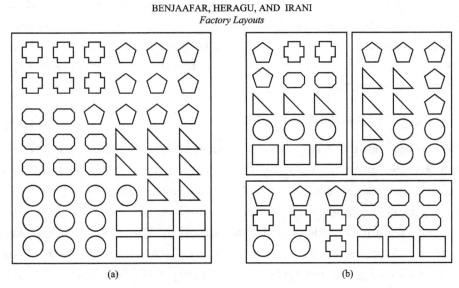

Figure 7-1 In a functional layout, resources of the same type are placed in the same location, while in a cellular layout, resources are partitioned into cells, each dedicated to a family of products

(a) Functional layout; (b) Cellular layout

An alternative to a functional layout is a cellular configuration, in which the factory is partitioned into cells (Figure 7-1), each dedicated to a family of products with similar processing requirements. Although cellular factories can simplify work flow and reduce material handling, they are generally designed to produce a specific set of products whose demand levels are assumed to be stable and product life cycles sufficiently long. In fact, cells are usually dedicated to single product families with little allowance for intercell flows. Cellular factories are inefficient when the demand for existing products fluctuates or new products are introduced often. Some authors have proposed alternative cellular structures to overcome these problems, such as overlapping cells, cells with machine sharing, and fractal cells. Although an improvement, these alternatives remain bounded by their cellular structure.

Layout design procedures, whether for functional or cellular layouts, have been largely based on a deterministic paradigm. Such design parameters as product mix, product demands, and product routings are assumed to be known with certainty. The design criterion is often a static measure of material-handling efficiency (a total adjacency score, total material-handling cost, or a combination of both), which does not capture the need for flexibility and reconfigurability. In fact, the relationship between layout flexibility and layout performance is poorly understood and analytical models for its evaluation are lacking. The structural properties of layouts that affect their flexibility are also not well understood. Current design criteria do not capture the effect of layout on such performance measures as congestion, cycle time, and throughput rate. They also ignore the impact of such operational parameters as setup, batching, and loading and unloading at work centers. More important, they measure only average performance and in so doing cannot guarantee effectiveness under all operating scenarios. Clearly, we need a new class of layouts, new evaluation criteria, and new design models and solution procedures.

7.2 Emerging trends in industry

Several important trends are emerging in industry that could transform the layout design problem or even eliminate it. We focus on five of these trends to highlight the interaction between new business practices, new technologies, and layout designs.

7.2.1 Contract manufacturing

In many industries, outside suppliers are increasingly doing most of the manufacturing and assembly for original equipment manufacturers (OEMs). Along with just-in-time deliveries, outsourcing has led to firms reconfiguring their final assembly facilities to accommodate closer coupling between suppliers and OEMs. For example, many automobile manufacturers allow suppliers to deliver components directly to the points of use on their assembly lines. They have designed multiple loading docks and multiple inventory drop-off points throughout their factories. To support modular plants, designers are using spine layouts (Figure 7-2), with the product moving along a main artery, or spine, through the plant. Linked to the spine are mini-assembly lines owned by the suppliers, each attaching its own module to the moving product. The hybrid layout has the features of a flow line and multiple, autonomous cells. The configuration allows the plant to add and remove suppliers without changing the main layout. It also gracefully accommodates the growth and contraction of supplier operations. Facility planners had to choose the layouts that make material handling efficient not only in each individual plant but also throughout the complex. The challenge for facility planners is then to develop a layout and a material-handling system to permit high efficiency at the core and flexibility and reconfigurability at the periphery. The design metrics should certainly be different depending on the area of the plant, but the design tools should also support a variety of layout types within the same facility. The modular layouts we discuss later address in part the challenges of constructing such hybrid layouts.

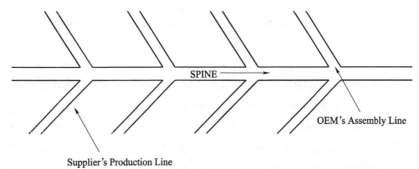

Figure 7-2 **In a spine layout, products move along a main artery through the plant. Linked to the spine are mini-assembly lines owned by independent suppliers who attach additional modules as needed**

7.2.2 Delayed product differentiation

Increased product variety and the need for mass customization have led many companies to delay product differentiation, postponing the point in the manufacturing process when products are assigned individual features. Companies do this, for example, by building a platform common to all products and differentiating it by assigning to it certain product-specific features and components only after actual demand becomes known. They create hybrid facilities consisting of flow-line-like components where they build the common platforms and job shop-like components where they customize the products. If final products are easily grouped into families, the job-shop structure could be replaced by cells, each dedicated to one of the product families (Figure 7-3). Taken to the extreme, delayed differentiation can eliminate the problem of designing layouts altogether. For example, if customization takes place at the point of sale or in distribution warehouses, as is increasingly the case for computers, the factory becomes a single high-volume, low-variety production line. Hewlett-Packard has implemented such a strategy by carrying out the localization steps for its computers and printers in its overseas distribution centers (For example, its distribution warehouses install country-specific power supplies and power cords).

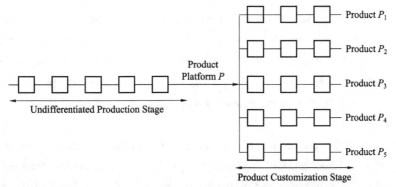

Figure 7-3 **A plant with delayed differentiation has a hybrid layout consisting of two stages. In the first stage, the plant makes undifferentiated products in a make-to-stock fashion. In the second stage, it customizes the products based on actual demand (make-to-order production)**

The blurring of the lines between warehousing and manufacturing raises interesting questions. How does transforming warehouses from pure storage facilities to the facilities that also do light assembly affect their design? How should the layout of warehouses change to accommodate both the needs of efficient storage and efficient manufacturing and assembly? In industries where the differentiation steps are carried out inside the factory, there is clearly a need for design tools that support hybrid layouts that may have the features of product, cellular, and functional layouts all under one roof. The modular layouts we discuss later could be a step in that direction.

7.2.3 Multichannel manufacturing

The increased emphasis on quick-response manufacturing and minimum finished-goods inventory has led many manufacturers and suppliers to invest in additional capacity, often by running parallel production lines. By having duplicated flexible production lines shared across products, companies hope to ensure a seamless flow of material. Depending on downstream congestion, products can move in and out of neighboring production lines, creating multiple paths, or channels, minimizing queueing and congestion. The designers of multichannel systems face such challenges as determining how many duplicate paths to have and how to organize the resource duplicates on the plant floor.

7.2.4 Scalable machines

In the last few years, there has been a concerted effort in the metal cutting industry to develop the machines that are highly flexible and scalable and that can perform many functions and be adjusted for various capacities. The functionality and efficiency of the machines can easily be upgraded by plugging in additional modules or acquiring additional software. If successful, such efforts could lead to the facilities that use one machine for most processing with little material handling and movement. Because a machine can be rapidly configured for different mixes and volumes, the changes in production requirements would have little effect on the layout.

Such scalable machines could transform layout design. If material movement became minimal, factory layouts would be greatly simplified and their design would be less important. The emphasis in factory design would then likely shift from the detailed design of each processing department to the higher level integration of these departments (for example, integrating machining with assembly or the assembly with inspection and packaging).

7.2.5 Portable machines

Several equipment manufacturers are marketing portable machines that are easily and dynamically deployed in different areas of the factory as production requirements change. The portable machines go to the workplace and mount on the workpieces — instead of the other way around (That is, workpieces are stationary and movement is incurred by the machines). Hence, factories would have to be laid out to facilitate the flow of machines instead of parts.

7.3 Next generation factory layouts

Three approaches to layout design address three distinct needs of the flexible factory. The first two approaches present novel layout configurations, namely distributed and modular layouts. In the third approach, we use operational performance as a design criterion to generate what we term agile layouts.

7.3.1 Distributed layouts

Distributed layouts disaggregate large functional departments into the subdepartments distributed throughout the plant floor (Figure 7-4). The duplicate departments strategically located throughout the factory allow the facility to hedge against future fluctuations in job-flow patterns and volumes. In turn, disaggregated and distributed subdepartments reduce material-travel distances for many production flow sequences. Planners can easily find efficient flows for a wide range of product mixes and volumes. Such layouts are especially appealing when demand fluctuates too frequently to make reconfiguring the plant cost effective. In these settings, a fixed layout that performs well for many demand scenarios is desirable.

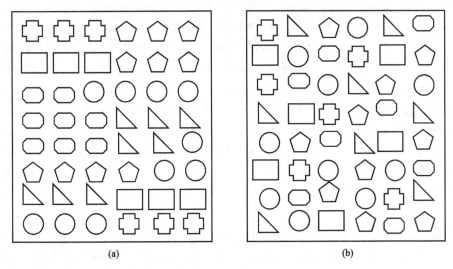

Figure 7-4 In a distributed layout, not all equipment of the same type (represented by a particular shape in the figure) is placed in adjoining locations. Instead, equipment of the same type is either grouped in multiple clusters (partial distribution) or placed individually throughout the plant (maximal distribution)
(a) Partially distributed layout; (b) Maximity distributed layout

In designing a distributed layout, a firm faces several challenges. How should it create subdepartments, and how many should it have of each type? How much capacity should it assign to each subdepartment? Where should it place the subdepartments? How should it allocate workload among similar subdepartments? How will department disaggregation and distribution affect operational performance (for example, material-handling times, work in process, and queueing times)? How should the firm manage material flow, now that there is greater routing flexibility? How should it coordinate the competing needs for material handling of similar subdepartments? What performance measure should the firm use when designing distributed layouts? Should it measure expected material-handling cost over possible demand scenarios, or should it seek a measure of robustness that guarantees a minimum level of performance for all scenarios? More important, how sensitive are the final layouts to the adopted performance measure? Although duplicating departments might increase flexibility, it could also increase and diminish economies of scale (For example, operators and auxiliary resources must be duplicated). The firm must trade off the material-handling benefits of disaggregation and duplication against cost increases in other areas.

7.3.2 Modular layouts

Modular layouts are hybrid layouts for systems with complex material flows that cannot be described as functional, flow line, or cellular. Several of the emerging trends in industry are leading to such configurations. For example, the automobile industry builds modular factories around flow-line-like cores with connected supplier production lines in various forms. The firms that delay product differentiation also use the layouts that combine product, process, and cellular features. With such modular layouts, manufacturers can scale their activities up or down quickly. In their research on modular layouts, Irani and Huang (2000) sought to answer the following fundamental questions. Could a layout other than the three traditional layouts better fit the material flows of multiproduct manufacturers? Perhaps a combination of the three traditional layouts? Could a network of layout modules provide a metastructure for designing multiproduct manufacturing facilities in general? Would grouping and arranging resources into the modules corresponding to specific traditional layouts minimize total flow distances or costs?

7.3.3 Agile layouts

In the facilities that permit frequent reconfiguration, layouts could be designed to maximize operational performance rather than to minimize material-handling cost. As production-planning periods shrink, factories shift their focus from long-run cost efficiency to short term responsiveness and agility. Such performance measures as cycle time, work-in-process (WIP) accumulation, and throughput become especially important. Unfortunately, capturing the relationship between layout configuration and operational performance is difficult. Meller and Gau (1996) reviewed over 150 papers on factory layout and found only one paper on the subject. Recently Benjaafar (2002) introduced an analytical model capable of capturing the relationship between layout configuration and operational performance. He embedded the model in a layout-design procedure in which the design criterion can be one of the several measures of operational performance. Heragu et al. (2000)

expanded Benjaafar's (2002) model to include set-up time, transfer, and process batch size and developed a method that can estimate operational performance measures of functional and cellular manufacturing systems.

7.4 Research challenges

Several research challenges remain. In designing distributed layouts, the designers of the current models assume that the number of department duplicates and the capacity of each duplicate are known. In practice, facility designers must make these decisions before developing a layout. Current models do not account for the cost of disaggregating and distributing departments nor do they capture the economies of scale associated with operating consolidated departments. The infrastructure typical of a single consolidated department in a job shop (for example, operators, computer control systems, loading and unloading areas, and waste-disposal facilities) must be duplicated in a distributed layout across all department duplicates. Thus, while department disaggregation and distribution may yield material-handling benefits, a firm must trade off these benefits against the advantages of operating consolidated facilities. We need an integrated model that combines department duplication and capacity assignment with layout design and flow allocation. In our initial flow-allocation model, we assumed full flexibility in assigning workload among the duplicates of the same department. In practice, this could mean splitting orders for a single product among several duplicates, smaller batches, and longer and more frequent setups. Order splitting could also delay shipping completed orders because the batches of the same order were not synchronized. To address this problem, one would need to capture setup minimization in the objective function or place additional constraints on flow allocation to prevent order splitting.

For modular layouts, several important issues need to be addressed: ① After identifying all common substrings, one would need to aggregate several of the substrings into a single module to minimize machine duplication costs based on a measure of substring dissimilarity and a threshold value for aggregating similar substrings. This is related to the problem of determining the optimal number of modules in the final layout. One idea is to develop measures of connectivity and transitivity of the directed graph we obtain from aggregating a set of common substrings. ② We need to establish feasibility criteria for allocating machines to several modules subject to machine availability and criteria for minimum machine utilization. An iterative loop should be incorporated in the design to absorb any module rejected because of these criteria. ③ The current approach treats each residual substring as a sequence of operations performed on machines located in process departments. It seems logical to cluster these substrings and aggregate their machines into cell modules based on user-defined thresholds for string clustering. ④ We must compare the performance of this new layout with those of flow line, cellular, and functional layouts for the same facility.

For agile layouts, we need the models that account for different routing and dispatching policies of the material-handling system. These models could then be used to study the effects of different policies on layout performance. Furthermore, we could use the queueing model to evaluate and compare the performance of classical layout configurations under varying conditions. We might identify new configurations that are more effective in achieving small WIP levels. In particular, the identifying configurations that reduce distance variance without affecting average distance can be valuable. Such configurations might include the star layout, where departments are equidistant from each other, or the hub-and-spoke layout, in which each hub consists of several equidistant departments and is served by a dedicated transporter. In many applications, differentiating between WIP at different departments or different stages of the production process is useful. WIP tends to appreciate in value as it progresses through the production process. We should favor layouts that reduce the most expensive WIP first, for example, those in which departments that carry out the last production steps are centrally located. Another important avenue of research is to integrate layout design with the design of the material-handling system. For example, we could simultaneously decide on the material-handling capacity (number of transporters or transporter carrying capacity) and department placement, with the objective of minimizing both WIP-holding costs and capital investment costs. We could then examine the trade-offs between capacity and WIP.

Professional Vocabularies and Expressions

factory layout	工厂布局
product layout	产品式布局
process layout	工艺式布局
functional layout	功能式布局
cellular layout	单元式布局
modular layout	模块式布局
layout/facility design	布局/设施设计
work-in-process (WIP)	在制品
material handling	物料搬运
cell	制造单元
throughput	生产量，生产率
reconfigurability	（布局的）可重组性，可重塑性
work center	工作中心
contract manufacturing	契约制造
original equipment manufacturer (OEM)	原始设备制造商
delayed product differentiation	产品延迟差异化

multichannel manufacturing	多通道制造
scalable machine	可扩展的机器
portable machine	便携式机器
workpiece	工件
distributed layout	分布式布局
agile layout	敏捷布局
waste-disposal facility	废物处理设施
capacity assignment	能力分配
threshold value	阈值
directed graph	有向图
machine utilization	设备利用率
routing and dispatching	路径规划和调度
consolidated facility	联合设施，公用设施
star layout	星型布局
hub-and-spoke layout	轮辐式布局

Notes

1. While grouping resources based on function provides some economies of scale and simplicity in allocating workloads, it makes the layout susceptible to manufacturing inefficiencies when there are changes in product mix or routings.

尽管根据能够实现的功能将资源分组能够获得一定的规模效应并能简化工作量的分配，但当产品的组合或工艺路径发生变化时很容易造成功能式布局的制造效率低下。

2. Layout design procedures, whether for functional or cellular layouts, have been largely based on a deterministic paradigm.

无论是功能式布局，还是单元式布局，其设计过程大体上都是基于确定性假设的。

3. In fact, the relationship between layout flexibility and layout performance is poorly understood and analytical models for its evaluation are lacking.

实际上，人们对于布局灵活性与布局绩效之间关系的理解很有限，而且缺乏用来评价这些关系的分析模型。

4. Facility planners had to choose the layouts that make material handling efficient not only in each individual plant but also throughout the complex. The challenge for facility planners is then to develop a layout and a material-handling system to permit high efficiency at the core and flexibility and reconfigurability at the periphery.

设施规划者必须选择那些不仅在每个工厂内部，而且在整个综合企业中就物料搬运来说都是有效的布局。因而，这里的挑战在于如何开发布局和物料搬运系统使得每个工厂在内部都很高效，而在其与其他工厂的交界处则具有很高的灵活性和可重组性。

5. They create hybrid facilities consisting of flow-line-like components where they build the common platforms and job shop-like components where they customize the products.

他们建设由通用和个性化平台组成的混合型设施。前者以流水线方式生产通用零部件，而后者则用专业化车间的方式生产体现产品个性化的零部件。

6. Depending on downstream congestion, products can move in and out of neighboring production lines, creating multiple paths, or channels, minimizing queueing and congestion.

根据生产线下游的阻塞情况，产品可以在相邻的生产线之间相互调配，这样就产生了多个生产路径或通道，同时可以最小化排队等待和阻塞（时间）。

Discussion Questions:

1. In the 20 years before 2007, vast amount of foreign manufacturing companies flushed into China. One of the common problems facing most of the companies is that the continuously rapid economic growth of China renders their plants outdated. Therefore, they have to either relocate or redesign their plants or even build new ones. From factory layout perspective, what suggestion do you have for these companies?

2. Since the global financial crisis in 2007, lots of manufacturing factories in China have been dealing with excess manufacturing capacity problem. From the perspective of factory layout planning, what suggestions do you have to these factories?

3. How can the next generation factory layouts help Chinese enterprises gain competitive advantages?

CHAPTER 8

Operations Management

8.1 Celebration of history and accomplishments

It is difficult to pinpoint the origins of the field of operations management. The search for rigorous laws governing the behaviors of physical systems and organizations has throughout history featured bursts of activity and periods of quiet. The classes of problems that we are most familiar with today came into high relief after the Industrial Revolution, when managers of large, vertically-integrated businesses faced coordination problems of unprecedented scope. The treatises on organizing, measuring, and managing production in these challenging settings were published by a range of professionals from business and industry. The rise of "scientific management" is usually associated with the work of Frederick Taylor, Frank and Lillian Gilbreth, and others in the late 19th and early 20th centuries. The Ford Harris EOQ model dates at least as far back as 1915.

During World War II these efforts continued, and were amplified, in the form of operations research groups largely initiated and funded by government and quasi-governmental organizations. These mission-focused mathematicians modeled the classes of problems and developed the foundational theories to address them, which created the Big Bang in our discipline. The applied problems motivating the work were concerned with the efficient allocation and control of resources; these were analyzed via mathematical models. Although some papers written in this era focused on the descriptive models of system behavior, the dominant paradigm was the optimization of system performance in the presence of constraints.

Management Science published its first volume in 1954 and helped to promote and catalog the explosive expansion of optimization theory fueled by interest in these applied problems. Indeed, the first issue of Management Science was dominated by the topics that are clearly related to the important issues in operations management. In the 1950s and 1960s the pages of Management Science displayed seminal articles by the scholars now recognized as giants in the field. These included contributions by G. Dantzig on the development and uses of linear programming; by L. R. Ford and D. R. Fulkerson on network flow problems; by A. J.

Clark, S. Karlin, H. Scarf, H. M. Wagner, T. M. Whitin, A. Veinott, and D. Iglehart on inventory theory; by R. Bellman, A. Manne, C. Derman, A. Veinott, and E. Denardo on dynamic programming; by C. Derman and S. Ross on machine maintenance; by J. Jackson on queueing networks; and by J. C. Harsanyi on game theory. Many of the methodological developments listed above were motivated by operations management problems and were described in those contexts. For example, Dantzig applied linear programming to machine-job scheduling and aircraft routing. Bell-man applied dynamic programming to a warehousing problem while Manne analyzed capacity expansion problems formulated as dynamic programs.

Most of the early research focused on developing algorithms and methodologies to solve optimization problems that arose in a broad range of functional areas. With a few notable exceptions such as the Dantzig-Wolfe decomposition and Harsanyi's work, much of this work involved mathematical analysis and algorithms within the context of a single decision maker. Most of the optimization problems also involved a single objective though there were early exceptions featuring multicriteria problems. The striking feature of this early research is the broad range of areas — including operations, finance, organizational design, economics, and marketing — from which problems originated. The first volume of Management Science, for example, included papers on executive compensation, linear programming under uncertainty, the impact of communication nets on task-oriented groups, and the axiomatization of utility. The common theme, however, was the use of a mathematical model to identify how the status quo could be improved.

Much of the initial work within the domain of operations management focused on tactical issues such as line balancing, scheduling, production planning, inventory control, and lot sizing. In some ways these tactical problems were ideally suited for the methodologies that had been developed up to that point. For these problems, the constraints and objective were usually well defined and involved a single objective with centralized control. These early successes resulted in the birth of operations research groups at many corporations, tasked with finding the ways of improving performance. Within the academic community, most of the research in these areas initially took place in engineering departments. Gradually, during the 1960s, researchers in business schools began to study more scientific and rigorous approaches for decision making, instigated in part by recommendations emanating from studies by various private foundations to make business education more rigorous, and efforts by universities to prepare faculty for this task.

8.2 The challenges of the 1970s and 1980s and the response

The period from the late 1960s through the 1970s saw a number of changes in the landscape of scientific computing, technology transfer of operations research tools, business education, and business practice that precipitated important changes in the field of operations management.

Operations research faced two types of challenges during this era. First, whereas the 1950s and 1960s provided a glimpse of the promise of management science to industry, the next two decades saw less success in delivering on this promise to industry. The speed and cost of computing continued to improve dramatically, but data storage and computation remained as practical hurdles to the implementation of many algorithms. Also, in some cases, the models did not keep pace with the evolution of business challenges and practice, and firms began to question the value of these models and methodologies. Second, academic researchers in functional areas such as accounting, finance, and marketing, had increasingly internalized the optimization theory and technology developed by operations researchers in the previous two decades and were using it as part of their research. This period saw many operations researchers move into other functional areas because those were the sources of their problems. As a result, the application of operations research ideas to marketing, for instance, began to be viewed more as marketing. By the 1980s, most corporate groups focused on operations research had shrunk or disappeared. At the same time, the academic research in operations research cum operations management became somewhat less focused on the problems arising in a broad range of functional areas and more on the problems that were internal to the theory developed in the field.

Simultaneously, industry was seeing the introduction of material requirements planning (MRP) systems, then later concepts such as just-in-time (JIT), the Toyota production system (TPS), and total quality management (TQM), which were having a significant impact on business practice and performance but were not strongly tied to the then-current academic research. Indeed, the ascendancy of the Toyota production system in business practice suggested that the locus of creativity had shifted away from academia.

During this period, researchers began examining operations management issues using non-operations research perspectives, seeking to explain the phenomena that could not be explained by the existing theory. The Toyota production system provided one focus for such research; although it contains the features that are compatible with classical theory, it is also a holistic system of physical and human processes that extends its reach into the whole firm in a cross-disciplinary manner. Other researchers were beginning to examine higher-level issues in manufacturing strategy using an empirical approach. By the end of the 1980s, researchers and practitioners were using a broader set of methods and paradigms in their quest to improve operations.

The changes and challenges of the 1970s and 1980s generated a sense of identity crisis in the discipline. This was felt at some level by all of the researchers who lived through this era, but there is no consensus on the totality of its causes or characteristics. Some contributing factors included the natural maturation of the classical problem classes, and a need to reach for the next higher level of complexity. There was also an evolution within business from centralized to more decentralized organizational forms. The theory base for the discipline was expanding and diversifying dramatically. Whatever the causes of the identity crisis, the challenge to the field at this stage was to return to the original mission of using theory to inform current practice.

The first literature to develop in response to this challenge focused on trying to explain JIT and other industry practices in the context of theory that had been developed earlier. This research was valuable because it brought the attention of the field back to the issues that were of concern to practicing managers. This refocusing of research questions has been a crucial driver of growth of the field in the 1990s.

Two important developments occurred as a result of this refocusing. The first was a move back toward interdisciplinary research. The second was an explicit recognition of decentralized loci of control and local incentives, and hence the re-emergence of economic equilibrium in addition to sole-owner optimality as criteria of central interest to our community. Both of these influences can be seen in the recent literature on supply contracts. The first papers in this area were motivated by contract forms actually in use by companies for sharing forecast risk, and examined the optimal response of a single party to a particular contract form. Thus, researchers focused on how capacity and replenishment decisions need to be modified for different contract contexts. It was only later that operations management researchers asked questions about appropriate (or optimal) contract forms. The initial papers featured relatively modest refinements to existing economic intuition by adding resolution to some general economic models (e.g., replacing general revenue or cost functions with more operational detail) and, by so doing, refining the claims that can be derived.

We will speculate as to the future of the supply chain subliterature later in this article, but here it is worthwhile to trace some broad outlines of its development. First, business practice called the existing research paradigm into question. Second, addressing the new problems in some cases required the importation of technology developed elsewhere (e.g., economics). Third, the research focus became more managerial (e.g., focusing on system design, information, and incentives) and less on tactical execution. For example, very simple inventory policies, such as base-stock policies, have often been used as the elements of higher-level system-design models. The development of this subfield has been very beneficial to our discipline, at least if one counts research papers, company sponsorships, and popular university courses. In response, the editor-in-chief of Management Science created the Supply Chain Management Department in 1997 to promote the cause, rather than assuming that the existing operations department would naturally embrace this new research agenda.

Each of these observations helped inform our department's response to the challenges of the time. Some broad themes are clear. First, the field needs to continually check its research against evolving industrial reality. This is sympathetic with the classical mission: The academic forefathers in war-time OR teams were very focused on reality out of mission-critical necessity. The elegant mathematics that energized the field responded to real problems and can do so again. Second, as a consequence of the first, the research will likely become more explicitly interdisciplinary, as it was in the early years, because actual business practice is not cleanly divided into functional problems. As we do this, we need to maintain the focus on the core agenda that defines the field: the design and management of the transformation processes that create value for society.

The department needs to embrace new, exciting research directions while protecting the brand equity of the journal. If we are sufficiently proactive, new departments will not be needed to raise the visibility of new and exciting subliteratures. This requires a delicate balance at times. Some of the classical research themes are relatively mature, with very clear barometers of research excellence well known to a large community of scholars. This is not so with some of the newer areas. We might anticipate a period — albeit short — of technology transfers from other disciplines that will naturally raise the question of how we judge the novelty of a paper. This is already happening.

We anticipate that a focus on the issues central to operations management will soon carry us beyond existing technologies and provide the catalyst for developing new ones. The set of challenging problems is without bounds, as is the upside potential for the field in this new era.

8.3 The department's history and current editorial mission

The history of the Operations and Supply Chain Department reflects a constancy of core mission and an evolution in its interpretation. The department has consistently focused on the operations function. The department title, editorial objectives, and implementation policies, however, have evolved with our understanding of what that mission entails.

The first volume of the journal in 1954 featured no separate departments, but rather six editors from a range of disciplines, drawn both from academia and industry, with C. West Churchman as managing editor. The stated mission of the journal was to identify, extend, and unify scientific knowledge that contributes to the understanding and practice of management. By 1959, the number of editors had grown to 11 (5 from industry), and to 40 (12 from industry) by 1968 when Robert Thrall was editor-in-chief. Martin Starr took over as editor-in-chief in 1969, and introduced the departmental structure. This featured separate departments for production management and logistics. Professor Starr published an interesting editorial letter in the 20th anniversary issue in 1974. He emphasizes a consistency of purposes since Volume 1, yet acknowledges the criticism of the field based on an inability to solve very complex problems, lack of implementation capabilities, and an overemphasis on optimization.

These issues remain with us today. The healthy tension, preordained in the practical world of management, between the purity of abstraction and the relevance of detail is not new, nor can we expect it to go away any time soon. It is part of the territory inherent in striving for a theory of management, and an integral driver of our cyclical attractions to theory, then practice, then theory again as we continually adjust to a changing world. This healthy tension is the correcting force that prevents the discipline from becoming too academically self-referential, or too focused on specific rather than universal insights. It is, in short, what makes this business so much fun.

Over the decades since its formation the department has regularly changed titles and editors as it searched for the boundaries of the operations function. Clearly, the transformation process can include input and output logistics, although intermittently one or more of these had separate departments. Does our mandate include design? What is the boundary between design and planning, the latter activity being central to all management? Where do operations end and finance begin, given that (at least in manufacturing firms) most capital investments are operations related and working capital has a large inventory component? Where do operations end and human resources begin, given that no good manager would ignore the social dimension of the operating system?

The challenge of defining workable boundaries between departments is an inevitable constant. Management is a holistic exercise, and attempting to draw definitive boundaries between its various aspects is a fool's mission. The definition of departmental boundaries turns on the dual attractions of refining existing knowledge via well-established subliteratures and encouraging new integrative ways of thinking about management and, hence, new subliteratures. It will always be so.

We offer some example punctuation points in this evolution. In 1974 there were separate departments for production management — Logistics, Dynamic Programming and Inventory Theory. In 1981, these three departments became two: Production and Operations Management; and Logistics, Distribution, and Inventory. By 1985, these two departments seemed to move closer in their missions, being titled Production and Operations Management; and Manufacturing, Distribution, and Inventory. Then, in 1987, all of the above were subsumed into a single department: Manufacturing, Distribution, and Service Operations. The editorial policy of this large department stated that

of particular interest are the papers that deal with strategic concerns such as the choice and impact of new production or information technology, and papers that may provide insight or simple models for guiding manufacturing or service policy. The department encourages the papers that examine the planning and coordination of activities and resources within a manufacturing, distribution or service operation.

With this, the department anticipated the current editorial philosophy of focusing on senior management issues, which can be seen as a natural extension of this earlier sentiment.

In 1997, the separate Supply Chain Management Department was added to provide a home for what was already a substantial and rapidly growing literature in this area. In 2002, the Manufacturing, Distribution, and Service Operations Department was renamed Design and Operations Management. There were two reasons for this. First, as our understanding of operations matured, we no longer required the detailed articulation of its parts (manufacturing, distribution, and services). Second, the substantial overlap among many design and operational issues argued against trying to define a boundary between the two. Finally, in 2003, another redistricting activity resulted in Supply Chains joining Operations to form the current Operations and Supply Chains Department, and some aspects of design included in another renamed department: Technological Development, Product Development, and Entrepreneurship.

Throughout this history, regardless of its name, the department's core mission has been to identify, extend, and unify scientific knowledge that contributes to the understanding and practice of operations management, defined as the design and management of the transformation processes that create value for society. The current editorial policy continues a trend discernable as far back as 1987, when the (then) new macrodepartment for operational and logistical issues adopted a mission focusing on higher-level system design issues, and encouraged the use of parsimonious models analyzed for insights. The current editorial posture reinforces that policy.

The current philosophy differs from the past only in the stringency with which we enforce these stated aims. We specifically encourage articles addressing decisions typically made by senior managers, and retarget to other journal articles that focus primarily on methodological contributions or issues of tactical execution. This policy is not intended to make a statement about the relative value of alternative research missions, as some tactical issues are of interest to upper management. Rather, we recognize the availability of other high-quality outlets under the INFORMS umbrella for outstanding research on classical problems, and wish to encourage new research directions for which the supporting academic infrastructure may not be as complete. When revising the editorial mission and considering how to implement it, we sought to consider Management Science not in isolation but rather as part of the portfolio of high-quality, operations-related INFORMS journals.

One simple test of consistency with our current mission is to ask whether an upper-level manager, rather than a scheduler or technician, would be interested in the results presented in the paper. Although we do not expect managers to read Management Science papers (Our language is too compact and arcane), the research ideas contained in an article should, perhaps with some translation into management vernacular, be of high interest to a senior manager. These will be predominantly the issues of investment, system design, and operations strategy rather than of tactical execution. Another intuitive filter is whether one can take the ideas in an article and prepare a one-page summary of the key take-away that would be of interest to senior managers. In fact, these deliverables should be apparent early in the article, reinforced by the presentation. High levels of rigor are, as always, needed to mount a convincing argument to defend the conclusions, but it is crucial to articulate the significance, applicability, and limitations of the results.

The recent changes in how we implement the editorial policy have not been without controversy. In the early days of our discipline we were energized by asking questions that needed answers in practice, and bringing clear logic (primarily mathematically represented) to bear on those problems. Many of the problem classes forged 50 years ago are still with us and remain important. However, as described above, the natural maturation of those problem classes and the evolution of industrial thinking and practice suggest that we can stand on the firm foundation of the past and reach up to the next level of organizational complexity.

We believe that there are opportunities to encourage important new work that does not yet have its own momentum and needs a high-octane kick-start, like Management Science, to help get it off the ground. Lacking that, natural institutional inertia encourages the maintenance of the status quo.

By pursuing this path, it is our intent to proactively encourage the research community to extend its reach without devaluing the traditional strengths that made the discipline what it is. There are dangers. As noted, the standards of excellence are not mature in novel areas of research. The challenge before us, editors and referees alike, is to protect the very high brand equity of the journal, while using the same brand equity to encourage work in new areas.

If we do our job well, this period will be recognized as one of great forward movements and the origination of important subliteratures that help define the future of our discipline. Recognizing the clear successes of the past, we embark upon this path with humility and with recognition of, and respect for, contrary views.

8.4 The way forward

We have already mentioned several anticipated consequences as we embark on this new journey. Our research will by necessity become more cross-functional in scope, which will require facility with the tools and concepts that have been developed in other research disciplines, and we hope and expect that we will pass through a stage of technology transfers to a new period of novel synthesis.

Although ultimately it is the problems facing real managers that will define our objectives and techniques, we can already see the broad outlines of potentially new and exciting subliteratures. We provide this list not to limit the scope of innovation, but to provide a necessarily incomplete set of examples to demonstrate the challenges and potential in our discipline.

(1) Supply Chains: Supply chain management, like operation itself, has ill-defined boundaries. In its broadest sense, it has come to be defined as the management of all aspects of providing goods to a consumer, from extraction of raw materials to end-of-life disposal and recycling, including manufacturing, physical logistics, and after-sale service and warranty

issues. With such a broad scope, combined with the rapid rate of evolution of supply chain structures in both physical and organizational dimensions, the evolution of legal structures that constrain the terms of trade and pollution, and trade structures that raise challenging issues of globalization, vast opportunities remain to address unanswered and as-yet-unposed questions, many of which involve broader decision scope, more decision makers, inclusion of risk and greater recognition of business realities that have traditionally been ignored. We anticipate that the waves of the interest in specific issues will come and go, just as they have in the past. The most valuable contributions, however, will involve addressing real problems in real supply chains, and developing the theory to support the managerial decision making in those contexts.

(2) OM-Marketing Interface: Marketing is the key information gatekeeper between operations and product markets. Marketing is charged with determining what customers value (including cost, quality, and delivery characteristics) prior to product development; product positioning, pricing, and forecasting both before and after product launch; and promotions after product launch. The interdisciplinary research involving operations and marketing decisions goes back many decades, but there is ample opportunity to develop the models that are more comprehensive and have greater fidelity than the current state of the art. Many of the key questions at this interface involve behavioral aspects, providing opportunities to incorporate results from the growing bodies of empirical research on related topics.

(3) OM-Finance Interface: Capital equipment and inventories constitute a sizable portion of the assets of most manufacturing companies. Companies have long recognized the role and impact of these assets in their financial decision making, but it is only relatively recent that operations management researchers have begun to relate financial models and financial instruments to the procurement and management of these assets. Also, as secondary markets for a range of commodities and other products mature, there is increased potential for applying the financial insights developed in the context of complete markets to more traditional operational issues.

(4) OM-Organizations Interface: No plant manager anywhere would ignore the role of good people management in running an efficient operation. Yet, the research in our discipline has remained largely disjoint from the social science literature on human resource management and organizational behavior (OB). Our heritage has emphasized constructing normative mathematical models, and the OB literature is dominated by positive empirical findings. Operations management models have historically invoked oversimplified models of motivation, learning, creativity, and other such aspects of human behavior that are vital to the success of management policies in practice. Models that can maintain high levels of rigor while incorporating these elements will be richer and more realistic. In this area and other, high-quality descriptive and empirical work, including experimental analysis of behavior and decision making, often precedes prescriptive models. We see this integration as a critical need,

but recognize that its evolution will be slow. One initiative we have taken is to add to our editorial staff the ability to apply social science standards to empirical research.

(5) Service Operations: Service organizations are a large and growing part of the world economy. Operations management academics have struggled with a clear definition of what services are — and what research challenges they pose — relative to more traditional manufacturing contexts. Services are difficult to inventory so that variability must be buffered by capacity or time. Also, in many cases, a service transaction features simultaneous production and consumption with the customer as an integral part of this activity. This may amplify the human perceptual component of service quality relative to the consumption of manufactured goods. The search for the distinctive attributes of service operations continues, but may be taken up in specific service contexts. Financial services and call centers already have their own subliteratures. It is clear that health-care operations will be of increasing economic importance with the aging of the post-war baby boom. There remain many opportunities for research, not only on how to make existing service operations more effective and efficient, but on how to design, deploy, and operate systems offering new services, or old services via new technologies.

(6) Operations Strategy: There is a large literature on firm strategies in different competitive environments. There is currently less literature on functional strategies and how they interact with each other. There is considerable scope for research on which mosaics of functional (including operations) strategies are self-consistent and aligned with firm strategies in different competitive environments.

(7) Process Design and Improvements: Many quality programs have process improvement as their core theme, and the key applied tactic is managing the innovation process. Where do new ideas come from? How are they encouraged, nurtured, screened, and implemented? Process design poses similar challenges, but with fewer constraints on the eventual outcome. Earlier we alluded to the critical relationship between operations and organizations. A good process design must merge the physical flow system, social system, and information system into a self-consistent whole.

As the research community moves into these new areas and others, we have full faith in the classical tools of our trade and the classical objective of applying those tools to help real people make real decisions. We also recognize that we will need to augment these tools to address new challenges as they arise. As these few examples have demonstrated, the challenges before us are great, and they will call for the same sort of creativity and dedication to the task demonstrated by the scholars of the Big Bang. The upside potential for novel, seminal research has never been greater. We hope and expect that years from now an overview will be written acknowledging the significance and contributions of papers now being written.

Professional Vocabularies and Expressions

operations management	运作管理
vertical integration	纵向集成
scientific management	科学管理
linear programming	线性规划
network flow problem	网络流问题
inventory theory	库存论
dynamic programming	动态规划
machine maintenance	机器维护
queueing network	排队网络
game theory	博弈论
line balancing	平衡生产线
scheduling	调度
production planning	生产规划
inventory control	库存控制
lot sizing	批量问题
material requirements planning (MRP)	物料需求规划
just-in-time (JIT)	准时化
Toyota production system (TPS)	丰田生产系统
total quality management (TQM)	全面质量管理
economic equilibrium	经济均衡
organizational behavior (OB)	组织行为学

Notes

This is sympathetic with the classical mission: The academic forefathers in war-time OR teams were very focused on reality out of mission-critical necessity.

（将运作管理领域的研究与工业发展的现实相对应）这种做法与运作管理领域传统的使命是吻合的，因为战争年代的运筹学小组里的学术先驱们就在使命所必需的关键（问题）之外非常关注现实问题。

Discussion Questions:

1. Many researchers who have made their contributions to shape the area of operations

research or operations management are mentioned in this article. Please surf on the Internet and learn more about those in whom you are most interested.
2. The organizations such as Management Science and INFORMS are mentioned. Do we have similar journals or organizations that are dedicated to the development of the field of OR/OM?
3. What is your perception about the gap between research and the industrial reality of the field of OR/OM? As researchers or practitioners, what can we do to bridge the gap?
4. What do you think might be the future research areas in the domain of OR/OM based on the industrial reality of China?

CHAPTER 9

The Role of IE in Engineering Economics

9.1 Introduction

As we are now in a global economy with ever-increasing competition, the need for world-class performance cannot be ignored. This need implies, among other things, the continued emergence of world-class quality, information systems, ergonomics, and manufacturing systems. It also means that more firms are likely to invest in such areas to reach their strategic objectives. Of course, this brings us to a very specific topic — project justification.

It may seem trivial to state that an industrial project must be evaluated in order to justify it. However, the kinds of the projects that are needed today to survive in our competitive environment are quite different from their counterparts 20 or 30 years ago. They differ in terms of their technological content and in terms of their strategic implications for the firm. Whereas yesterday we were dealing with single machine replacement problems, we are now confronted with overall systems, programs, and processes.

The consequence of such complexity is that the traditional investment justification process fails to measure the proper value of projects such as computer-integrated manufacturing systems, information systems, and even ergonomics projects. It is well known that such a failure may result in wrong decisions. Poor investment justification processes may lead to poor decision making with respect to today's projects: Good projects might be rejected, and bad ones might be accepted. This seems to be the fate of several new technologies (including industrial ergonomics) that are not implemented because their prospective return is not satisfactory. Among the causes of such poor ratings is the inability to properly estimate the benefits and costs of today's proposal.

As a result, management must resort to the "leap of faith" approach to justify new systems that are intuitively sound from a strategic point of view but that are not convincing economically. From such considerations it may seem that firms don't have any other choices other than to spend their capital, whatever the cost, and go ahead with implementing the resulting changes that come with these projects. Such a strategy would be dangerous.

If it is true that the firms that do not invest in strategic projects due to poor investment analyses may be in a serious predicament in the future, it also would be risky for them to systematically go ahead with such projects when their rate of return is not acceptable. It may also be true that under certain conditions strategic projects may not be the right thing to do. After all, investments such as information technology or computer-integrated manufacturing systems are only as good as their contributions to the overall strategy of the firm.

9.2 Engineering economics

The role of engineering economics is to correctly assess the appropriateness of a given project, estimate its value, and justify it from an economic standpoint. If projects are not acceptable, then the evaluation process that has been used to reach this conclusion should also explain their poor returns. That same process should also indicate ways to improve the investment proposal to make it more attractive to management.

Engineering economy has been part of engineers' training (and of IE curricula, of course) for a long time. Historically, it was used for the projects that had only operational implications for the firm. However, as noted above, today's projects may have strategic implications as well. As a consequence, engineering economy is likely to be important for both engineers and management.

However, engineering economy cannot do it alone. It must be part of the process that includes not only engineers but also management accountants; marketing, quality, and health and safety specialists; and others within the firm. Such a process should foster interdisciplinary thinking, not unlike the parallel or concurrent engineering used in product design.

At this point it is certainly worthwhile to emphasize the role of IEs in this process. As industrial engineers are trained in both technology and engineering economy, they are able to bridge the gap between mechanical, electrical, and computer engineering and ergonomics, on the one hand, and management accounting on the other. The highly qualified engineers designing equipment for flexible manufacturing systems (FMS) or information systems, while aware of the technology with which they are dealing, are not necessarily trained to translate technological characteristics into economic and strategic terms.

At the other end of the spectrum, management accountants may be well aware of the business needs, strategic aims, and their organization's financial position, but cannot understand the capabilities of new technologies. Not surprisingly, communication barriers occur. Industrial engineering's main contribution to the economic evaluation process is linking technology to economics. That is where engineering economy comes into the picture. The background of IEs in engineering economy provides them with cost models that link technology with the economics of accounting (Figure 9-1).

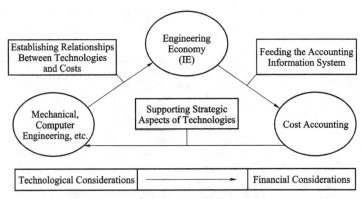

Figure 9-1   The role of IE in project evaluation

As the industrial environment has changed drastically, engineering economy has evolved accordingly. Indeed, its aim is not only to compute net present values (NPVs) or internal rates of return (IRRs), but also to design cost models and evaluation processes that can be used within decision support systems for a variety of technological projects.

Armed with the economic models tailored to specific technologies, industrial engineers are able to measure, for instance, the cost of flexibility and, in turn, help integrate this figure in accounting cost systems and financial justification models. By including engineering economy in the justification process, firms are therefore better equipped for solving the complex justification problems that involve the technical and financial specialists working together in an interdisciplinary group.

Such a successful group is likely to shed light on such questions as: What is the rate of the return of ergonomics? What is the payback of a six-sigma program? What are the benefits of this new information technology? What is the value of flexibility associated with this FMS? It is unreasonable to think that one person would be able to answer such difficult questions satisfactorily. The need for a project evaluation group thus seems more appropriate in the face of the competitive environment within which firms must compete, on the one hand, and the complexity of the projects involved, on the other.

Such a concept is certainly compatible with open accounting, which is implemented by firms and aimed at sharing financial information inside the organization. There is another practical advantage of starting a group that has diversity: The persons involved agree to have a unified vision of costs and benefits related to a new technology (if they want to work effectively). Lack of agreement on the nature of costs and benefits may lead to controversies over the project and failure of the justification effort.

A project evaluation group, like any group or task force in the firm, should follow a process. In a way, economic justification itself is a process. This may not be obvious, but to evaluate a project, especially one of those proposed today, a great deal of analysis must be done. The justification process can be defined in terms of steps as illustrated in Figure 9-2.

86 CHAPTER 9

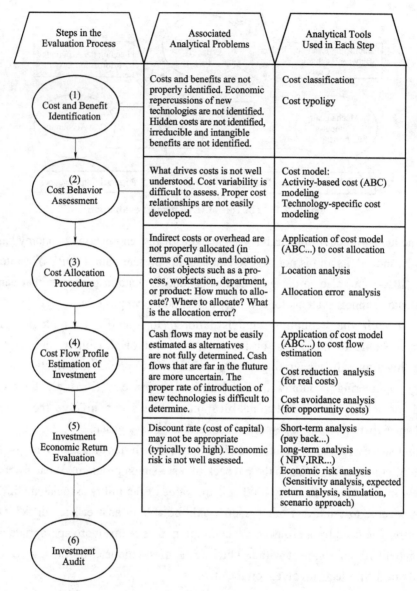

Figure 9-2 Evaluation process for technological investments

9.3 Steps in the evaluation process

An important advantage of such a process is that the overall evaluation problem is divided into smaller subproblems that can be tackled more easily. Moreover, this process is able to give a sense of direction to engineering economy analysts and to the nonspecialists who are confronted with justifying their proposals and have nowhere to start. Such a process is needed for the kinds of the projects that are found in today's proposals (e.g., new manufacturing technologies, new computer/information systems, total quality programs, and ergonomics projects).

Ideally, all of the steps in Figure 9-2 should be performed; however, depending on the specific situation, some of these steps may require more or less effort. But the implicit or explicit in any justification procedure is the fact that the nature of costs and benefits be identified. Then their behavior is modeled in one way or another (Engineering economists, cost estimators, and traditional and management accountants all use some cost models). Afterward, costs are allocated to specific cost objects such as a production/assembly line, department, workstation, or product. Then, an estimate of future benefits resulting from the project is performed. The evaluation of the project is done in terms of both short-and long-term standpoints along with a risk analysis (which should be done, if possible).

These steps result in an estimate of the return of a project. Another step is sometimes done after project implementation, namely a project audit. This last step is not part of project evaluations *per se*, but it is wise to include it. The correctness of future cash flow estimations depends on the reliability of the evaluation process. Improvements in this area come from recognizing and avoiding past errors in cash flow estimation. This is the main purpose of a project audit.

9.4 Analytical problems encountered

Not surprisingly, the steps described here represent a challenge for the analysts confronted with a thorough evaluation of a strategic investment. Each of these steps helps define the particular problems that must be solved within the justification process. These problems are common to several kinds of projects. They have been found in justifying investments in new manufacturing technologies, new computer/information systems, total quality programs, and ergonomic interventions — the very projects with which IEs and other engineers are typically confronted.

Take, for instance, the problem of identifying the costs and benefits of a project. Many studies have been done to identify, describe, classify, and quantify the economic value of the flexibility of new manufacturing systems such as FMS. Flexibility is one of the main economic advantages (or strategic benefits) of such systems; yet its definition is multidimensional and covers many aspects of organizations. It is a classic example of cost identification that requires special analysis. Another example of difficult cost identification is that of quality, especially the costs related to poor quality. Classifying certain quality costs is not straightforward. Also, it is not obvious to show that some overhead or so-called indirect quality costs are due to quality problems.

But the most challenging experience associated with cost and benefit identification is probably with information technology (IT). This class of investment has proved to be complex and somewhat elusive, even for IT specialists. There are several reasons for this. Without going into detail, let's say that IT has far-reaching implications for firms in general, as its enabling capabilities can significantly modify business processes. This step of cost identification is far from trivial and should not be taken lightly.

The same can be said for the other steps of the process. In the second step, cost behavior analysis, the main problem is how to correctly model specific costs in terms of their drivers. In the area of new manufacturing systems (e.g., FMS), special models and approaches need to be used if the cost of flexibility is going to be modeled. Information technology is another example that shows the importance of performing this step. Take programming costs for instance. The drivers of this cost are likely to be the programming language, quality of the software tools, complexity and size of the system, and number of functions to be programmed.

In the third step, cost allocation, much has been said on properly allocating overhead (indirect costs) to specific products and workstations. This is because traditional allocation procedures do not take into account the complexity of these costs when automation projects are involved and therefore use wrong drivers. This allocation problem has been found especially crucial for new manufacturing systems (which involve high automation), information technologies, and ergonomics, where health and safety costs are not easily traced to workstations.

The main difficulties for the analyst are to determine the proper amount of cost to allocate, where to allocate it, and to make sure the allocation error (if any) is kept to a minimum. The allocation error depends on the quality of the cost model used. It is well known that the improper allocation of indirect production costs (e.g., setup, warehousing, production planning and control, and tooling) impedes the implementation of automation and flexibility within the firm.

In the fourth step, cash flow profile estimation, the analyst is faced with another set of problems. The importance of having a valid cost model cannot be overemphasized at this point, as future cash flows are to be estimated. It is also here that all proper alternatives should be determined. This is one of the fundamental principles of engineering economy. Its application is particularly important for cash flow computations, since cash flows are determined from the differences between alternatives (another fundamental principle), including the "do nothing" alternative, which can be very costly and risky in certain situations. Applying these engineering economy principles becomes crucial when dealing with strategic technological projects.

9.5 Tools of engineering economy

As seen here, the evaluation process can be overwhelming to the individuals who attempt to justify their projects. Fortunately, significant research has been made in this area for the kinds of the projects mentioned here. Without claiming that engineering economy has solved all problems, it can be said that help is available. Engineering economy can contribute to several steps of this evaluation process.

For instance, cost typologies for quality control, computerized information systems, ergonomics interventions, and new manufacturing systems give a comprehensive view of pertinent costs. In the area of manufacturing, several flexibility typologies are used to define the costs that are related to the flexibility of new manufacturing technologies. A summary of cost typologies for these typical investments is given in Figure 9-3.

Total Quality Processes and Programs	Computer and Information Systems	Ergonomics Interventions Programs	Manufacturing Systems
• Prevention costs • Appraisal costs • Internal failure costs • External failure costs	• Technological costs • System costs • Support costs	• Insurance costs • Work-related costs • Perturbation costs	• Technological costs • Operational costs • Support costs

Figure 9-3   Simplified cost typologies for different classes of projects

These typologies start by pooling costs in families so that similar costs are grouped together for further analysis. For instance, quality costs are usually classified into four categories. Prevention costs cover those related to the activities aimed at preventing quality problems. Appraisal costs are related to detection and measuring activities necessary to assess quality. Failure costs are associated with the quality problems that occur inside and outside the organization.

Computer and information system costs can be classified into three categories: technological costs, system costs, and support costs. Technological costs are related to computer hardware, opportunity costs due to equipment obsolescence, technological risk associated with new information technology, and the cost of complexity in terms of reach (the number of the people that are connected) and range (interactions provided by the new system). System costs are more software related and include the cost of studies, software development costs, training costs, and business reorganization costs. Finally, support costs are those necessary to operate and maintain the system; they include installation costs, facility layout costs, debugging costs, security costs, and insurance costs.

Likewise, manufacturing system costs are classified into three categories: technological costs, which include the cost of manufacturing and/or material-handling equipment and the cost of studies; operational costs, which include direct labor costs and the costs related to flexibility; and support costs, which include engineering, planning and control, setup, tooling, maintenance, and material handling. Support costs are also related to flexibility. For instance, engineering, tooling, and material handling costs due to parts revision are measured by the time and cost for these changes; the lower the costs, the more flexible the system.

Once the main cost categories are defined, then more comprehensive cost descriptions are developed; the overall picture of costs is then available for analysts. These full-blown typologies give extensive cost classifications in terms of discrete vs. periodical costs and in terms of tangible, irreducible, and intangible costs. They also include real costs vs.

opportunity costs. This last type of cost is usually part of the projects such as those mentioned here.

As IEs are exposed during their training to new manufacturing technologies such as information technology (IT), total quality management (TQM), and ergonomics, they can certainly contribute to cost and benefit identification of related projects. Furthermore, their background in systems optimization provides them with an overall perspective on such technologies whose effects are organization-wide and cross-functional. This overall picture is important when prospective technological projects must be aligned with business strategy.

Tools also have been developed for cost modeling (step 2 of the evaluation process). Major approaches include activity-based costing (ABC) and technology-specific cost modeling. Activity-based accounting came into being as a result of poor allocation methods. Traditional accounting methods could not determine the proper amount of indirect costs to cost the objects such as products and workstations. ABC was then devised as a new allocation method. But ABC is also used as a tool for modeling costs in general. ABC explains what drives support costs such as scheduling, maintenance, and material handling. As indirect costs are most important in new technologies, ABC has proved to be a useful cost modeling approach for decision making, including project justification.

Again, IEs can make unique contributions here. ABC modeling is as much an industrial engineering tool as an accounting one. Formal ABC cost models are written from an engineering point of view and can be readily understood and used by IEs. In fact, ABC can be viewed as an extension of operation, workflow, and process analyses.

ABC is also used in step 4, where cash flows are estimated. Cost improvement or reduction and cost avoidance are part of that step. The quality of the cost model will determine the effectiveness of the estimation of future cash flows. Cost reduction analysis determines the real (out-of-pocket) cash flows of alternatives with respect to the *status quo* (the "do nothing" alternative). Cost avoidance analysis determines the cost avoided, including the lost revenues (opportunity costs) resulting from the investment.

Step 5 is the evaluation itself, where the criteria such as the NPV, the IRR, and payback are used. The cost models tailored to specific technologies are usually integrated in the NPV calculations. For instance, the NPV of new manufacturing systems (such as FMS) includes the value of flexibility. This value translates, in dollar amount, all the kinds of the flexibility of the new technology. The overall flexibility value depends on the cost of this flexibility and the revenues they generate.

Finally, it is in this step that economic risk analysis is performed. The economic risk can be substantial and depends, among other things, on the technological risk of the investments such as those discussed here. Engineering economy provides tools (e.g., sensitivity analysis, risk analysis, and simulation) to assess such a risk. These tools, of course, are part of the IE domain.

9.6 The potential of IE for the firm

Attempting to evaluate and justify complex and strategic capital investments is far from simple. Not only does it require the expertise of several members of the firm, but also all this knowledge must be funneled through a systematic process. Industrial engineers are uniquely positioned to contribute to such a process. Their technical background makes it possible for them to bridge the gap between purely technical and financial aspects of an industrial project. Because they are well versed in the topics such as total quality, ergonomics, information systems, and manufacturing systems (all essential in today's competitive environment), their ability to play key roles in complex capital investment justification is likely to make them attractive assets to management.

Professional Vocabularies and Expressions

engineering economics	工程经济学
information system	信息系统
ergonomics	功效学
manufacturing system	制造系统
project justification	项目论证
computer integrated manufacturing system	计算机集成制造系统
investment analysis	投资分析
rate of return	收益率
internal rates of return (IRR)	内部收益率
concurrent engineering	并行工程
flexible manufacturing system (FMS)	柔性制造系统
net present value (NPV)	净现值
risk analysis	风险分析
project audit	项目审计
overhead	企业一般管理费
indirect cost	间接成本
cash flow	现金流
profile estimation	轮廓评估
quality cost	质量成本
prevention cost	预防成本
appraisal cost	估价成本
failure cost	失败成本
technological cost	技术成本

system cost	系统成本
support cost	辅助成本
equipment obsolescence	设备老化
direct labor cost	直接劳动力成本
tangible cost	有形成本
irreducible cost	既约成本
intangible cost	无形成本
real cost	实际成本
opportunity cost	机会成本
total quality management (TQM)	全面质量管理
activity-based costing (ABC)	基于活动的成本分析
sensitivity analysis	灵敏度分析

Notes

1. It may seem trivial to state that an industrial project must be evaluated in order to justify it.

为了论证某一项目，必须对其进行评价，这样一个论断可能显得无足轻重。

2. As a result, management must resort to the "leap of faith" approach to justify new systems that are intuitively sound from a strategic point of view but that are not convincing economically.

结果，管理层不得不求助于"信任的跳跃"，以便从战略的高度论证那些直观上感觉可行，但经济上不能令人信服的新系统。

3. Armed with the economic models tailored to specific technologies, industrial engineers are able to measure, for instance, the cost of flexibility and, in turn, help integrate this figure in accounting cost systems and financial justification models.

掌握了适应各种特定技术的经济模型后，工业工程师就能够对诸如柔性成本等指标进行度量，并且能够反过来协助将这些数值与会计成本系统和金融论证模型集成起来。

4. Without going into detail, let's say that IT has far-reaching implications for firms in general, as its enabling capabilities can significantly modify business processes.

简言之，信息技术对一般的企业都具有深远的影响，因为它有能力对企业的业务流程进行重要修正。

5. Without claiming that engineering economy has solved all problems, it can be said that help is available.

尽管不能说工程经济学已经解决了所有问题，但可以对问题的解决起到帮助作用。

6. These full-blown typologies give extensive cost classifications in terms of discrete vs.

periodical costs and in terms of tangible, irreducible, and intangible costs.

这些成熟的成本类型学根据离散成本和周期性成本以及有形成本、既约成本和无形成本对项目中所涉及的成本进行了广泛的分类。

7. Activity-based accounting came into being as a result of poor allocation methods.

质量低劣的成本分配方法导致了基于活动的会计统计方法的产生。

8. Attempting to evaluate and justify complex and strategic capital investments is far from simple.

评价和论证复杂的战略资本投资方案绝对不是一个人可以单打独斗的事。

Discussion Questions:

1. This article outlines three roles of IE in the engineering economic evaluation of a project. They are: feeding the accounting information system, establishing the relationships between technologies and costs, and supporting the strategic aspects of technologies. Further elaborate on these roles of IE.
2. Cost analysis is essential to engineering economy. How can IE methods and techniques facilitate engineering economists with regard to cost analysis?

CHAPTER 10

Systems Engineering and Engineering Management

With the globalization of our manufacturing base, the efficiencies derived from advances in information technology (and the subsequent decrease in mid-management positions), and the shifting of our economy to be service-based, the roles of the technical organization and engineering manager have changed. The 21st century technical organization must be concerned with ① maintaining a strong business base of products or services in a fluctuating economy, ② keeping a highly qualified and trained staff of engineers, scientists, and technicians in a rapidly changing technological environment, and ③ demonstrating a high level of capability maturity.

Meanwhile, the 21st century engineering manager must now be able to understand and operate in this new paradigm. Systems engineering (SE) is a key aspect of this paradigm. Outsourcing, reduced time to market, customer-driven requirements, and just-in-time inventory are just some of the business practices required to achieve the concerns just outlined. The engineers who practise in the services and manufacturing domains must be able to understand the tools and processes available in defining the fuzzy front end associated with generating conceptual ideas and developing the architectures of innovative and efficient product solutions.

In the academic world, SE and engineering management (EM) are typically taught in the same academic department. The principles of SE are invaluable for enabling practicing engineering managers to deliver effective products on time and within the budget that meets customer expectations.

10.1 Nature of system development

A system is the integrated composition of the elements, which provides a capability to satisfy a stated need or objective. These integrated elements can be the products of hardware and software, people, facilities, and procedures. To develop a system successfully, engineers must first define the problem that exists, identify the mission requirements (or business drivers) of the organization(s) needing the problem to be solved, evaluate high-level concepts for solving the problem, select the concept that makes the most sense in light of the mission requirements, develop an operational concept around the selected concept, create system-level requirements, create architectures and derived requirements for the subsystems, components, and configuration items consistent with the decomposition of the system, design the integration and test processes for the parts of the system, conduct the integration and test processes for the parts of the system, manufacture/assemble the parts of the system, deploy the system, train operators and maintainers, operate/maintain the system, refine the system, and finally, retire the system. All of this life-cycle activity is focused on the product or system to be delivered and used by the organization(s) with the driving need. The system development activities must be brought to bear on the development system, manufacturing system, deployment system, training system, maintenance system, refinement system, and retirement system throughout the life cycle.

The front end of this system development process (definition of the problem through the delivery of an operating system) has typically taken years (often five to ten) in many market segments. There has been substantial pressure from stakeholders, marketers, and managers to decrease this time to months or a couple of years. The increasing rate of technological development has both helped and hindered this effort to reduce time to market. More and more system components exist, waiting to be integrated; yet technological churn and competition increase the selection and integration of the right components.

The last decade has seen the trends of the products or systems having more versions available (though there is often a reduction of feature explosion available to the customer for each version). Also, products are living longer via more upgrades, often quite frequent upgrades to the product. Finally, the concept of a product platform is gaining acceptance in industries from power tools to automobiles to software products to military systems. A product platform is an integrated and interoperable set of components that can be used to create many different products, e.g., power saws, sanders, and drills.

These changes in system development are taking place while many technical organizations are being reorganized. The resulting organizations are flatter and provide reduced flexibility in the career path of the engineers (Figure 10-1). Industry is making far greater use of multidisciplinary teams and asking academia to provide increased experience in teamwork at the undergraduate level.

Figure 10-2 is a commonly used generalization to explain the importance of good SE. The system life cycle is shown on the horizontal axis. The total life-cycle cost of the system is shown on the vertical axis; any overruns are built into this 100% life-cycle cost as well as reworks due to design mistakes and testing failures. The lower curve in Figure 10-2 shows how the money is spent over the life cycle, rising slowly in the beginning but at an increasing rate. Most of the money is spent in the construction and early operational period.

96 CHAPTER 10

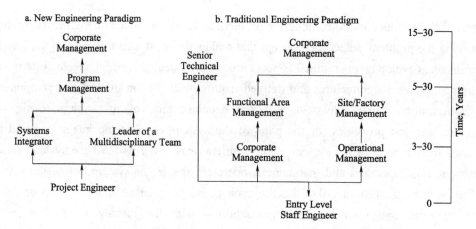

Figure 10-1 Traditional versus new engineering paradigm

The expenditures slow down again as the system is being retired. The upper curve shows the rate at which cost expenditures are committed by design decisions that get made; these commitments rise rapidly as early decisions with far reaching impacts are made and slow down as more and more detailed decisions get made. Many decisions are made implicitly as design alternatives are ignored or disappear due to the focus of the engineers on other problems. This is clearly a major concern of engineering managers.

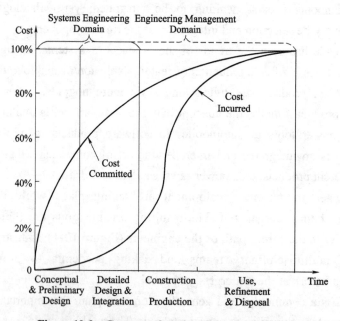

Figure 10-2 Costs as a function of product life cycle

10.2 Systems engineering and engineering management

There is a substantial overlap between the disciplines of engineering management and systems engineering, and yet, there is substantial confusion in the two professions about what comprises the other.

10.2.1 Systems engineering

Buede (2000) presents seven different definitions of SE. We chose the definition used by the U.S. government because it is still relevant and is the most descriptive for the purposes of this article. Military Standard 499A (1974) defines systems engineering as the application of scientific and engineering efforts to:

(1) Transform an operational need into a description of system performance parameters and a system configuration through the use of an iterative process of definition, synthesis, analysis, design, test, and evaluation;

(2) Integrate the related technical parameters and ensure the compatibility of all related, functional, and program interfaces in a manner that optimizes the total system definition and design; and

(3) Integrate reliability, maintainability, safety, and survivability, human, and other such factors into the total engineering effort to meet cost, schedule, and technical performance objectives.

World War II was the first time people needed to integrate and coordinate the complex organizations focused on materials, people, and information in order to accomplish the prescribed objectives. After the war, many felt the techniques could be generalized and applied to other fields. Many other types of "quantitative management" techniques also grew out of World War II. By the late 1950s, systems thinking focused on the methodologies and processes needed to define the SE discipline. Numerous formal systems design processes currently exist.

10.2.2 Engineering management

Few formal definitions exist in the literature for EM. Kocaolgu (1984) defined EM as a field of study in five interrelated categories, namely:

(1) Management of Engineering and Scientists: Motivation and leadership in engineering, technical obsolescence, communications transition from technical specialty to technical management.

(2) Management of Research, Development, and Engineering (RD&E) Projects: Selection, evaluation, scheduling and control of technical projects.

(3) Management of Technical Organizations: Design of technical organizations, authority/responsibility patterns in functional project, matrix, and venture organizations, the role of participative management in technical organizations.

(4) Management of Technical Resources: Use of statistics, operations research, decision theory and computer simulation in resource optimization, management of raw materials, technical manpower planning, financial management in engineering.

(5) Management of Technological Systems: Management of innovation, entrepreneurship,

98 CHAPTER 10

technological planning and forecasting, technological risk management, engineering law, research and development management, and productivity.

Babcock (1996) perhaps best describes the role of the traditional engineer versus that of other types of management in that "the engineering manager is distinguished from other managers because he or she possesses both the ability to apply engineering principles and a skill in organizing and directing people and projects. He or she is uniquely qualified for two types of jobs; the management of technical functions (such as design or production) in almost any enterprise, or the management of broader functions (such as marketing or top management) in a high technology enterprise."

10.3 Overlap, difference, and synergies

10.3.1 Functional perspective

If you build upon Babcock's definition, an engineering manager must be able to apply engineering principles such as SE. The role of a system engineer within a product life cycle is graphically demonstrated in Figure 10-3. Whereas the EM can be responsible for any of the steps in the product cycle or even the total product life cycle, the SE is usually more focused on the early stages of the product cycles as shown in Figure 10-3.

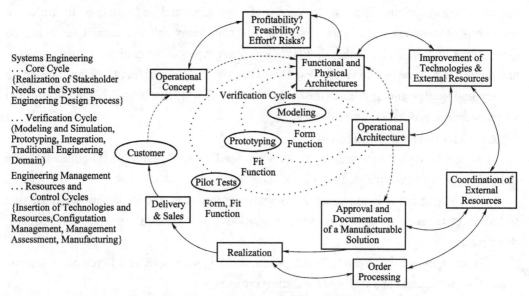

Figure 10-3 Product life cycle

10.3.2 Career development perspective

The career paths of the system engineer and engineering manager are very different. The EM often comes from the ranks of the traditional engineer. The EM career path is typically characterized by progressive responsibility for larger systems (See Figure 10-1). These are typically larger systems within the same product line (e.g., gears for a transmission, power train, etc.). Most system engineers also come from the ranks of traditional engineers. Like EM, there are few undergraduate programs in SE; however, the number of SE programs at the undergraduate level is on the increase. After an initial apprentice position, they typically move into the role of system integrators. Within most organizations, the SE functions as part of an interdisciplinary effort.

 Professional Vocabularies and Expressions

systems engineering	系统工程
engineering management	工程管理
outsourcing	外包
system/product life cycle	系统/产品生命周期
iterative process	反复/迭代过程
reliability	可靠性
maintainability	可维护性
quantitative management	定量化管理
innovation management	创新管理
entrepreneurship management	企业家管理
technological risk management	技术风险管理
research and development management	研发管理
operations research	运筹学
decision theory	决策理论
computer simulation	计算机仿真
apprentice position	见习职位，实习岗位

 Notes

1. To develop a system successfully, engineers must first define ... the system.

句中 must 后面的部分为一系列的并列结构，详细阐述了系统开发生命周期过程中需要完成的各项活动。

2. A product platform is an integrated and interoperable set of components that can be used to create many different products, e.g., power saws, sanders, and drills.

一个产品开发平台是指一组可以集成和互换的零件，基于这些零件可以产生多种不同的产品，如电锯、打磨机和电钻等。

3. Military Standard 499A (1974) defines systems engineering as ... and technical

performance objectives.

这里给出了系统工程的定义。可翻译为：

1974年的美国军方标准499A把系统工程定义为将科学和工程知识用于实现如下功能的应用：

（1）经过从定义、合成、分析、设计、测试到评价的不断反复过程，将运作需求转换为对系统行为参数的描述以及系统配置；

（2）以能够优化整个系统的定义和设计的方式集成相关的技术参数并确保所有相关的功能和程序界面相互兼容；

（3）在满足成本、交期和技术要求的情况下从工程角度综合考虑可靠性、可维护性、安全性、生命力、人因学以及其他因素。

4. Kocaolgu (1984) defined EM as a field of study in … and productivity.

这里给出了工程管理的定义。可翻译为：

1984年Kocaolgu将工程管理定义为一个面向如下5种相互关联的管理类型的研究领域：

（1）工程和科学管理：研究工程领域的动机和领导、技术的废弃、从技术专业化到技术管理的过渡等。

（2）研究、开发与工程项目管理：研究技术项目的选择、评价、规划和控制。

（3）技术型组织的管理：研究技术型组织的设计和功能型、项目型、矩阵型和风险型组织的职能模式设计以及全员参与管理在技术型组织中的角色。

（4）技术资源管理：将统计学、运筹学、决策理论和计算机仿真应用在工程领域的资源优化、原材料管理、技术人员规划和金融管理。

（5）技术系统管理：研究创新管理、企业家管理、技术规划和预测、技术风险管理、工程法律、研发管理和生产率管理。

Discussion Questions:

This paper has made it clear about the relationship between systems engineering (SE) and engineering management (EM). Try to set up the relationship between IE and SE, and between IE and EM. Further identify the overlaps, differences and synergies among them.

第三篇

现代工业工程

CHAPTER 11

Concurrent Engineering

11.1 Introduction

According to Department of Defense (DoD) Regulations 5000.1 and 5000.2, concurrent engineering (CE) will be used for the development of all future military systems. The primary requirements for successfully implementing a CE philosophy are management support, enhanced communication, team building and appropriate tool use. Where CE has been successful, much credit is attributed to the involvement of senior management in establishing the goals of the improved quality, cost and schedule; in forming the teams of the qualified people; and in providing the teams with the necessary tools and resources. Management must commit the necessary funding and resources for a successful CE program, and they must allow ample time for the new philosophy to generate benefits.

To ensure that the U.S. Army Missile Command (MICOM) managed weapon systems adhered to the CE design philosophy, a CE steering committee was formed. This steering committee, consisting of command-wide representation, examined current design environments at MICOM, and determined some impediments to CE implementation. The committee determined that most personnel had not received adequate information about CE, and in general there were many misconceptions concerning its requirements. Therefore, it was decided that additional training should be provided to both MICOM and project management personnel. The production engineering division (PED) of the Systems Engineering and Production Directorate was tasked by the steering committee to develop a training program to assist in the advancement of the CE concept and provide guidelines for CE implementation.

11.2 The training philosophy

The content of the CE training modules presents a well-rounded knowledge of all important aspects of CE. Training, which addresses a philosophy, can often digress into an intense training course on a specific tool or technology that supports that philosophy. That was a pitfall which was avoided with the formation of this training. While tools and methodologies were given adequate coverage, more philosophical aspects of CE (i.e. improving communication, organizational and team structure, etc.) were not slighted. To achieve the right mix of training, seven training modules were created. Each module addresses a different, equally important aspect of CE implementation:

Module 1: Introduction to MICOM CE steering committee;
Module 2: CE overview;
Module 3: Team building for CE;
Module 4: CE tools and methodologies;
Module 5: The MICOM CE design process;
Module 6: Government/Contractor roles/responsibilities;
Module 7: Program specific CE activities.

11.2.1 MICOM CE steering committee

The first module used in the CE training course serves to inform the training participants of the existence and mission of the MICOM CE steering committee. This was considered an important first step in the training process. It is imperative that the recipients of this training realize the commitment of top management to the CE design philosophy. By demonstrating this commitment at the outset of the training program, participants should realize the dedication and determination of MICOM management to successfully implement CE.

The CE team that will be trained using these modules will consist of managers and engineers representing many functional areas of MICOM. To reinforce this idea of multi-disciplinary teamwork, the CE steering committee consists of representatives from these same diverse areas. By emphasizing that the steering committee "practises what it preaches," the point will be made from the outset as to what is required for CE success.

11.2.2 CE overview

The CE overview module is used to give all participants a set of common definitions and terminology for the ensuing training. One of the most prevalent problems in implementing CE is the lack of a commonly agreed upon definition for the term. For the purpose of the training modules, the definition as developed by the Institute for Defense Analysis was used. Many other misconceptions are related to CE. In some cases, these misconceptions have become the barriers to successful CE implementation. This module discusses the confusion commonly noted throughout the MICOM and DoD community. Common misunderstandings, such as the difference between CE, systems engineering and total quality management, are explained.

In preparing this training module, the lessons learned and critical factors for success were captured from CE leaders in industry and the government. From this information, as well as MICOM's own lessons learned, CE implementation guidelines were developed and included. This portion of the training discusses the importance of management-driven implementation, adequate funding profiles, multi-functional teaming, training, customer/supplier involvement, integrated require-merits definition, integrated product/process design, and CE tools and computer-based support initiatives.

Upon completion of the CE overview module, participants should have a good understanding of what CE is and is not. With everyone working with a common set of assumptions, the training moves to the importance of team building.

11.2.3 Team building for CE

Multi-disciplinary teams are at the very heart of CE because, when properly constructed, they contain the intelligence base for a successful program. CE involves integrating the contributions of diverse specialists. These teams facilitate the optimization of all important measures of a product's function — performance, producibility, ease of maintenance, reliability, cost and quality. Management forms a team of specialists who have knowledge in the different phases of the product's life cycle to concurrently engineer both the product and downstream processes for production and support.

The problem with developing and maintaining a CE team is that most people are not accustomed to working (or trained to work) in teams. The first lesson of the module establishes how CE team members are selected, what part they play as individuals, and how they become a working unit. A team dynamics discussion and group exercises are an important aspect of this lesson. The second lesson focuses on the mechanics of the team in order to facilitate an increase in effectiveness.

This module also stresses that the voice of the customer must be represented to ensure requirements are correctly stated and understood by the CE team. All program requirements should have their foundation in a need or the expectation of the customer, internal or external. At the same time, CE teams must maintain a balance between the customer's needs and expectations and a reasonably scoped program.

11.2.4 CE tools and methodologies

Throughout industry and government, there are many proponents for the use of multi-disciplined teams for successful CE implementation, or for the use of CE-related tools and methodologies as the needed ingredient for success. MICOM believes both are required to truly optimize the design process. During discussions on CE tools with various sources in industry and government, it became obvious there were several misconceptions and barriers associated with CE tool/methodology implementation. First, most technical personnel appeared interested only in computer-based tools. This led to management's misinterpretation that all CE tools required new computer systems and software. One of the objectives of this training module was to inform the MICOM design community of the array of tools and methodologies available to them.

This module included an examination of a number of technologies currently being used in government and industry, and how these technologies have or can be more fully integrated into more comprehensive design tools. The technologies researched and analyzed included, but were not limited to Taguchi methods, quality function deployment, rapid prototyping, computer-aided design, computer-aided manufacturing, computer-aided process planning, design for assembly/manufacturability, design for reusability, design for maintainability and design for reliability.

Technological innovations have vastly improved the arsenal of tools available to the system engineer. However, there is still a lack of required integration of the design tools. The first step in integrating the design tools is to understand where they should be utilized in the product life cycle. Training addressed this issue by identifying various technologies and relating those to the system life cycle phases.

11.2.5 MICOM CE design process

The MICOM CE design process module was developed to provide a CE design process specific to MICOM's organizational structure and mission and functions. The module is intended to be used as a handbook to assist new project leaders in understanding each organization's area of expertise and the level of the input they have during each life cycle phase. Stressing the importance of the communication and knowledge of one's own organization, this module presented the life-cycle model with each MICOM organization's role defined. For example, 23 directorates/offices within MICOM worked with the CE steering committee to define their primary activities, major areas of input, and milestone design review (MDR) required documents into which they provide input.

The module instructs participants on the steps required to ensure that all necessary players are used appropriately in each life cycle phase of the project. For example, the project manager first uses the CE design team functional makeup model to determine the functional areas typically represented on the CE team during the particular life cycle phase of the program. The project manager then utilizes the module handbook to obtain the detailed information on each of the MICOM organizations that would be involved. This information includes the organization's mission, function, and major activities during the life cycle phase. From these tools and program-specific information, the project manager can determine the team's necessary makeup, and determine how each member will support the team.

11.2.6 Government/contractor roles and responsibilities

The successful implementation of CE will require communication channels to be established and used not only between functions, but also between the contractor and the government. In recent years, the DoD and its contractors have been willing to reexamine the traditional roles each has historically played in design process. Most notably, they have shown willingness to openly share information, and work as partners to solve problems rather than to establish blame. This has been a keystone to their successes.

The stereotypes attributed to both government and contractor personnel have contributed to the difficulty in defining CE integration into a project encompassing government and contractor CE teams. In order to understand these stereotypes, training module developers asked both types of personnel the following: "If you were drawing a caricature of a typical government/contractor person, what would you include?"

Industry personnel stated that the government person would be wearing a sign stating that "He/she was the government"; would be carrying a multitude of specifications and standards with a label saying "Just do it"; and would have a red ink pen in hand to mark up program deliverables.

The government personnel stated that the contractor person would be holding a bottle of snake oil for sale, would have their hand stretched out wanting more money, and have information hidden in their back pocket. Although this was a humorous way to obtain information, it did provide vast insight into the mistrust and negative views which can be involved.

Contractor personnel also highlighted concerns over a lack of definitive requirements in requests for proposals (RFPs) and funding variations over the course of a program. Conversely, the government personnel stated that, due to the reduction in defense funding, contractors will agree to anything in order to win a contract, while knowing that they may not have the expertise to adequately complete the contract within the cost and schedule. The fundamental mistrust that underlies contractor-government relations results in a lack of cooperation and undermines attempts to work as a team.

Although these broad-based concerns were highlighted by many different sources, it was evident that many government/contractor programs had managed to eliminate the issue of mistrust. The personnel in these programs worked at developing long-term relationships based on respect. All members of the project team believed that if the program failed, they failed. It was also noted that, in these programs, government personnel always brought something to the table. Typically, the government is viewed as an overseer, but in these cases they brought previously performed research, military parts experts, industrial base knowledge, lessons learned, and other information to the team.

This training module strives to take this concept of teamwork one step further through implementation of CE throughout the project. Most DoD contractors, at least at the prime level, are attempting to utilize CE teams. The government is now attempting to do the same. This training module provides the participant with a simplistic model that serves as the framework for this new teamwork. The model describes the lines of communication between the two teams and addresses information flow. For example, currently it is common for most of the information flow between the government and the contractor to be between two engineering specialists (low-level communication) or through the project managers (high-level communication). With the advent of CE, many sources believe that all work should be performed in the team environment and that government engineering specialist to contractor engineering specialist communications should be reduced or eliminated. The MICOM CE steering committee does not believe this is appropriate or realistic. Although design decisions and problem resolutions will be handled in the team environment, the one-on-one relationship is absolutely necessary to achieve the trust and resolve the day-to-day issues necessary for a successful program. The model also provides for the creation of supporting teams made up of the government and contractor personnel to address critical problem areas, on an basis as needed.

11.2.7 Program specific CE activities

The last training module, program specific CE activities, is used to put the participants to work on their program, using the CE design philosophy that was covered in the previous modules. This serves several purposes. First, as training is completed, team members have the opportunity to immediately employ what they have learned. There is no time delay so that confusion can cloud the lesson. Second, instructors are still available to facilitate the activities of the group, and to answer any question that may arise. And finally, the team has just shared the common training experience. People are familiar with their team members, and are more inspired to tackle the task at hand.

The successful implementation of CE within DoD requires its practitioners to have a common understanding of the philosophy. Team building, managerial support, and government/contractor cooperation are additional key ingredients, along with numerous tools and methodologies that can smooth the transition to the CE design environment. CE requires a cultural change, with new tools, roles and responsibilities. Its implementation will not be easy. That is why training is important.

MICOM has seen the need for an innovative approach to training its managers and design teams in CE. The undertaking not only was successful, but also used the CE philosophy in its own creation. The CE steering committee, bringing together the collective knowledge of the MICOM design environment, used many of the same tools and techniques to create a set of training modules to address all aspects of CE, and integrate those lessons into the models that could be used within MICOM and DoD.

 Professional Vocabularies and Expressions

concurrent engineering	并行工程
Department of Defense (DoD)	美国国防部
the institute for defense analysis (IDA)	防御分析研究所
management support	管理层支持
enhanced communication	强化沟通
team building	团队建设
U.S. Army Missile Command (MICOM)	美国战术导弹指挥部
steering committee	控制委员会，指导委员会
taguchi methods	田口法

quality function deployment	质量功能展开
rapid prototyping	快速原型
computer-aided design	计算机辅助设计
computer-aided manufacturing	计算机辅助制造
computer-aided process planning	计算机辅助工艺规划
design for assembly/manufacturability	面向装配/制造的设计
design for reusability	面向可重复使用的设计
design for maintainability	面向维护的设计
design for reliability	面向可靠性的设计
technological innovation	技术创新，技术革新
product life cycle	产品生命周期

Notes

1. According to Department of Defense (DoD) Regulations 5000.1 and 5000.2, concurrent engineering (CE) will be used for the development of all future military systems.

并行工程的概念是 1986 年由美国国防部防御分析研究所提出的。可以定义为集成地、并行地设计产品及其相关的各种过程（包括制造过程和支持过程）的系统方法。这种方法要求产品开发人员在一开始就考虑产品整个生命周期中的、从概念设计到产品报废的所有因素，包括质量、成本、进度规划和用户要求。

2. While tools and methodologies were given adequate coverage, more philosophical aspects of CE (i.e. improving communication, organizational and team structure, etc.) were not slighted.

在给予各种工具和方法足够重视的同时，对诸如沟通、组织和团队结构的改善等并行工程的哲学层面的内容也给予了相应的尊重。

3. Contractor personnel also highlighted concerns over a lack of definitive requirements in requests for proposals (RFPs) and funding variations over the course of a program.

契约商对建议书中缺少明确的需求信息以及项目进行过程中资助的变化也很担心并予以强调。

Discussion Questions:

Summarize the development track of CE in China and analyze what we can benefit from the practice mentioned in this article.

CHAPTER 12

New Product Development

12.1 Introduction

The failure to integrate a product strategy, a well-planned portfolio, and a facilitating organization structure with clearly identified customer needs, a well-defined product concept, and a project plan can severely hamper new product development.

Many companies formulate product strategies, routinely choose among new product concepts, and plan new product development projects. Yet, when asked where the greatest weakness in product innovation is, the managers at these companies indicate the fuzzy front end. They recite some familiar symptoms of front-end failure:

(1) New products are abruptly canceled in midstream because they don't "match the company strategy."

(2) "Top priority" new product projects suffer because key people are "too busy" to spend the required time on them.

(3) New products are frequently introduced later than announced because the product concept has become a moving target.

Times have changed since 1983 when Donald Schön described product development as a "game" in which "general managers distance themselves from the uncertainties inherent in product development and...technical personnel protect themselves against the loss of corporate commitment. Since then, new product development has become a core business activity that needs to be closely tied to the business strategy and a process that must be managed through analysis and decision making. Now, general managers cannot distance themselves from the uncertainties of product development, nor can technical personnel protect themselves against corporate commitment.

As enhanced capabilities for concurrent engineering, rapid prototyping, and smoothly functioning supplier partnerships have helped reduce product design and development times, management attention has begun to shift to the cross-functional, front-end strategic, conceptual, and planning activities that typically precede the detailed design and development of a new product. Here, new product ideas gain the shape, justification, plans, and support leading to their approval and subsequent execution. Yet, despite the widespread recognition of the front end's importance, there has been limited systematic examination directed at improving its effectiveness.

12.2 What is the "Front End"?

Prior research has focused on the success factors for new product development (NPD). While many of these factors relate to design execution and project management issues, some pertain to the front end. Consistent with Roberts's model, we classified the front-end-related success factors identified in prior research into foundation and project-specific elements. The distinction is important because the two require different skills and levels of effort. Also, without adequate foundation elements, product and project success becomes a matter of luck. Project-specific activities focus on the individual project and require the project team's effort to ensure a useful product definition and project plan. These include a product concept statement and evaluation, product definition, and project planning. Foundation elements, on the other hand, cut across projects and form the basis for project-specific activities. Thus they typically require enterprises' wide support, senior management participation, and a cross-functional effort.

12.2.1 Foundation elements

Without a clear product strategy, a well-planned portfolio of new products, and an organization structure that facilitates product development via ongoing communications and cross-functional sharing of responsibilities, front-end decisions become ineffective. Achieving these preconditions provides a foundation for the streams of successful new products.

Key product strategy elements include the formulation and communication of a strategic vision, a product-platform strategy, and a product-line strategy to support the go/no-go decision for a new product. Previous research suggests that familiarity with the product strategy enables appropriate decisions on NPD timing and target markets and also an assessment of the fit between the product and the core competence of the business unit.

In addition to a product vision, business units need to plan their portfolio of new product development activities, which goes beyond the traditional marketing view of having a product for every segment, market, and price point. Portfolio planning should map all new product initiatives across the business to balance risk and potential return, short and long time horizons, or mature and emerging markets. At the same time, the portfolio plan should ensure consistency with the product and business strategy. If well done, it facilitates the allocation of scarce resources to new product development projects.

An essential precondition is establishing the organization structure for new product development. Decisions on structure, communication networks, and roles are made at a business-unit level. Research has highlighted several requirements for the product development organization and its functioning, such as using a matrix or project form, organizing NPD around core business/product teams rather than traditional functions, using design and communication tools including information systems, and establishing controls and incentives as rewards.

12.2.2 Project-specific elements

Product-specific front-end activities help clarify the product concept, define product and market requirements, and develop plans, schedules, and estimates of the project's resource requirements. However, they stop far short of creating detailed designs and specifications for the product and its components.

The product concept is a preliminary identification of customer needs, market segments, competitive situations, business prospects, and alignment with existing business and technology plans. Research suggests that the product concept should be clear so that managers can sense whether the newly defined opportunity seems worth exploring. Managers need to understand customer needs and identify the potential technologies and applications to satisfy them. For tangible products, the product concept is usually illustrated with a sketch or three-dimensional model. Because such concepts are relatively inexpensive to produce, managers often create several before selecting one to fully design and develop. Early targets — measured in product cost, product performance, project cost, and time to market — set the stage for generating various product concepts.

The product definition, an elaboration of the product concept, incorporates judgments about the target market, competitive offerings, and the time and resources for bringing the new product to market. The definition activity includes identification of customer and user needs, technologies, and regulatory requirements. These lead to a choice of product features and functions, target market segments, and design priorities. Research on the implementation of the front end indicates that an explicit, stable product definition and an understanding of the trade-offs among customer requirements, technology, and resource/cost constraints are important factors for success.

Project planning includes project priorities and tasks, a master schedule, projected resource requirements, and other supporting information. Here, it is critical to communicate the project priorities, provide adequate resources, and anticipate contingencies. And, despite progress in new product development practices, typical systems do not adequately address these critical issues.

12.2.3 The front-end process

We take a process view of the front end because earlier studies and our preliminary research suggested that the individual activities, while logically interrelated, often are treated independently. Accordingly, we present a system view of the front end (See Figure 12-1). This process description is consistent with the growing empirical evidence of the need to simultaneously consider overall product strategy (foundation elements) with project-relevant input such as product ideas, market analysis, and technology options. Thus understanding the interrelationships between the activities is as important as the activities themselves.

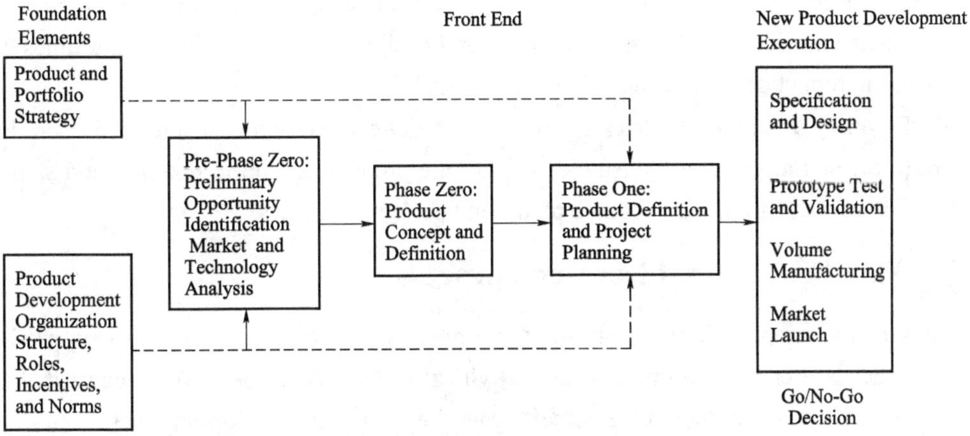

Figure 12-1 A model of the new product development front end

Product strategy and portfolio plans should drive the complete new product development effort, in conjunction with the capabilities and competencies of the product development organization, with its inherent assumptions about roles, communications, and culture. These elements are thus preconditions or foundations for the explicit activities in new product development. Many companies implement a formal phase-review management system to define and guide the explicit project-specific activities; this review process involves the process itself, the roles that make it work, and primary deliverables.

(1) **Phases of the Front-End Process.** Companies generally begin work on new product opportunities (often called "pre-phase zero") when they first recognize, in a semiformal way, an opportunity. If the newly defined opportunity is worth exploring, the company assigns a small group, sometimes including suppliers, to work together on the product concept and definition (phase zero).

In phase one, the company assesses the business and technical feasibility of the new product, confirms the product definition, and plans the NPD project. Thus the development team identifies the new product, its development, and the business rationale for proceeding. The front end is complete at the end of this phase when the team presents the business case and the business unit either commits to funding, staffing, and launch of the project or kills the project.

(2) **Front-End Roles.** A core team (including the project leader) and an executive review committee of senior functional managers responsible for making the go/no-go decision typically conduct the process we've described. During phase one, if not sooner, companies assign individuals from all functional areas as the members of the core team for the product development project. Normally, if a company approves the project at the end of phase one, a full complement of people to design, develop, test, manufacture, and launch the new product

supplements the core team. Previous studies have indicated that team structure varies in composition, size, and leadership. Often, the core team includes the selected suppliers as partners; their knowledge of technology, costs, and design and manufacturing lead times can contribute to product definition and project planning.

(3) **Primary Front-End Deliverables.** The front-end activities result in the product concept (clear and aligned with customer needs), the product definition (explicit and stable), and the project plan (priorities, resource plans, and project schedules).

12.3 A well-engineered front-end process

How can a company improve its front-end practices to achieve success in new product development? Is it enough to improve the activities we have described? We suggest that the best practice in new product development goes beyond simply adopting these activities. Success depends on how companies integrate the dimensions and elements of product development.

Our research highlighted certain challenges in integration of the front end beyond the obvious need for cross-functional effort. First, because project-specific activities build on foundation activities, companies should ensure that the foundation elements are aligned with the product development process and project-specific activities. Second, they should ensure consistency between strategic and operational activities. The challenge is to make strategy explicit enough to guide day-to-day choices for new product development. We found the integration of these two factors was rare but extremely potent. At the companies studied, we observed several kinds of integration problems:

(1) Senior managers sometimes delegated the formulation of a product strategy to product and R&D managers.

(2) The product development staff often made the decisions that affected other products and business unit strategy. (While the core team faces technical uncertainty about the product and manufacturing and distribution processes, resolving cross-project issues or providing guidelines should be senior management responsibilities.)

(3) Managers in various functions and organizational levels rarely ensured consistency and links among R&D activities, product strategy, and current product development.

(4) Managers frequently took on product development projects without committing adequate resources. (Often there is a misconception that product development staff working on multiple projects improves efficiency. The result is long delays in product launch and lost revenues. With ongoing downsizing in many companies, this kind of neglect is becoming chronic. Senior managers need to help product and R&D managers understand a project's relative importance.)

(5) Senior managers did little to measure and reward cross-functional teamwork. (Front-end participants need to know that management values their contributions.)

12.4 Balancing front-end explicitness and flexibility

The management of the front end also requires a balance between getting things right and being flexible during NPD execution. Other front-end elements and activities should also be balanced. There is a natural tension between planning to reduce risk and responding to inherent uncertainties. For example, we suggest that product strategy and portfolio planning be explicit, yet we recognize that some subsequent shifts in the product definition are inevitable, forcing contingent actions. Furthermore, postponing the final decisions at the front end by continuing the development of parallel concepts or solutions may reduce uncertainty. While our research did not focus on this issue, we believe that there must be a balance between front-end planned activities and ongoing iteration during the NPD project, between making "final" decisions early and intentionally keeping open parallel alternatives, and between establishing product development targets through analysis and working by instinct alone.

12.5 Diagnosing front-end activities

Based on our study findings, we propose that companies evaluate their front end on the degree of formality and the integration of activities. The dimensions — formality and process integration — can be measured on a checklist. The diagnostic statements evaluate the explicitness and formality of front-end practices. The statements on integration document how well these and other front-end activities are integrated.

A senior business unit manager such as the vice president of R&D, chief technology officer, or director of new product development should assess business practices and then calculate the score of the business unit, counting a check for any item as one point. The sum of the scores on the formality statements gives the formality score; the sum of the integration statements, the integration score. The manager can then map the score on each dimension on the front-end capability map (See Figure 12-2).

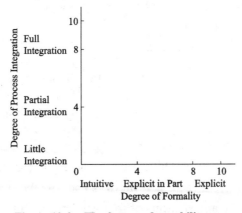

Figure 12-2 The front-end capability map

The mapping indicates how well (or poorly) a business unit is doing along the two dimensions of formality and integration. Research indicates that world-class companies score eight or more on both dimensions. The companies that score three or less on either dimension have a deficient front end and are likely to have major problems with their product development efforts. Senior management needs to find the ways to improve these efforts; the checklist is the first step to understand where and what to improve. What is more difficult is to understand how. In the next section, we discuss how companies and business units can plan a transition to a better-managed front end.

12.6 Managing the transition

All the companies studied were moving toward a more explicit, integrated front end. They were trying to build complementary capabilities to support the critical go/no-go decisions and development plans for new product concepts. Yet each was taking a different path at a different rate.

We see three stages in the product development front-end, not including the stage in which a company has no formal front end — the pre-emergent stage. The next stages are "awareness," "islands of capability," and "integrated capability" (See Figure 12-3). The triggers to reach the awareness stage from the pre-emergent stage are typically growth, additional product line complexity; or competitive pressures for either more product innovation or lower product development costs. In any case, at the awareness stage, companies recognize the significance of the front end but have little capability associated with it. They score poorly on both the formality and integration dimensions.

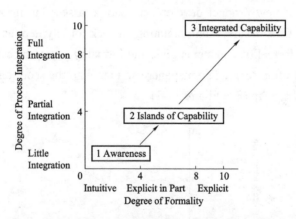

Figure 12-3 **Stages in the transition to a mature front end**

(1) Islands of Capability (Stage Two). Study suggests that most leading product innovators are at the islands of capability stage. These companies realize the potential of having a well-managed front end and have some of the required capabilities, but inconsistently. Missing are many elements of front-end process integration. Companies find it

easier to improve the formality of this process than to address the subtle gaps in integration.

How can companies evolve from "awareness" to "islands of capability"? That depends on what the business unit has already achieved and what capabilities it needs, given its industry and company. We identified two broad approaches to achieving Stage Two. First, those companies that have barely begun to understand the importance of the front end should recognize that product development is a senior management responsibility. Managers should carry out several structured activities, such as the diagnostic test. Second, those companies that recognize the importance of the front end should formally and systematically conduct various front-end activities. Those activities include having an explicit product definition, estimating technology requirements early, and planning resources.

(2) Integrated Capability (Stage Three). Front-end product development integration, the hallmark of stage Three, is quite rare. We believe that most companies don't understand that this stage is significant in terms of required capabilities, and achieving it takes concerted effort. At the few companies with this degree of process integration, analysis and decisions have been both explicit and rigorous, and all front-end activities are managed as a single process. Stage Three companies execute NPD projects better and faster than their competitors and are more likely to introduce a winning product. One can honestly say of these companies that "well begun is more than half done."

How can companies make a transition from "islands of capability" to "integrated capability"? Some Stage Two companies have much of the required formality but not necessarily the degree of integration to yield substantial benefits. Most Stage Two companies should focus on understanding the various dimensions of integration. Among our sample, we identified three clusters of companies that required somewhat different approaches to get to Stage Three. These three clusters represent the generic front-end states and problems that many companies face.

While the companies in the first cluster have passed Stage One, they still have a long way to go. They need to focus closely on senior management involvement in creating a product vision. The improvements in front-end formality and integration, while not easy, will be easier if the product development group can understand its purpose better.

The second cluster of companies will realize improvements from refinements in the front-end process. They need to make their front-end activities more explicit and, in particular, understand how to better manage their technology and resource requirements. Once they progress on these dimensions, they can focus more on cross functional and integration problems.

The third cluster of companies were the most advanced among the Stage Two companies. Front-end explicitness is not their main problem. Instead, their challenge is to work on cross-project issues and technological uncertainties. By having close ties among strategic planners and project personnel, they will understand the links among projects and anticipate matches or mismatches between future market needs and current technology and product plans. They need to establish closer connections between their R&D and product development groups so that they can anticipate overall technological progress and product-specific technological uncertainty.

(3) Sustaining Stage Three. Clearly, reaching Stage Three is not easy; even those companies that have achieved it continue to require improvements. The changes in competition, technologies, tools, and organizational structures and relationships may need changes in at least some front-end practices.

12.7 Conclusion

Most companies have unnecessarily fuzzy front-end systems. The best way to integrate the front-end process is to use an overall system perspective and thoroughly assess the current state of the front end. Fixing what appears to be broken requires the ability to see the interrelatedness of issues and the development of a coherent agenda.

We caution against oversimplification: not all companies should adopt the same front-end solution, and most will need to adopt more than one. For example, we found that companies used executive reviews in different ways with mixed success; some case study companies changed the role of the executive review group for different products. In general, company size, decision-making style, operating culture, and frequency of new product introduction are some factors that are critical to a preferred front-end solution. We discourage companies from importing a particular process or procedure that has worked well for others unless their contexts are clearly similar.

Managing to become less fuzzy means integrating seemingly disparate but related strategic and operational activities, typically crossing functional boundaries. The solution must be balanced with the emerging realities of business and the environment. With proper diagnosis, consensus, and commitment, companies can enhance product development performance over the long term.

 Professional Vocabularies and Expressions

new product development	新产品开发
research and development (R&D)	研究与开发，研发
product strategy	产品策略
product portfolio	产品汇总表
customer needs	顾客需求
product concept	产品概念

project plan	项目计划
concurrent engineering	并行工程
rapid prototyping	快速原型
product concept statement	产品概念陈述
product definition	产品定义
project planning	项目规划
foundation element	基本要素
project-specific element	项目特有要素
tangible product	实物产品
sketch	草图
three-dimensional model	三维模型
product feature and function	产品特征和功能
target market segment	目标市场部分
design priority	设计优先级
resource constraint	资源限制
important factor	关键因素
project priority	项目优先级
task	任务
projected resource requirement	资源需求预估

 Notes

1. As enhanced capabilities for concurrent engineering, rapid prototyping, and smoothly functioning supplier partnerships have helped reduce product design and development times, management attention has begun to shift to the cross-functional, front-end strategic, conceptual, and planning activities that typically precede the detailed design and development of a new product.

随着能力增强的并行工程、快速原型和与供应商的和谐伙伴关系对产品设计和开发时间的缩短，（产品开发）管理的注意力已经转向交叉职能性的、前期策略性的、概念性和规划性的活动。这些活动通常在新产品的详细设计和开发之前（展开）。

2. Also, without adequate foundation elements, product and project success becomes a matter of luck.

而且，如果不具备充分的基本要素，产品和项目的成功与否就靠运气了。

3. However, they stop far short of creating detailed designs and specifications for the product and its components.

然而，产品特有的前期活动早在产生详细的产品设计（方案）和规格以及产品的构成零件之前就结束了。

4. We found the integration of these two factors was rare but extremely potent.

我们发现就两者有机集成起来的（公司）很少，但这种集成具有相当大的潜力。

5. Fixing what appears to be broken requires the ability to see the interrelatedness of issues and the development of a coherent agenda.

弥补缺陷需要具备识别问题间的相互依赖性和制订紧凑的行动计划的能力。

Discussion Questions:

1. How to tell whether a company has a fuzzy front end as far as new product design is concerned?
2. Product lifecycle management (PLM) is popular in the domain of product development. Find out what PLM is and further analyze whether the ideas proposed in this paper are compatible with those of PLM.

CHAPTER 13

Computer Integrated Manufacturing (CIM)

The goal of CIM is to integrate and coordinate, via computer hardware and software, all aspects of design, manufacturing and related functions. CIM may be viewed as the management technology that makes feasible the fully-automated factory-of-the-future.

Certain computer-based technologies falling within the broad realm of CIM have been sufficiently well developed to merit specific attention. These include computer-aided design (CAD), computer-aided process planning (CAPP), material requirement planning (MRP), manufacturing resources planning (MRP II), capacity requirements planning (CPR) and shop-floor control (SFC). Also of importance is group technology (GT), which significantly facilitates computer-aided process planning (CAPP), and computer-aided manufacturing (CAM). The topic of networks (telecommunications between computerized elements) pervades many of the specific technologies listed above, and hence deserves special consideration.

13.1 Computer-aided design

Computer-aided design (CAD) allows the designer to draw a design on a visual display unit (VDU), or computer monitor screen. Computer graphics is the term applied to the combination of hardware and software that makes this possible. Completed designs are stored in a design database.

Most CAD systems allow the designer to draw a model of the design by making available a set of primitives. These are simple geometric figures such as lines and circles in two-dimensional modeling. Primitives may be brought onto the screen and re-sized, re-oriented, partially trimmed or otherwise adjusted to create the desired drawing. In other words, each more complex part in the design is broken down into a set of simpler figures that, when appropriately positioned, create a graphic image of the whole part. The use of different colors in different portions of the design display helps make drawings even clearer and easier to understand. Another aspect of CAD graphics that substantially enhances clarity is that a drawing may be rotated so the designer can view it from many different angles. This is accomplished by having the computer calculate a large number of coordinate transformations — a repetitive mathematical process that a computer is well-suited to do quickly. Some CAD systems can also simulate the movement of the part if, for example, a piece of it is hinged. The ability to rotate or cause movement in the design allows testing for clearance and frequently leads to a major reduction in the cost of prototyping.

Having access to a computerized design database makes it easy for a designer to quickly modify an old design to meet new design requirements — an event that occurs quite frequently. This enhances designer productivity; speeds up the design process; reduces design errors resulting from hurried, inaccurate copying; and reduces the number of the designers needed to perform the same amount of work. It also means the designers can focus on doing work that is mostly non-routine, while the CAD system does most of the routine work. Another advantage associated with a CAD database is that all of the designs are based on the same standards: standard primitives, standard colors and other standard design rules. This reduces unpleasant surprises for a designer attempting to modify a previous design that might, under a manual system, be based on a different set of rules or assumptions that the ones (s)he is following.

13.2 Computer-aided engineering

Computer-aided engineering (CAE) enables engineers to do complex engineering analysis on the computer. Once CAD work had been completed, a designer can use CAE to analyze the design and determine if it will work like the designer thought it would. For example, if a simulation of a circuit design shows that the circuit produces a few unanticipated and undesired outputs, some re-design is clearly necessary. Likewise, if a stress analysis shows that a particular design would break down if subjected to more than 15 pounds of pressure, and the specifications call for withstanding 30 pounds, it is back to the drawing board.

Electronic computer-aided engineering (ECAE) is primarily used to design the integrated circuits and printed-circuit boards. The term computer-aided software engineering (CASE) is sometimes used to distinguish software development tools from hardware development tools. Circuit-design, circuit-checking and project management software are the major elements of CASE. Mechanical computer-aided engineering (MCAE) deals with the mechanical aspects of design, making sure that all of the pieces fit together and that all of them actually fit into the box as planned. When these designs are subjected to spreadsheet-like "what if" analysis based on the engineering equations contained in the software, the essentials of the design can be optimized before the design engineer spends a lot of time getting down into the fine details. Part of the optimization can include manufacturability.

With any kind of CAE, detailed engineering analysis provides data, which will probably be useful when actually manufacturing the product. Such data not only include product specifications, but also process the information on the design of tools or molds, and the programs used for controlling the motions of numerical control (NC) machines or robots. Thus a database created as a result of CAD/CAE may then be used to support computer-aided manufacturing (CAM).

13.3 Computer-aided manufacturing

Computer-aided manufacturing (CAM) encompasses the computer-aided techniques that facilitate the planning, operation and control of a production facility. Such techniques include computer-aided process planning (CAPP), numerical control part programming, robotics programming, computer-generated work standards, material requirements planning (MRP), manufacturing resources planning (MRP II), capacity requirements planning (CRP) and shop-floor control (SFC).

Computer-aided process planning (CAPP) creates the sequence of the steps that must be followed to produce a given part or product. It instances where a variety of similar products are to be produced. Process planning is typically a sophisticated, but largely repetitive task. Hence, it is a task for which a computer is well suited, provided a well-organized system is devised for the computer to follow.

Group technology (GT) is the methodology that usually provides the basis for the well-organized system required by CAPP. GT classifies parts quite efficiently by dividing the parts into the families that exhibit similar characteristics. One common basis for similarity is the characteristics of the part itself, such as its shape, its size, or the material from which the part is made. Another common basis for similarity is the characteristics of the manufacturing process for the part, such as the process sequences or routings the part must follow, or the types of the equipment used to make the part.

Any of a variety of coding schemes may be applied to uniquely identify each part by a number of an alphanumeric (letters plus numbers). These may range from less than 10 to more than 30 characters in length. Each character adds a little more information about the part.

Once all parts have been coded, standard process plans may be developed for each family of parts. After this phase has been completed, process planning for a new but similar part may be accomplished by slight modifications to the standard plan for the part's family. If the part has been built before, the plan is simply called up from the CAPP database.

The system just described is called variant CAPP because human users get involved to deal with variants of the standard plans retrieved from the CAPP database. A more sophisticated approach is generative CAPP, wherein CAPP more accurately stands for computer-automated process planning. Generative CAPP allows the computer to automatically generate optimal process plans based on a series of algorithms imbedded in the system software. The algorithms can take into account a variety of relevant concerns, including differences in speed, quality and cost for various alternative methods, prior results, the age of the equipment involved (if tool wear or potential for breakdown is factors), etc. In current practice, the capabilities of generative CAPP systems are rather limited.

Material requirements planning (MRP) is a computerized system for the timely planning and control of inventory. MRP requires the estimates of the demand for a particular finished product in a particular week be developed based on forecasts, available capacity and other factors. MRP then analyzes the bill of materials (BOM) — the list of all of the parts needed to build the product — and calculates when each of these parts should be ordered so that enough of them will be on hand when they are required by manufacturing. This sounds logical and straightforward, but can actually get quite complicated in practice.

For example, a particular finished product may contain a number of complex subassemblies, which are in turn made of less complex sub-assemblies, which are made of simple subassemblies, which are made of a variety of parts! Then, in addition to these levels of complexity, imagine that the lead-times required to order and receive certain parts in simple sub-assembly #127 are 12 weeks instead of the more typical five, six or seven weeks. Compound this problem with the possibility that the 12-week lead-time for those parts might suddenly rocket up to 20 weeks due to an unexpected increase in supplier demand or problems in the supplier manufacturing process. Then suppose that in-house manufacturing difficulties could cause a temporary slowdown in the anticipated production rate for simple sub-assemblies in general. Given this degree of variety and complexity, the tremendous appeal of a computerized technique for keeping track of all these interdependent factors is obvious.

Also obvious from the hypothetical scenario outlined above is that the MRP program must be supplied with the best possible estimates for both the lead-times required to manufacture any of these parts, sub-assemblies or final assemblies in-house and the leadtime required to purchase any of these items from outside suppliers. The changes in the original schedule are then noted by the computer, which issues change notice to relevant factory personnel. The MRP systems that take into account feedback from manufacturing and other functions are often referred to as closed-loop MRP systems, since the feedback serves to close information loops between concerned parties.

Manufacturing resources planning (MRP II) is basically an extended version of material requirements planning (MRP). Parts are required at various times and MRP II determines the costs of the parts and the cash flows required to pay for them. It also estimates cash flows for the related expenditures such as wages, tools, equipment repairs and even the power bills. Sophisticated MRP II programs can predict cash requirements, by departmental unit, for a year or more in advance, thus accomplishing computerized budgeting. Also, because MRP II converts all of its inputs into equivalent cash flows, it can be used as a simulator to answer a variety of "what if" questions about the actions that may be taken by any given department. The results of such simulations can then be used as a basis for more complex analyses to determine how proposed changes would impact the other parts of the organizational system.

Capacity requirements planning (CPR) is a different variation on the MRP theme. Instead of focusing on the timely acquisition of inventory or controlling cash flows, CRP analyzes available capacity to perform the manufacturing function. Important concerns are people and equipment. How much output can each person or machine provide per hour or day? The factors such as break-times, fatigue, absenteeism and so forth affect a plant's people-related capacity, which can be further modified by special arrangements such as overtime work. Equipment-related capacity is an interactive function of the speed of the machine; the rate at which inputs can be supplied to the machine, and output removes; planned or unplanned maintenance; how many machines of a particular type are on hand; etc. Since these capacities are likely to vary in complexity over time in a manner similar to the lead-times and levels issues of MRP, the computerized tracking of capacity is another logical addition to CAM.

Shop floor control (SFC) is another aspect of CAM to be considered. SFC systems make use of the computer to monitor and control what occurs on the factory (shop) floor. The key functions of SFC include prioritizing shop orders; monitoring the status of current shop orders; and comparing the data on actual work-in-process (WIP) with MRP and CRP plans. If WIP does not match the MRP/CRP plans, SFC facilities adjustments as necessary.

13.4 Networks

Thus far a substantial number of computer-aided techniques that contribute toward computer integrated manufacturing (CIM) have been reviewed, but nothing has been said about how they might be computer integrated. Integration may be achieved through one or more networks, which electronically link together all of the various computerized entities or systems in the factory.

Getting different types and makes of computers to talk to one another is not a problem readily resolved. Attempts are being made at the international level as well as at the national level within the United States to develop the standards that will make this possible. The open systems interconnection (OSI) model is currently the most well-developed standard. It features a seven-layer system, each layer dealing with a different aspect of data communications compatibility. Layer 1 is concerned with standards for the actual physical linkage of one machine to another, such as the kinds of the hardware connectors that should be used. As another example, layer 6 is concerned with the form of data representation; i.e., whether the data is coded in the American standard code for information interchange (ASCII), extended binary-coded-decimal interchange code (ECDIC) or some other code. It also is responsible for converting any incoming stream of data into a common code format.

A pair of industry-driven network systems based on the OSI model are manufacturing automation protocol (MAP) and technical and office protocol (TOP). MAP was initially developed by General Motors, but is now gaining the support of a large number of CIM suppliers and users. TOP is a similar networking standard developed by Boeing computer services for business office and engineering applications. MAP and TOP are now being integrated into a single MAP/TOP network system.

Networking is further complicated by the need to have the networks that operate at different hierarchical levels within a CIM environment, such as a substantially or fully automated factory. For example, the highest-level networking might integrate an entire factory, much like a plant manager does. At the next level down several networks might act like middle managers to plan and coordinate activities within and between various functions within the factory. The level below might consist of the networks that monitor and control the activities of various groups of automated machines (departments), such as a flexible manufacturing system. Additional levels might contain the networks responsible for activities like material handling between workstations, and finally the networks that cause the action of individual workstations.

The actual physical networks that link together various computers and computer controlled equipment (e.g., robots, and automated test equipment) within a single plant site are called local-area networks (LANs). These typically consist of coaxial and fiber-optic cables, which interconnect the machines and network computers that manage the flow of data through the network. The larger-scale networks linking a variety of locations are termed wide-area networks (WANs).

13.5 Other key elements of factory automation

The factory automation technologies discussed thus far have, for the most part, consisted of computer hardware and software. Other key technologies, while also computerized to at least some extent, are more recognizable as physically active machines. Hard automation will be contrasted with the forms of flexible automation such as numerical control, programmable logic controllers (PLCs), automatic test equipment (ATE) and robots. Various systems, including flexible manufacturing systems (FMSs), automated storage and retrieval systems (AS/RS) and pathways for automated guided vehicles (AGVs) are also the important aspects of factory automation.

13.5.1 Hard automation

Automation may be defined as the replacement of manual labor with machine labor. In the simpler forms of automation, the machine does the work while a human guides the machine. Examples include drilling a hole with an electric drill, cleaning up a dusty workbench with a miniature vacuum cleaner, or assembling a metal or plastic box with a power screwdriver. In the more sophisticated forms of automation, a human need not guide the activities of the machine continuously. Instead, the machine is programmed to perform tasks in appropriate ways.

A machine designed to cycle through only one specific set of motion is an example of fixed or hard automation. A toaster is such a machine. It automatically exposes bread to heat, converting it into toast. A dishwasher, a coffee-making machine and a traffic light are also the forms of hard automation.

13.5.2 Numerical control

Numerical control (NC) machines consist of the combinations of cutting and shaping tools, such as lathes and drill presses, which are controlled by instruction coded onto a paper tape. As the tape passes through a paper-tape reader, the various tools reshape the work piece according to the pattern prescribed by the instructions on the tape. Any described change in the pattern is accomplished by simply changing a new version of the paper tape.

Modern approaches to numerical control are computer numerical control (CNC) and direct numerical control (DNC). In CNC, a small computer replaces the conventional controller unit of the NC machine.

DNC differs from CNC in that a larger computer controls a number of NC machines simultaneously. A combination of CNC and DNC is also possible. In this hybrid approach, the larger computer stores the NC part programs. These are downloaded as needed to the smaller CNC computers, which then control the NC machines.

13.5.3 Programmable logic controllers

Programmable logic controllers (PLCs) are, in essence, small and simple computers that can be programmed to control industrial equipment in relatively simple ways. They differ from other types of computers in that they are specifically designed to cope with an industrial environment, which may exhibit relatively extreme temperatures (for computers), high humidity, significant vibration and substantial amounts of electro-magnetic interference (EMI).

The applications of PLCs include monitoring the output of production equipment; monitoring tool wear; monitoring reporting and controlling plant power and energy usage; controlling temperature and pressure for plastic injection-molding machines; and controlling the materials handling equipment (transfer-line machines). As personal computers (PCs) become smaller and more ruggedly built, they will probably replace PLCs in many applications.

13.5.4 Automatic test equipment

Automatic test equipment (ATE) currently plays a very significant role in testing integrated circuits (ICs) and printed-circuit boards (PCBs), both of which are key elements in computer and telecommunications equipment. Once properly programmed, ATE can rapidly and accurately perform a large number of tests on the circuit in question. This is really a form of computer-automated inspection (CAI). So ATE plays an important role in assuring high levels of quality. Most ATE systems consist of:

(1) a general-purpose microcomputer or workstation;

(2) a hardware interface that connects the circuits being tested to the circuits under the control of the computer; and

(3) a variety of testing software, which must be frequently updated. Some customization is typically required to meet the needs of each specific application.

13.5.5 Robotics

Robots, according to the Robot Institute of America, are the "reprogrammable, multi-functional manipulators designed to move material, parts, tools or specialized devices through variable programmed motions for the performance of a variety of tasks." While the traits of reprogrammability and multi-functionality apply to numerical control (NC) machines as well, the latter consists of the combinations of specific tools rather than of one of two very general-purpose manipulators to which a wide variety of tools might be attached. Robotic manipulators are typically more mobile than the tools in NC machines. Industrial robots consist of four basic components:

(1) manipulators;

(2) end-effectors;

(3) sensors; and

(4) controllers.

Manipulators are the counterparts to human arms and wrists. They require joints or articulations in order to move. Robotic manipulators are hydraulically- (liquid-), pneumatically- (gas-) or electrically-powered. The lengths of most industrial robots' manipulators range from a few inches to about 10 feet.

End-effectors are attached to the ends of manipulators. An effector is a device that effects in action, like picking up part of manipulating a tool. Thus an effector attached to the end of a manipulator is called an end-effector.

Sensors convert information concerning what is happening in the robot's world (e.g., workpiece-reflected light rays for vision) into the electronic signals that can be analyzed by the computer(s) controlling the robot. The robotic sensors of greatest interest include vision, tactile (touch) and force sensors.

Controllers are robotic brains, the computers that tell the robot what to do next. Robotic controllers vary from simple to complex. The level of the controller intelligence required by a robot is dependent upon the sophistication of the manipulator(s), end effector(s) and sensor(s) to be incorporated in that robot.

The simplest robots do not actually require a computer at all. They just move their arms or grippers in a direction until pressure or the arm or gripper triggers a halt in motion. These pick-and-place robots, and those on the next highest level of sophistication, may be classified as point-to-point (PTP) robots.

The most sophisticated modern robots are controlled by one or more computers. Such robots may be programmed to follow a continuous path or contour rather than simply moving directly from one point to another, and hence are known as continuous path robots. They exhibit considerably greater accuracy and dexterity than PTP robots. Continuous path robots may be taught their tasks via the lead-through method — using a remote controlled box called a teaching pendant — or via off-line programming.

Some major applications of robots in high-technology operations include material handling, parts positioning and assembly. Robots are also commonly used in welding, drilling and spray-painting applications.

13.5.6 Flexible manufacturing systems

In general, a flexible manufacturing system (FMS) is a major grouping of computer controlled manufacturing devices linked to a computer that acts as their manager. An FMS is intended to operate with little or no human intervention. The key attributes of an FMS are:

(1) flexible work stations that can make a wide variety of parts with very short set-up times;

(2) a flexible materials handling system that moves the parts between work stations; and

(3) computer control in real time.

A typical FMS might consist of a half dozen numerical control (NC) machines that are loaded and unloaded by robots, all of whom report to a minicomputer. The NC machines would most likely operate under distributed numerical control (DNC II), a hybrid combination of CNC and DNC. The robots would probably be continuous path robots, for greater flexibility. The lowest three levels of the network system hierarchy discussed earlier would be applied within such an FMS. Broadly speaking, an FMS is a work group or department within an automated factory. An FMS may be considered an evolutionary step towards a truly fully-automated factory.

Related to flexible manufacturing systems is the concept of flexible manufacturing cells (FMCs). FMCs are usually smaller and less automated than FMSs, typically involving two to four machines plus at least one human operator. The operators monitor the equipment, inspect the output of the cell for quality, perform maintenance, cope with any unusual situation, and may also get involved in changing programs for some of the equipment, such as NC machines.

13.5.7 Automated storage and retrieval systems

An automated storage and retrieval system (AS/RS) essentially functions as an automated warehouse, though it should be noted that some AS/RSs are considerably closer to warehouse-size than others. Parts are stored in the bins that can be delivered to one or more collection and distribution points, where more parts may be added or needed parts may be removed and sent on to manufacturing. A computer keeps track of how many of which kinds of parts are stored in which bins, and controls the mechanical system that selects the desired bin and moves it to a collection or distribution point.

Besides enhancing the accuracy of material pulls (i.e., the removal of material to fill an internal or customer order), an AS/RS is space efficient, providing better use of the available volume of storage space.

13.5.8 Automated guided vehicles

Automated guided vehicles (AGVs) are a form of the truck that does not require a human driver. Guidance is provided by a system of pathways in or on the factory floor. In some AGV systems, the pathways consist of a grid of wires embedded in the concrete floor, through which radio signals may be sent to be picked up by the sensing units in the undersides of the AGVs. In another approach, the pathways consist of painted strips, and the units in the undersides of the AGVs are designed to detect or activate the special paints (e.g. photoreflective paint). Whatever method is used, the basic idea is that a computer can send its fleet of AGVs to the right places at the right times in order to transfer materials to other locations on the factory floor.

An AGV can be designed to contain additional microprocessor-based intelligence, useful for coping with unanticipated events — such as some unintelligent person crossing the AGV's path while it goes about its assigned tasks. AGVs can be designed to transport a wide variety of containers, or even standard wooden pallets on which containers are stacked.

Professional Vocabularies and Expressions

computer integrated manufacturing (CIM)	计算机集成制造
computer-aided design (CAD)	计算机辅助设计
computer-aided process planning (CAPP)	计算机辅助工艺规划
material requirement planning (MRP)	物料需求规划
manufacturing resources planning (MRP II)	制造资源规划
capacity requirements planning (CPR)	能力需求规划
shop-floor control (SFC)	车间控制
group technology (GT)	成组技术
computer-aided manufacturing (CAM)	计算机辅助制造
computer graphics	计算机图形学
primitive	基本构图元素
coordinate transformation	坐标变换
prototyping	原型
computer-aided engineering (CAE)	计算机辅助工程
stress analysis	应力分析
integrated circuit board	集成电路板
printed-circuit board	印刷电路板
computer-aided software engineering (CASE)	计算机辅助软件工程

numerical control (NC) machine	数控机床
numerical control part programming	数控零件编程
robotics programming	机器人编程
computer-generated work standard	计算机生成的工作标准
variant CAPP	变异式计算机辅助工艺规划
generative CAPP	生成式计算机辅助工艺规划
bill of materials (BOM)	物料清单
change notice	变更通知单
closed-loop MRP system	闭环 MRP 系统
open systems interconnection (OSI)	开放系统互联
American standard code for information interchange (ASCII)	用于信息交换的美国标准编码
extended binary-coded-decimal interchange code (ECDIC)	扩展的十进制二元编码交换码
manufacturing automation protocol (MAP)	制造自动化协议
technical and office protocol (TOP)	技术和办公协议
flexible manufacturing system	柔性制造系统
automated test equipment (ATE)	自动检测设备
local-area network (LAN)	局域网
coaxial cable	同轴电缆
fiber-optic cable	光纤电缆
wide-area network (WAN)	广域网
factory automation	工厂自动化
hard automation	刚性自动化
flexible automation	柔性自动化
programmable logic controller (PLC)	可编程逻辑控制器
automated storage and retrieval system (AS/RS)	自动存取系统
automated guided vehicle (AGV)	自动导航设备
computer numerical control (CNC)	计算机数控
direct numerical control (DNC)	直接数控
distributed numerical control (DNC II)	分布式数控
electro-magnetic interference (EMI)	电磁干涉
plastic injection-molding machine	塑料注塑机
computer-automated inspection (CAI)	计算机自动检测
manipulator	操作器
end-effector	执行件
sensor	传感器
controller	控制器

hydraulically-powered	液动的
pneumatically-powered	气动的
electrically-powered	电动的
vision sensor	视觉传感器
tactile sensor	触觉传感器
force sensor	压力传感器
point-to-point (PTP) robot	点到点机器人
flexible manufacturing cell (FMC)	柔性制造单元

Notes

1. Certain computer-based technologies falling within the broad realm of CIM have been sufficiently well developed to merit specific attention.

计算机集成制造这一广博领域中包括一些已经得到充分发展并且值得注意的基于计算机的技术。

2. Most CAD systems allow the designer to draw a model of the design by making available a set of primitives.

大部分的计算机辅助设计系统都向设计者提供一组基本构图元素（如二维绘图中的线、圆等）。基于这些基本构图元素，设计者可以绘出（零部件）设计的（计算机）模型。

3. When these designs are subjected to spreadsheet — like "what if" analysis based on the engineering equations contained in the software, the essentials of the design can be optimized before the design engineer spends a lot of time getting down into the fine details.

当需要用包含在软件中的工程方程对这些设计进行类似于电子数据表格的"如果……会怎么样……"的分析时，设计的本质内容在没必要等到设计工程师花费许多时间以得到详细设计的情况下就能够得到优化。

4. It instances where a variety of similar products are to be produced.

计算机辅助工艺规划系统基于已有零部件产品的工艺方案通过实例化来生成新的相似零部件的工艺方案。

5. Any of a variety of coding schemes may be applied to uniquely identify each part by a number of an alphanumeric (letters plus numbers).

各种编码方法中的任何一个都可以利用一个字母数字串来唯一地标识每一个零件。

6. Given this degree of variety and complexity, the tremendous appeal of a computerized technique for keeping track of all these interdependent factors is obvious.

考虑到这样的变化程度和复杂程度，能够用来跟踪这些相互关联的变量的计算机技术就显得非常有吸引力。

7. Sophisticated MRP II programs can predict cash requirements, by departmental unit, for a year or more in advance, thus accomplishing computerized budgeting.

复杂的制造资源规划系统能够提前一年甚至更长时间预测每一个功能单元的现金需求，因此可以用来实现预算的计算机化。

8. Getting different types and makes of computers to talk to one another is not a problem readily resolved.

使得不同类型和构造的计算机之间能够通信畅通不是一件容易的事情。

Discussion Questions:

1. Based on the first three articles in this section of the book, write a comprehensive essay that streamlines the concepts proposed in these papers. The emphasis should be focused on the relationships among concurrent engineering, integrated product design and computer integrated manufacturing.

2. Summarize the evolution process of computer integrated manufacturing in China.

CHAPTER 14

The Evolution of Simulation

14.1 Introduction

An understanding of the evolution of simulation is assisted by applying categorizations according to various criteria. One such categorization is based on the objectives of the simulation study. By far, the early work in simulation and what has been dominant in management science and operations research over the history is system analysis, where the intent is to mimic behavior to understand or improve system performance. A second objective is education and training, where the former addresses the broader understanding of concepts and the latter, more specific behavior in the application of concepts. A third objective is acquisition and system acceptance, where the simulation model is intended to answer the questions related to "Does the system meet the requirement?" or, "Does a subsystem contribute significantly to the improvement of the larger system performance?." A fourth objective relates to the research which can involve the creation of an artificial environment. In such an environment, systems' components can be tested or the behaviors of an individual or groups can be compared, contrasted, or categorized. Entertainment is the most recent objective: using a simulation model in a real-time interactive mode to derive pleasure and enjoyment.

A second categorization relates to the representation of time and state in a simulation model. A Monte Carlo model requires state sequencing but no explicit representation of time. Discrete event models specify state changes at discrete points in time. Continuous simulation portrays state changes as continuous over time, and the discretized approximate solutions of differential equations are the most common examples. The combined discrete event and continuous models enable both techniques to be applied within the same study. Hybrid simulation models generally incorporate an analytical submodel within a discrete event model.

Related to simulation models are games and gaming, a topic of considerable interest in the early history. Stimulated by the entertainment objective, games are experiencing a strong resurgence, but the earlier batch mode of play is now replaced by real-time interaction with human players.

The use of simulation precedes computers, either analog or digital. Described by some authors as "artificial sampling," a manual Monte Carlo method was employed to estimate π in a study documented in 1777. Hammersley and Handscomb (1964) identify "Student" (a pseudonym) as using artificial sampling to calculate exact expressions for the distribution of the sample correlation coefficient and to derive what is now called Student's t-statistic.

Computer simulation began during World War II in the case of the continuous and Monte Carlo models. Discrete event simulation probably originated in the late 1940s; however, we have no evidence as to the exact date. During the remainder of this paper we focus on computer simulation with discrete event models and simply use the term "computer simulation" or "simulation."

14.2   The early days

Simulation books published in the 1960s present a rather uniform set of steps for conducting a study: problem formulation, system data collection and conceptual model formulation, validation of the conceptual model, construction of the simulation program, execution of the simulation program, operational (results) validation, experimental design, output data analysis, and documentation. To give a feel of how the earliest steps were accomplished, we examine the form of input, the content of the input, the execution of the program (running the model), and the output.

The early simulation program consisted of a model description and an auxiliary set of simulation functions, including a random number generator, random variate generators, list processing routines for queue insertion and deletion, a time flow mechanism, forms of model data collection and analysis, and a report generator. A Simulation Programming Language (SPL) representation of the model would include a library that the translator would access to provide these functions. If programmed in a General Purpose Language (GPL), the simulation modeler would have to rely on a GPL library routine or include a program to perform each necessary function.

The content of the model, referred to as the model specification, requires a world view. The early works identify differences in world views that distinguish SPLs.

The implementation step (programming) of the model relied on simple techniques for creating uncertainty (random number and random variate production), about which little in terms of randomness properties was actually known. Arrays were used for simple list processing, and variable — or fixed-time incrementing was used in the time flow mechanism. Data collection methods used simple statistical accumulations, again relying on the array data structure. A deck of 80-column (also called "IBM") cards represented both programs. Debugging of programs was often tedious and not infrequently required the decoding of "core dumps" with values in octal or hexadecimal representation. Storage limitations and costly processor time required conservation on both fronts.

Output analysis often took the form of multiple replications with different random number streams or simply reliance on an estimation of the mean without concern for variance estimation. Report generation was limited to a rather restricted set of output variables; however, the early versions of the SPLs did supply some rudimentary forms of dynamic error checking.

The teaching of simulation in the 1960s was inhibited by the lack of textbooks. Often based on experience from practice, instructors used the techniques that had no identifying source, and students were expected to know (or to learn) the basic fundamentals of computer programming, list processing, and statistics as needed.

Excitement and expectation characterized both the academic and industrial sectors of the simulation community in the 1960s. SPL developers were interested in sharing ideas and understanding different approaches, and this interest is reflected in a number of conferences and papers comparing simulation languages. The first book on simulation appeared (Tocher 1963), and a number of others followed thereafter. A healthy tension existed between research and practice, and the methods and techniques for modeling and simulation created during that period have had a lasting influence.

14.3 Technical factors in simulation development

Examining the first few pages of a contemporary simulation book in comparison with one published 30 years ago, one notices strong similarities in the steps described for performing a simulation study. Essentially, what characterizes the modeling and simulation activities today seems little different; however, how those steps are performed differs considerably. We have chosen to separate the factors marking the evolution of simulation into two categories: ① external — those emanating from computing technology that set directions or shaped the progress of simulation research and practice; and ② internal — those generated by the communities of simulation researchers and practitioners. Within each factor below, the development is described in a loose chronological order.

14.3.1 External factors shaping the evolution

The early pervading view of simulation as a problem-solving technique stems from the development of Monte Carlo techniques well before the appearance of either analog or digital computers. Monte Carlo computation performed on electromechanical calculators by a host of operators was the common solution procedure in the 1950s for numerical models (approximate solutions of differential equations). Yet simulation, and in particular discrete event simulation, could never have been a major problem-solving technique without the emergence and rapid development of the digital computer. Consequently, our view is that the external influences on simulation are dominated by those associated with digital computing technology.

The Revolution in Computer Hardware. Youthful faces and sprightly gaits aside, we are made even more conscious of the huge gaps in computing history separating us from our students when we realize that most today do not recognize the terms: "mainframe computer," "core memory," or "keypunch." Since the ENIAC in the late 1940s, progress in computer hardware has advanced at a revolutionary pace. Processor speeds and storage sizes (both primary and peripheral) have increased by several orders of magnitude, while component size has decreased to a like degree as the succession of hardware technologies has transitioned from the mainframes of the 1960s to the minicomputers of the 1970s, the parallel processors of the 1980s, networks of processors in the 1990s, and the desktops and laptops joined by wireless connections of today. While the time intervals stipulated above are imprecise, the impact on modeling and simulation has been pervasive.

For the vast majority of the OR community, the recognition of the hardware influence needs little justification, but we believe that the effects are more pronounced for simulation than for most areas. That claim aside, the incredible advances in computer hardware must be acknowledged as making simulation a viable problem-solving technique for some and the preferred technique for many.

Advances in Computer Software. The machine language representations of the early 1950s gave way to the assembly language of the mid-1950s. The improved representational capability, supporting the list processing and functional library organization needs for simulation, made a significant contribution to the development of the first packaged simulator: the General Simulation Program (GSP). By the late 1950s FORTRAN had extended the semantics helpful for understanding model representations. While FORTRAN emerged as the dominant language for engineers and scientists in the United States throughout the next two decades, its limited data structures (the array) in the early versions had some lasting effects. FORTRAN simulation packages such as GASP and MILITRAN provided functional capabilities, but in general inhibited the acceptance and widespread the use of SPLs that were appearing in the mid-1960s.

In Europe ALGOL was the dominant language, and its failure to achieve widespread acceptance in the United States was in part due to the hardware influence: the domination of IBM in the mainframe market at the time. SIMULA 67, as an extension of ALGOL, ushered in the object-oriented programming style. Popularized by Smalltalk in the 1980s, object-oriented programming would become the dominant software methodology in the 1990s.

A burgeoning interest in SPLs stimulated a number of representational issues related to specification and abstraction in model development. Graphical representations were prominent in some early languages, notably the flow chart symbology in GPSS and the Activity-Cycle Diagram (ACD) (or wheel chart) in the Control and Simulation Language (CSL), popular in the United Kingdom.

The recognition of software engineering as an area of study had its own effects on simulation in the late 1960s and early 1970s. Model documentation, stimulated by issues in program documentation, became an important concern as did the life-cycle perspective and the user involvement in model development. Two government reports (U.S. General Accounting Office 1973, 1976), identified major deficiencies in "computerized models" (Many were simulation studies). Sensitivity to good software engineering practices became a requirement for major simulation modeling efforts. Arguments were advanced that model representation should generate model documentation, and that the common consideration of documentation as an after-the-fact "activity" was a major detriment to the effective use of the model.

Influences by Other Computing Technologies. The influences cited in this section derive from the technical areas that do not fit within either hardware or software. A brief description serves to support the assertion that these technical areas have had notable influence on modeling and simulation.

(1) Computer Graphics. Utilizing the capabilities to discriminate based on color, perspective, and motion, advances in computer graphics have led to the use of animation for model output and increased the credibility of simulation results. Interestingly, the early emphasis on graphical input (the flowchart symbols in GPSS and the Activity-Cycle Diagrams) did not persist with the major advances in the 1980s. An early development that never reached commercial use was the RAND Tablet that transformed the drawing of GPSS flow-chart symbols automatically into a GPSS program. GPSS/NORDEN demonstrated the use of output animation using vector graphics. The NORDEN version also provided a graphical depiction of transaction queuing in the GPSS flow diagram to assist in program debugging, which, coupled with the capability for user interrupts, permitted some interactive corrections and changes. Graphical interests in the late 1970s and early 1980s centered on output animation. Color and motion were prominent in depicting product transformations during the execution of the simulation model. Visual Interactive Simulation (VIS) became a prominent technology in the mid-1980s. The current work in graphics is pushing the development of the three-dimensional displays of output behavior.

(2) Human-Computer Interaction. Significant developments in human-computer interaction (HCI) would not have been possible without hardware and software advances that enabled time-sharing operating systems and interactive programming. HCI has the goal of making interactive software efficient, effective, safe, and satisfying in its use. A major consequence of the conjunction of HCI with other advances is an ever-increasing user relief from the requirement to have detailed knowledge of the underlying computing technology. The result has greatly expanded the population of productive users of the ubiquitous digital technology. However, a concomitant result is that, unless the user forces revealing actions, the modeling software hides how the function is performed. An unsettling consequence is that simulation

model users need not be those who developed the model, and users are likely to have little understanding of how the model results are being produced. Furthermore, model developers sometimes lack a sufficient understanding of the internal logic of SPLs to enable the recognition of the erroneous results produced by incorrect models.

(3) Computer Networks. The dumb terminal interface enabled by time-sharing systems of the 1970s, and first used for simulation purposes by the OPS project at MIT in the 1960s, was displaced by the networking of terminal interfaces in the 1980s. Several terminals connected to a minicomputer, supplemented by networked communications among several other minicomputers, were a typical architecture. As the minicomputers gave way to the microprocessor workstations, the growth of networks accelerated. The National Bureau of Standards (now National Institute of Standards and Technology) was a major factor through its leadership in the international arena that led to the creation of local area and metropolitan area networking standards. The preponderance of networked computing, coupled with the emergence of the Internet, provided the enabling factors for the distributed interactive simulation.

(4) The World Wide Web. In this past decade, network computing has expanded to a global level. Web-based simulation is now an implementation issue rather than a research concept. The potential in web-based simulation is for a model to be constructed and provided as a commodity. Users can define a set of parameter values and select alternate structures internal to the model in configuring an experiment. Remote execution is invoked to produce the simulation output. The maintenance and modifications are left with the model producer, and the simulation activity assumes the role of receiving service from a utility. The responsibilities of model producers and simulation experimenters are clearly distinguished.

14.3.2 Internal factors

Modeling. As the SPLs of the early 1960s emerged, each offered a conceptual framework derived from an application area, the influence of a GPL, or some combination of influences. Amidst the din of claims from the language disciples, a few sought to fathom the SPL differences in more fundamental language-independent terms. The world views for continuous, discrete, and combined (discrete and continuous) simulation were categorized. The representations for discrete event simulation included the event, activity, and process representations.

The graphical assistance in model specification accompanied the introduction of the languages for the transaction (GPSS) and activity (CSL) world views. For the latter, the activity-cycle diagram served several SPLs and was the basis for the interactive program generation work in the United Kingdom in the 1970s. Event Graphs were introduced to assist in model building using the event world view. A graphical model representation for the process world view, called Control Flow Graphs, was developed and later extended to Hierarchical Control Flow Graphs to aid in the control of representational complexity.

Model development environments that were research subjects in the 1980s have become the practitioner's initial modeling tool in the 1990s. In 1990, the renaming of the tutorial track "Software" to "Software and Modelware" in the program of the Winter Simulation Conference reflected the expansion of modeling tools beyond the SPL level. Today, visual interactive modeling employs icons, graphical depictions, or actual pictures of system elements imported to provide a more recognizable association with the system counterpart. Modeling methodology, which includes events list management, automated and semi-automated modeling techniques (diagnosis, agent-based approaches), time flow mechanisms, and validation and verification, is recognized as a primary research area. The transition to environments has relieved most practitioners from direct involvement with modeling methodology issues, relegating them to provided functions. This indirect involvement does exact a price: the inability of model users to recognize potential errors. Moreover, these simulation functions remain as essential contributors to the success of a simulation study.

Simulation Functions.

(1) Random Number and Random Variate Generators. Random number generation (RNG), tests for randomness, and transformation techniques (random variate generators) have been active research topics since the advent of the digital computer. The congruential generators displaced the ad hoc techniques in the 1960s, but various unsubstantiated methods for achieving better randomness properties can be found in publications into the 1980s. The field of random variate generation gained maturity in the 1980s after much research in the prior decades.

(2) Tune Flow Mechanisms and Event List Management. Early simulation programs used either a fixed-time increment (FFI) or variable-time increment (VTI) method as the basis for control of time. The developer of an SPL, influenced by application area or perception of run-time efficiency often chose between FTI and VTI inevitably creating the world view implemented in the language. Each world view promotes a particular way of characterizing the relationships among model objects and their attributes depicting time and state.

The event view imposes the implementation of time passing because events occur, and event list management (insertion, reordering, and removal) determines the execution time for a simulation model. A contentious issue in the 1960s was the comparative performance of FTI and VTI methods. It was shown that universal superiority could not be claimed by either method.

During the late 1970s and early 1980s the research in data structures for event list management received major attention. The three-phase extension to the activity scan method dominated in the United Kingdom and the SIMULA co-routine implementation of process interaction had major influence in Europe and a few United States locations. Both of these methods can transition between resembling a next event and an activity scan method. The process view treats the object as primary, but the (process) transactional view characterizes only the dynamic objects as processes. (Hence, the term "active resource" is also used to distinguish the "pure" process view from the transaction view.)

Verification and Validation. In the 1960s, simulation practitioners' major attention had been drawn to the validation issue. Is the model actually representing the truthful behavior of the referent system? The numerous techniques that can be used were identified or developed. While the issues of both verification and validation were of concern from the early days of simulation, often no clear distinction was made between the two terms.

Current views hold verification and validation to be separate processes, each employing the techniques appropriate to the differing objectives. Informally, verification focuses on the activities in developing the model ("producing the model correctly") and validation focuses on the comparison of the model with the referent system ("producing the correct model"). The formal statistical tests developed for model validation are difficult to apply in practice because of the required assumptions and/or the availability of system data. In practice, both verification and validation are often performed using subjective (inspection) approaches, with the validation being given the greater attention.

Analysis Methodology. Richard Conway (1963) initiated a research area that became characterized as analysis methodology. This paper was the first to take a holistic approach to simulation experimentation, identifying the two phases as "strategic planning" and "tactical planning." While this paper concentrates on tactical planning, in particular the difficulties inherent in steady-state parameter estimation, it also discusses the use of variance-reduction techniques and different statistical approaches for comparisons of the alternatives systems (or operating policies) using simulation. The analysis methodology area has been and continues to be an extremely active research area with papers on the subject numbering in the hundreds.

(1) Output Analysis. The analysis of simulation output is divided into two system classes: steady-state and terminating. The systems such as banks and many retail outlets can be modeled as terminating simulations if replications of a defined operating period can be assumed to constitute an independent and identically distributed random sample. The classical statistical analysis techniques can then be employed.

The systems modeled for steady-state analysis introduce the complexities of: ① removal of the bias of the imposed initial model state and ② definition of a sample that admits an accepted estimate of sample variance, which is needed to determine the precision of estimates of steady-state parameters. The removal of initial state bias (also called the initial transient problem), despite some innovative approaches, remains an unresolved problem (unless the regenerative process technique is employed). The estimation of sample variance by imposing assumptions to apply the method of replications and the batch means method (dividing one long series of output values into batches with the autocorrelation among them included in the variance estimate) were both addressed by Conway (1963). Theoretical and experimental research since that time has significantly improved the understanding of the behavioral properties of both methods. Developing procedures to determine appropriate batch sizes remains an active research topic.

Research in other approaches for variance estimation includes spectral analysis, autoregressive models, regenerative processes, overlapping batch means, standardized time series, and the combinations of different methods. Comparative behaviors have been investigated using theoretical and experimental approaches and each method has proponents. Generalized Semi-Markov Processes (GSMPs) have been proposed as a foundation for steady-state output analysis. Variance estimation for steady-state analysis remains an actively investigated problem.

While the discussion above dwells on the estimation of the mean and associated confidence interval for a single simulation model parameter, active research continues on other output analysis techniques. Included in this group are quantile estimation, multiple joint measures, the use of fixed-sample-size versus sequential-sample-size procedures, Bayesian statistics, jackknife and bootstrap sampling.

(2) Experimental Design and Comparison of Alternatives. From the early 1960s until today, considerable research has dealt with the use of the classical design of experiments in simulation for such applications as the comparison of alternatives, metamodeling, optimization, sensitivity analysis, and validation. Conway, in his 1963 paper, suggested that the newly proposed (at that time) ranking and selection (R&S) procedures were more appropriate for the comparison of alternatives than the techniques derived from the classical design of experiments. In the interim, considerable research has been conducted in R&S procedures in general and specifically for simulation. Software enabling the use of R&S procedures in simulation studies is now included in several commercial simulation products. The use of variance-reduction techniques with the design of experiments and with R&S procedures is the subject of numerous articles.

(3) Metamodels and Optimization. Metamodels — (simple) mathematical models of the output response surface of a simulation model — have been studied in terms of both the metamodeling role and the types of the models that can be used.

The optimization of simulation model output has a number of complexities. The number of model variables is often large, and a variable (or parameter) can take on a large or infinite number of values. Sometimes the response surface is multimodal. Various approaches have been suggested over the years, including the use of gradient-based optimization methods, response surface methodologies (including metamodels), pattern search methods, and random search. Much of the attention to these methods involves the convergence to a local or global optimum. The sophistication and computational intensity of these methods limit their use in practice.

More recent research (1990s) has taken a different tack towards optimization: expressing the objective so as to obtain a "good" but not necessarily optimal solution. These approaches use some type of metaheuristics such as tabu search or a genetic algorithm. Several commercial simulation software systems today contain "optimization" packages based on one of these approaches.

(4) Variance-Reduction Techniques. Variance-reduction (or reducing) techniques (VRTs) received much attention in the early days of simulation since computer time was extremely expensive, and reductions in run time represented valuable savings. The extensive use of VRTs in Monte Carlo studies suggested similar efficiencies in (discrete event) simulation. Using VRTs in the collection and analysis of data has been a focus. While a few VRTs are simple to use, most VRTs are sophisticated and model dependent, which limits their general use. A counterexample is common random numbers, often found in commercial simulation products because they are easy to understand and simple to apply. The two cases where (sophisticated) VRTs are justified: ① simulation models investigating rare events and ② simulation models that exact excessive computation time.

Theory of Simulation. As early as 1964 Lackner had proposed the use of system theory as a basis for simulation modeling. First with a journal paper in 1972, then with his book in 1976, Zeigler built an explanatory theory of simulation based on systems-theoretic concepts. This work had a major impact on those who sought to separate the expression of simulation concepts from their implementation in SPLs. The theoretical structure applied to discrete event, continuous, and combined models provided a linkage that heretofore was difficult for many to conceive.

Factors Contributing Jointly to Simulation and Computer Science. Although originating in simulation, at least three concepts have had a major influence in the areas of computer science and the advancement of computing technology.

(1) The Process Concept. Embodied restrictively in the GPSS transaction representation and expanded more elegantly in the SIMULA process interaction world view, the process concept is a lasting contribution to both simulation and operating systems. Its influence in simulation was to provide the realization of an entity whose dynamic behavior it sought to mimic. In the operating system context the process presented a quasi-independent program segment in execution, and served as a major concept underlying computational models. The process concept within the co-routine execution environment provided by SIMULA provided a powerful mechanism for expanding the ability to represent complex systems.

(2) The Entity/Attribute/Set Concept. Introduced by Kiviat et al. (1968) in SIMSCRIPT II, this modeling perspective provided a rigorous basis for describing the static relationships among objects. Entities could be the members of and owners of sets, yet each was described individually by its own attributes. Coupled with the recognition of the relationships among entities, the underlying concepts of the entity relational model of data were actually present in simulation for almost 10 years before their recognition by the database community.

(3) Object-Oriented Programming. The revision to SIMULA I, known as SIMULA 67, introduced the object-oriented paradigm (OOP) with the concepts of abstract data types, encapsulation, inheritance, and message passing. The co-routine concept from the earlier version, enhanced by the OOP capabilities, promoted a very powerful style of simulation programming, so powerful that after two decades the OOP became the predominant style for programming in general. This particular factor has exerted an effect far beyond simulation, substantiated by the fact that four of the eight most significant languages selected for the 1993 History of Programming Languages II Conference (HOPL II) traced their major roots to SIMULA (Ada, C++, CLU, and Smalltalk).

Combined Simulation. The evolution of GASP enabled combined continuous and discrete modeling in GASP IV through the work of Pritsker (1974). Pritsker and his students worked out the detailed transitional relationships between the continuous and discrete computations by adding the necessary subroutines to the earlier version of the language (GASP II) and providing an alternative definition of the term "event."

Parallel Simulation. Initiated by research in the late 1970s and early 1980s, parallel simulation became a major area of research in the middle to late 1980s and extending into the 1990s. Fueled by the time warp concept, the research using this optimistic protocol in which checkpointing with rollback and recovery is required, was contrasted with the conservative protocol where no events were executed unless correct temporal ordering was guaranteed. A series of conferences bearing the name PADS (Parallel and Distributed Simulation) began in 1985, and the Proceedings contains much of this research. Strong tensions between the proponents of the two protocols marked the early conferences, but now have all but disappeared. The intense early interest in the subject has also waned considerably.

A special issue of the ORSA Journal on Computing in 1993, guest edited by Richard Fujimoto and devoted to parallel discrete event simulation, raised the issue of why parallel simulation has not been accepted in the broader domain of simulation practice. Numerous answers were offered, both within and outside the PADS community, but no consensus has formed.

Distributed Interactive Simulation. Enabled by network computing advances, the concept of distributed interactive simulation originated in the military domain for training. Major funding by ARPA/DARPA permitted the demonstration that remotely executing simulation models could communicate, although major questions still remain regarding the correct representation of temporal causality and trade-offs between the level of model fidelity versus the cost of the training experiment. The early Distributed Interactive Simulation (DIS) and Aggregate Level Simulation Protocol (ALSP) are being supplanted by the High Level Architecture (HLA) protocol, intended to enable interoperability among DOD simulation models.

14.4 Organizational factors

14.4.1 Conferences and symposia

The interest in the new field of computer simulation and excitement about future prospects was high in the late 1950s. Meetings provided the prime venue for communications. One of the first was the System Simulation Symposium held in 1957, to be followed closely by the Second Symposium on System Simulation in 1959. Another of note was the IBM Scientific Computing Symposium on Simulation Models and Gaming held in December 1964 with 175 attendees. Workshops on simulation languages were held at Stanford University in 1964 and at the University of Pennsylvania in 1966, the latter having 110 attendees. The NATO-sponsored conference on digital simulation held in Hamburg in 1965 had 180 attendees. A symposium on "The Design of Computer Simulation Experiments," sponsored by the Institute of Management Sciences (TIMS) College on Simulation and Gaming, was held at Duke University in 1968 (250 attendees). IBM's SHARE User Group set up a System Simulation Project that held meetings where changes to GPSS were discussed. Three members of this group, H. Hixson, A. Ockene, and J. Reitman, feeling the need for a national conference on the applications of simulation, organized the "Conference on the Applications of Simulation Using GPSS" in November 1967 in New York City. A planned attendance of 225 and an actual of 401 encouraged a successor, held in December 1968. The follow-up conference was called "The Second Conference on the Applications of Simulation" (note the removal of GPSS); the proceedings were issued; and the attendance numbered 856.

The two application-oriented conferences above began what is now called the Winter Simulation Conference (WSC). See http://www.wintersim.org/article.htm for a regularly updated overview of the conference and its more recent history. The WSC, held each December, is the premier conference in simulation, attracting international attendees drawn from researchers, practitioners, and simulation software vendors. Considered a "model" conference, the WSC is sponsored by several societies, including INFORMS, and is run by volunteers. The conference attracts high quality papers, publishes electronic and hard-copy proceedings, and offers exhibits by vendors.

The Annual Simulation Symposium, initiated in 1968 by Ira Kay, is a single-track conference. Operating now under Society for Modeling and Simulation International (SCS) sponsorship, the symposium lays claim to being the longest continuously running simulation conference.

In response to growing interest in the modeling of computer systems for performance evaluation in the 1970s, the Association for Computing Machinery (ACM) Special Interest Group on SIMulation (SIGSIM) and the National Bureau of Standards cosponsored a series of symposia (with proceedings) and workshops on the topic. The specialized languages for computer systems simulation were developed during this period, and a Federal agency,

FEDSIM, was established for computer system performance improvement.

Two conferences on simulation research were held by SICSIM of NYC (Special Interest Committee for SIMulation of New York City) under Nabil Adam's leadership. Papers from the first led to the publication of a book, Adam and Dogramaci (1979), and those from the second to a special issue of Communications of the ACM (April 1981). Nabil Adam, Richard E. Nance and Robert G. Sargent organized a follow-up conference sponsored by ORSA and SICSIM of NYC that led to a special issue of Operations Research (November-December 1983).

Tuncer Oren was extremely active in the organization of meetings in Europe, notably a 1979 workshop on the standardization of simulation languages in St. Agata, Italy. Francois Cellier (1982) renewed the European model of the conference with the papers appearing in a book (as had the NATO conference proceedings earlier). Oren, Maurice Elzas, and Bernard Zeigler organized a series of four conferences following this model.

Described above as the areas of intense research activity, parallel and distributed simulation spawned a conference bearing the acronym "PADS" that since the mid-1980s has occurred (with proceedings) almost annually. Technically related to PADS is the Simulation Interoperability Workshop (SIW), a semiannual meeting encompassing a broad range of modeling and simulation issues, applications, and communities (see http://siso.sc.ist.ucf.edu/siw/).

A dozen or more conferences with simulation in the title or featuring simulation as a major topic are offered annually, sponsored by numerous organizations. The Summer Computer Simulation Conference (SCSC) is a complementary conference to the WSC. Sponsored by SCS and originally limited to continuous simulation, the scope in recent years has expanded to include discrete event simulation. Several multiconferences are sponsored or cosponsored by SCS, with a typical format of concurrent one — and two-day miniconferences involving different technical and applications topics.

14.4.2 Professional organizations

Simulation draws its professional lifeblood from special interest groups within larger societies. The principal group today is the INFORMS College on Simulation (CS), founded in 1963 as the College of Simulation and Gaming (CSG) within TIMS. Another group is SIGSIM of ACM, formed in 1967 and extremely active in the 1970s and 1980s. Preceding both TIMS/CSG and ACM/SIGSIM was SCS, originally founded as Simulation Councils Inc. in 1952 under the leadership of John McLeod. Originally limited to continuous simulation, SCS now includes all types and forms of simulation. Within the Institute of Electrical and Electronic Engineers (IEEE) are the Computer Society and the Systems, Man, and Cybernetics Society. Both have strong interests in simulation, and the former has a subgroup with the title Technical Committee on Simulation (TCSIM). Simulation is also an area of technical and publication interest for the Institute of Industrial Engineers (IIE).

14.4.3 Simulation coverage in journals

Various professional journals established departments to handle simulation papers in the mid-to-late 1970s: AIIE Transactions in 1976 with Richard E. Nance as editor, Management Science in 1978 with George Fishman as editor, Operations Research in 1978 with Richard E. Nance as editor, and the Communications of ACM (CACM) in 1980 with Robert G. Sargent as editor. (CACM transitioned from a focus on research papers to informative articles in the late 1980s.) When the ORSA (now INFORMS) Journal on Computing was established in 1989, it contained an area on simulation with Richard E. Nance as its editor.

SCS established an archival journal in 1984 called Transactions of the Society for Computer Simulation to handle both continuous and discrete event simulations. The journal Transactions on Modeling and Computer Simulation (TOMACS), devoted primarily to discrete event simulation, was established by ACM in 1990 with Richard E. Nance as editor-in-chief. The current publication venue offers numerous archival journals where simulation papers can be published.

From 1988 to 1994 Paul Fishwick maintained Simulation Digest, the first online publication devoted explicitly to simulation interests. Another online publication bearing the same name was launched during the 1988–1990 time frame jointly by Fishwick (Chair of TCSIM) and Stephen Roberts (Chair of SIGSIM) to serve as a joint organizational newsletter.

14.5 Concluding summary

In drawing this trace of the evolution of simulation to a close, comments on three aspects are offered. The first concerns the breadth and extent of simulation applications; the second relates to the differences in views of scholarly depth of simulation research; and the third pertains to the future of simulation.

14.5.1 Applications: What cannot be simulated?

From the beginning, the ingenuity and innovation with which simulation is applied have proved impressive. The adoption of simulation in numerous fields has created a disturbing side effect as well: The term is often inappropriately used. An early book, Shapiro and Rogers (1967), provides a fascinating collection of papers on self-reproducing systems, the use of graphics in studying dynamic system instability, associative processor design, and the simulation of the human aorta for studying artificial blood pumps, design of a parallel network computer, torpedo performance analysis, and so forth. A common misconception was, and still persists, that any computational process produces a "simulation." Nevertheless, the proper applications of the technique have abounded.

14.5.2 Simulation as a scholarly activity

Until the late-1960s, fundamental developments in simulation were readily accepted in the scientific literature. About this time an attitude of scholarly disrespect seemed to emerge. Many professionals in management science and operations research cast simulation as the "method of last resort" and expressed the view that "anyone could do it." Unfortunately, the belief that simulation was simply a programming exercise led to that conviction becoming widespread among those who understood neither simulation nor computer programming.

Did this pejorative view arise from the misuse of the term "simulation," the far-reaching applications in so many diverse fields, or the preoccupation of OR and MS with mathematical sophistication? Or did it stem from a combination of these factors? The answer is not obvious, but the emergence of simulation departments (or areas) in the archival journals in the late 1970s gave the evidence of a reputation regained. An increasing number of simulation researchers were finding outlets for quality publications.

14.5.3 The future of simulation

Computer graphics, virtual reality, and virtual environments are defining new vistas for simulation, but at the same time creating threats to overwhelm it. Entertainment uses and extensions of the technique offer the financial inducements that are mind-boggling. Real-time and web-based models can expand and extend the impact far beyond its current level. At the same time, simulation-based acquisition and medical training applications impose the requirements that appear daunting. Perhaps we are on the verge of achieving that which J. C. R. Licklider (1967) predicted some 35 years ago:

In their dynamic form, however, computer-program models appeal to the recipient's understanding directly through his perception of dynamic behavior. That mode of appeal is beyond the reach of ordinary documents. When we have learned how to take good advantage of it, it may — indeed, I believe it will — be the greatest boon to scientific and technical communication, and to the teaching and learning of science and technology, since the invention of writing on a flat surface.

 Professional Vocabularies and Expressions

simulation	仿真
Monte Carlo model	蒙特卡罗模型
state	状态
state sequence	状态序列
state change	状态变化
discrete event model	离散事件模型
continuous simulation	连续仿真
discretized simulation	离散仿真
hybrid simulation	混合仿真
submodel	子模型
batch mode	批处理模式

real-time interaction	实时交互
game	游戏
gaming	赌博
analog computer	模拟计算机
digital computer	数字计算机
artificial sampling	人工抽样
correlation coefficient	相关系数
Student's *t*-statistic	史蒂特氏 t 统计量
computer simulation	计算机仿真
conceptual model	概念模型
random number generator(RNG)	随机数生成器
random variate generator(RVG)	随机变量生成器
list processing routine	（事件）列表处理程序
time flow mechanism	计时机制
simulation programming language (SPL)	仿真编程语言
general purpose language (GPL)	通用语言
variable-time incrementing(VTI)	变动时间拨钟
fixed-time incrementing(FTI)	固定时间拨钟
octal	八进制（的）
hexadecimal	十六进制（的）
output analysis	输出分析
random number stream	随机数流
mean	均值
variance	方差
differential equation	微分方程
discrete event simulation	离散事件仿真
mainframe computer	大型计算机
core memory	存储器
keypunch	键盘打孔
mainframe	主机
minicomputer	小型机
parallel processor	并行处理器
networks of processors	处理器网络
desktop	台式机
laptop	便携机
machine language	机器语言
assembly language	汇编语言

general simulation program (GSP)	通用仿真程序
formula translation (FORTRAN)	公式翻译程序语言
simulation package	仿真软件包
algorithmic language (ALGOL)	Algol 算法语言
object-oriented programming	面向对象程序设计
general-purpose system simulator (GPSS)	通用系统仿真程序
flowchart symbol	流程图
activity-cycle diagram (ACD)	活动循环图
control and simulation language (CSL)	控制和仿真语言
computer graphics	计算机图形学
vector graphics	向（矢）量图
visual interactive simulation (VIS)	视觉交互仿真
human-computer interaction (HCI)	人机交互
time-sharing operating system (TSOS)	分时操作系统
interactive programming	交互式编程
computer network	计算机网络
microprocessor workstation	微处理器工作站
National Institute of Standards and Technology (NIST)	美国标准技术研究院
distributed interactive simulation	分布式交互仿真
network computing	网络计算
web-based simulation	基于网络的仿真
event	事件
activity	活动
process	流程
event graph	事件图
control flow graph	控制流程图
hierarchical control flow graph	层次（递阶）控制流程图
events list management	事件列表管理
agent-based simulation	基于主体的仿真
congruential random number generator	迭代随机数生成器
analysis methodology	分析方法
steady-state parameter estimation	稳态参数预算
variance-reduction technique	方差消减技术
output analysis	输出分析
steady-state output	稳态输出
terminating output	中止状态输出

initial transient problem	初始（状态）变化问题
regenerative process technique	再生流程技术
variance estimation	方差估计
spectral analysis	光谱分析（法）
generalized semi-Markov process (GSMP)	广义半马尔科夫链
confidence interval	置信区间
quantile estimation	分位数估算
Bayesian statistics	贝氏统计
jackknife sampling	刀切法抽样
bootstrap sampling	自助法抽样
design of experiment (DOE)	实验设计
metamodeling	元模型建模
ranking and selection (R&S)	排序和选择
response surface	响应表面
multimodal	多模的
gradient-based optimization	梯度优化
tabu search	禁忌搜索
genetic algorithm	基因算法
common random number	共同随机数
encapsulation	封装（压缩）
inheritance	继承（遗传）
message passing	消息传递
aggregate level simulation protocol (ALSP)	聚合级仿真协议
high level architecture (HLA)	高层体系结构
virtual reality	虚拟现实
virtual environment	虚拟环境

 Notes

1. Youthful faces and sprightly gaits aside, we are made even more conscious of the huge gaps in computing history separating us from our students when we realize that most today do not recognize the terms: "mainframe computer," "core memory," or "keypunch."

除了年轻的面孔和轻快的步伐之外，就计算机的发展历史而言，我们更清楚地意识到我们与学生之间存在巨大的代沟还表现在（作为长辈的）我们大多对大型计算机、存储器和键盘打孔等术语不甚了解。

2. Amidst the din of claims from the language disciples, a few sought to fathom the SPL

differences in more fundamental language-independent terms.

在（仿真）语言的信徒们正在争论不休时，少数（学者）开始寻求用更基本的、与（仿真）语言无关的术语来研究仿真编程语言间的不同。

3. In 1990, the renaming of the tutorial track "Software" to "Software and Modelware" in the program of the Winter Simulation Conference reflected the expansion of modeling tools beyond the SPL level.

1990年举行的冬季仿真会议将（传统的）"软件"部分重新命名为"软件和建模工具"，（这一变化）反映出建模工具已经超越了仿真建模语言的范畴。

4. This indirect involvement does exact a price: the inability of model users to recognize potential errors.

（仿真人员）不直接介入（编程）确实是要付出一定代价的，即建模者不能够识别潜在的错误。

5. Entertainment uses and extensions of the technique offer financial inducements that are mind-boggling.

（仿真）技术在娱乐界的应用和扩展产生财务上的诱惑，使人犹豫不决。

Discussion Questions:

1. Summarize the external and internal technical factors that have helped shaping simulation.
2. What are your comments on the argument that "simulation was simply a programming exercise"?
3. What are the situations or areas where, most likely, you will resort to simulation? Why do analytical or mathematical methods fail in those situations?
4. How much do you know about simulation systems like Arena, AutoMod, Flexsim Anylogic, Swarm or Netlogo? What do you think might be the future of simulation in China, from both industrial and academic perspectives?

第四篇

丰田制造模式

CHAPTER 15

Classification of JIT Techniques

This is an endeavor to understand JIT from the inside by analyzing its techniques, classifying them and examining their possible relations. More than 6 years of research devoted to the JIT system has led to tentatively distinguishing among its elements two main categories: JIT's industrial engineering techniques and Japanese management-related features of JIT. The interconnections among the elements are shown in Figure 15-1.

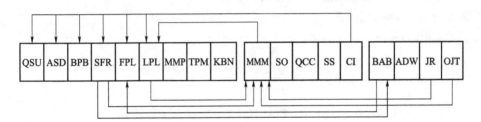

Figure 15-1 Interconnection among the groups

It is a question of JIT techniques that can be seen as belonging or related to the field of industrial engineering. They can be divided into two groups. There are pure industrial engineering methods and there are industrial engineering elements that are closely associated with the worker's actions.

15.1 JIT's pure engineering elements

In this category, one has to find the techniques that are universally valid like the laws of physics or mathematics. They have no close relationship with the social, cultural, economic or managerial environment in which they appear or are discovered for the first time. Those elements can therefore be applied anywhere and yield the same results. The following are the elements of the JIT production system identified as belonging to that group:

(1) Quick set-up (QSU);

(2) Automation (ASD) (poka yoke or automatic stopping device, full-work system);

(3) Breaking of physical barriers (BPB) between processes, sections or departments: Shop floor reduction (SFR);

(4) Flow-of-products-oriented layout of processes and machines (FPL);

(5) U-formed processing line (UPL);

(6) Mass production of mixed models (MMP)—on the same line;

(7) Total preventive maintenance (TPM);

(8) Kanban (KBN).

Those engineering elements constitute the "technical side" of JIT or "technical JIT." Applying them anywhere would unavoidably contribute to the reduction of cost, production lead time, defective parts (work), overproduction of work-in-process inventories and workforce.

15.2 Worker's operations/activities as JIT elements

The worker's operations can and do constitute some JIT elements. In other words, you have JIT techniques that are part of the worker's activities and that interact with the human being. Their application and realization or success depend also on the human factor. If they are accepted by the work force, then they can work, otherwise they cannot. In that group may be included the following JIT techniques or methods:

(1) Multi-machine manning working system (MMM);

(2) Standard operations (SO);

(3) Quality control circles (QCC);

(4) Suggestions system (SS); and

(5) Continuous improvement (CI).

15.3 Japanese management-related elements of JIT

The Japanese-management-related elements of JIT are JIT methods that are either imported directly from or highly conditioned by Japanese management. Included in that category are the following techniques:

(1) Breaking of administrative barriers (BAB) between processes from the point of view of the paper work and work function definition;

(2) Autonomation (ADW) (decision by worker to stop the line);

(3) Job rotation (JR); and

(4) On-the-job training (OJT).

BAB means eliminating the paper work that has to be completed before the move of products from one station or process to another or from one section to another takes place. ADW refers to an "autonomous" worker capable of stopping, based on his own judgment, the production line in case of trouble occurrence.

It is worth pointing out that autonomation and the breaking of barriers each have two assets: a technical and a managerial aspect. Therefore, they have been mentioned as JIT elements pertaining to industrial engineering as well as to Japanese management.

15.4 Is the classification justifiable?

One may wonder why the human-related elements have not been dealt with as a sub-group in the group of management features of JIT. The multi-machine handling seems to be too technical to be classified in the category of management-related features of JIT. It has been thought of as a set of technical actions, motions and operations requiring technical skills that do not have much in common with the pure management features. There is a strong influence from the Japanese management system on the multi-machine working system. This occurs because of the similarities of the situations one finds in both the Japanese management and JIT systems. But MMM remains a technique of industrial engineering.

The same question may be also raised about QCC, SS and CI. Are they not Japanese management-related elements of JIT? QCC, SS and CI are now so wide-spread in almost all kinds of Japanese companies, regardless of their respective industry, that they may be thought of as management features that JIT has adopted. That would be an error of perception. One should remember that QCC, for example, did not proceed or develop from the well-known small groups that are recognized as being specific to Japanese management. They have their origins in the quality control ideas introduced in Japan by Dr. Deming, and in the famous zero defects of NASA. The notions of zero defects and quality control evoke the shop floor environment and at the same time suggest the idea of CI. Suggestions for CI are closely related to QCC, and can even be seen as an emanation of QCC. The main difference between the two elements is that SS may involve either an individual or a group while QCC is always a matter of a group or a team.

This article attempts to put into the category of the management-related techniques of JIT only the "raw" features of Japanese management. Raw referring to the management characteristics that are found unchanged in JIT (e.g. JR). Those elements are found not only in the factory management but also in any kind of Japanese company regardless of the type of industry.

There are reasons the other side of autonomation among management features of JIT is included. At first, it is sure that autonomation, as a whole, may sound too technical. This is true when it refers only to machines and processes. But when applied to the person of the worker, it loses its technical resonance. An autonomous worker refers only to an officially recognized responsible and trusted worker. Such a worker is not the only one confined in the production shop floor and who deals primarily with machines. The Japanese office worker is also very autonomous because he is given the powers to perform many duties that in other countries are in the sphere of the management authorities. Take, for example, the simple case of student's academic record transcripts. Both in Zaire and in Japan, they bear the stamp and/or signature of the dean. The main difference is that in Zaire the dean signs it himself while in Japan the dean's name is stamped by a clerk.

15.5 Significance of the classification

Grasping the nature of JIT components is like understanding the individuals who belong to a community, an approach that helps in dealing with the community one wants to know about. In a similar manner, the comprehension of the nature of the JIT elements (and if possible their internal relationship) should prove an efficient way of:

(1) grasping JIT as a system itself; and

(2) examining the possibility of its transfer in another environment.

For a number of observers, JIT may look only like a pure production method having little or nothing to do with the surrounding environment. One should, however, keep in mind the fact that it was born and developed neither at a technical research center nor in an engineering department of some university. It took form on a shop floor. And in the shop, the work force and management are the most important role players. In fact, the work force performs its job within and through the company-defined management framework. That is why the work hypothesis has been that JIT as a production system draws many of its elements from three primary sources: industrial engineering, work force (worker's operations) and (Japanese) company management.

The different classes of JIT elements are not independent. They are part of the same reality (i.e., JIT), and they are closely related to each other.

In fact, one should have realized that JR and OJT, which have been classified as management-related features, are crucial factors in transforming the line workers into MMM operators.

Closely related to the MMM system is UPL. UPL becomes useful and effective if the work force accepts performing many operations simultaneously. Therefore its success depends also on that of the MMM acceptability by the work force.

On the other hand, the UPL should be viewed as a technical tool of making the MMM system more efficient thanks to the flexibility it offers. It helps increase or decrease the number of the processes or machines an operator can simultaneously handle. It can facilitate the checking or recording of the processing lead time of each item because of the fact that the starting and final points may be at the same position. If the work force resists becoming multimachine handlers, UPL would play only the role of a technical ornamentation.

15.6 Lessons

There are lessons to draw from the suggested classification of JIT elements. First, JIT pure-engineering elements can be applied efficiently anywhere. Second, both Japanese-management-related and worker's-operations-related features of JIT will not necessarily work in different contexts, due to their entrenchment in the Japanese socio-cultural environment. Third, due to the complexity of links between all elements of JIT, it seems that even the pure engineering JIT could not be as productive as it is in Japan unless it is accompanied by other

JIT elements or equivalently compensated for by local features.

Besides those overall lessons, it is necessary to point to the fact that within each class, JIT elements are linked to each other.

Five observations can be made concerning JIT's pure industrial engineering elements. First, QSU should be considered as having an order of precedence over the other elements especially while dealing with the introduction of JIT. In order not to be trapped by the famous economic lot size, the shortening of the changeover time should be the first thing to realize before starting. Furthermore, it is meaningless for machines to stop themselves in cases of slight malfunctioning or errors if changeovers take many hours. The wise option would be to correct errors by rework. ASD would not pay off, but would backfire if machines are not maintained. Frequent breakdowns and defective occurrences would trigger the autonomation mechanism, which would frequently shut down the entire production line.

Second, though SFR slashed the production lead time by curtailing the transportation time, that would not be so significant if there were no flow of products, and if the products had to go through twistedly complicated ways (absence of FPL). SFR gets more effective as it is sustained by FPL.

Third, BPB makes sense only if the production of defectives is neither allowed nor tolerated. And this is achieved through ASDs such as poka yoke. Otherwise, barriers would be required to check the acceptability of each lot before it moves to or enters another process. Barriers would be necessary as they would fulfill the role of inspection stations.

Fourth, UPL is impossible to realize if barriers between processes are not torn down. Such a layout would be neither useful nor effective if machines and processes are not arranged in the sense of the flow of products. Besides it would be impossible to join different processes to form a U-line if those processes are too far from each other.

Fifth, kanban is effective only if the kanban-controlled production and the kanban itself can flow smoothly between processes. TPM prevents machines from breaking down and/or malfunctioning during the production time and also contributes to the efficiency of kanban.

Though pure IE elements of JIT have been thought of as able to work in any environment, all isolated elements may not. The order of their implementation is crucial. Otherwise, the implementation cannot be brought into fruition. In order to be effective, the kanban needs the QSU. Figure 15-2 shows clearly that the mass production of the mixed models depends on both the implementation of the kanban and QSU. On the other hand, the QSU that is aiming neither at the MMM system nor at MMP does not seem necessary. And the kanban without the QSU will result in a failure with devastating effects.

As for workers' operations that are considered JIT elements, it should be noted first that the MMM system and SO are closely associated and their core is the multi-machine handling system. SO can be understood within the MMM system. In fact, SO can be seen as a method, a means for:

160 CHAPTER 15

(1) coordinating and harmonizing different actions or operations of an MMM worker; and

(2) synchronizing them with those of other multimachine handling operators working on the same production line.

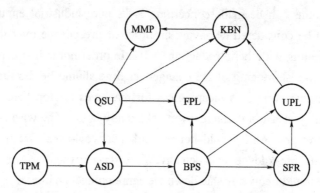

Figure 15-2   Interconnection between pure IE features

QCC and SS are the best instances of CI activities. And CI sustains the system dynamics that prevents it from ever being 100 percent satisfied with its own achievements by setting up reasonably unreachable goals such as zero set-up times, zero inventories, zero defects, one-at-a-time processing line, JIT delivery, etc. In such a context, SO is under CI, and the number of the machines an operator can handle varies continuously due to CI activities.

Figure 15-3 shows that QCC and SS contribute to the success of CI. The latter contributes to the multi-machine manning system and SO being effective. At the same time, SO sustains MMM.

For Japanese management elements that have become part of JIT, JR and OJT are directly related. JR could not work if there are no on-the-site-training programs. Besides, removing barriers facilitates JR. And both BAB and JR clarify to workers the fact that an operator can stop the entire processing line while some problem occurs in the process. Other line workers know that if they are in a similar situation they would use the same powers they are given to stop the entire processing line. The interconnections among management features are shown in Figure 15-4.

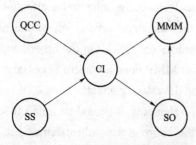 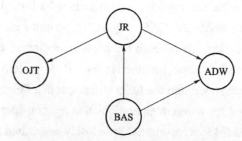

Figure 15-3   Interconnection between worker operations   **Figure 15-4   Interconnection between management features**

15.7 Summary

JIT's pure industrial elements seem to make up the core of that production system. However, workers' operations and management features that have become JIT elements also play an important role. JIT is a complex reality whose effectiveness depends upon a wide range of parameters.

Should one want to have the full JIT successfully carried out, he has a much harder task, since there are more steps to go through methodically and maybe simultaneously or sequentially. A partial implementation of JIT, say the "technical" JIT, is less demanding and it has more chances of being fruitful because there are fewer steps to undertake. It would, however, have only limited results.

In either case, it should be emphasized that skipping a conditioning step may have destructive effects. Switching to the mass production of mixed models would never work and would be costly if there is no quick setup and no defect-free production.

From the practical point of view, the figures can fulfill the role of either instruments for evaluating JIT or instructions for JIT implementation. Why did you succeed or fail, partially or completely, in implementing JIT at your company? The figures can provide some answers to this question. By showing causal links between JIT elements, the figures suggest some necessary steps to follow while switching to the JIT production and can prevent or minimize the risk of inadvertently skipping important steps.

Professional Vocabularies and Expressions

Just in Time (JIT)	准时制造
Japanese management	日式管理
quick set-up (QSU)	快速启动
automation (ASD)	自动化
poka yoke or automatic stopping device	自动停线设施
breaking of physical barriers (BPB)	打破物理分隔
shop floor reduction (SFR)	车间缩减
flow-of-products-oriented layout (FPL)	面向产品流动的布局
U-formed processing line (UPL)	U形生产线
mass production of mixed models (MMP)	混合型号产品的大规模生产
total preventive maintenance (TPM)	全面预防性维护
kanban (KBN)	看板
production lead time	生产提前期
defective part	次品

work-in-process	在制品
multi-machine manning working system (MMM)	多设备配员工作系统
standard operations (SO)	操作标准化
quality control circles (QCC)	质量控制圈
suggestions system (SS)	建议系统
continuous improvement (CI)	持续改进
breaking of administrative barriers (BAB)	打破管理界线
autonomation (ADW)	员工自治（有决定停线的权利）
job rotation (JR)	工作轮换，轮岗
on-the-job training (OJT)	在线培训，在岗培训
zero inventories	零库存
zero defects	零缺陷

Notes

They have their origins in the quality control ideas introduced in Japan by Dr. Deming, and in the famous zero defects of NASA.

戴明博士（Dr. W. Edwards Deming, 1900.10.14—1993.12.20），是近代著名的质量管理大师，1928年从耶鲁大学获得了数学物理学博士。他是一位教日本人提升品质的美国人。1950年7月，戴明受邀至日本对一群日本企业领导人讲述质量管理的重要性。他的理念鼓舞了日本产业的革新，并进而反过来给了美国经济沉重的打击。他被日本人尊称为"质量之神"。1951年起，以他的名字命名的戴明奖已被日本企业界视为最高荣誉。

Discussion Questions:

1. This paper classifies JIT techniques into three categories: pure engineering elements, worker's operations or activities elements and Japanese management related elements. Which of these elements are shared by Western and Japanese companies? And which ones are specific only to Japanese companies?

2. According to Michael Porter, "Competitive strategy is about being different. It means deliberately choosing a different set of activities to deliver a unique mix of value." Try to explain the success of JIT based on this statement.

CHAPTER 16

Industrial Engineering of the Toyota Production System

16.1 Introduction

This paper is intended to highlight the undervalued industrial engineering contribution of the Gilbreths to the Toyota Production System (TPS). As background we note that all evidence suggests Ohno[1] was the inspired industrial engineer responsible for conceiving the TPS architecture. Typical of all innovative engineering projects, TPS brings together, sifts, and successfully adapts the ideas from many sources. Critically, TPS is manifestly a system, in which case the totality is (much) greater than the sum of the constituent parts. Furthermore, effective linking of the latter is critical in enabling improved throughput. Finally, such large-scale systems take considerable time and effort to analyze requirements, plan, design, test pilot schemes, implement full-scale solutions, and manage start-up. This is the remit of the industrial engineering discipline, which is the TPS area linked (by just two handshakes at most) to Lillian Gilbreth.

The viewpoint here is that the Toyota Production System is an evolutionary output with some of its roots clearly traceable back to method study (and indeed to the construction of the UK Crystal Palace Exhibition Building of 1851). Historically method study detail then rapidly expanded into the university discipline of industrial engineering (IE) but still with a very narrow focus. Post WWII and the ensuing close association with OR (Operation Research) and systems engineering, the scope expanded to cover multi-processes and multiple flows together with more informed design principles and control strategies. The quality movement helped enable what was ordered to actually output useful goods (as distinct from making

---

[1] **Taiichi Ohno** (大野耐一 Ōno Taiichi, February 29, 1912–May 28, 1990) was a prominent Japanese businessman. He is considered to be the father of the Toyota Production System, which became Lean Manufacturing in the U.S. He devised the seven wastes (or muda in Japanese) as part of this system. He wrote several books about the system, including *Toyota Production System: Beyond Large-Scale Production*. Ohno's principles influenced the areas outside manufacturing, and have been extended into the service arena. For example, the field of sales process engineering has shown how the concept of Just in Time (JIT) can improve sales, marketing, and customer service processes.

scrap). There are three traceable pathways connecting method study and TPS, which we shall pursue. These include the Japanese Management Association, the lecture activities of Lillian Gilbreth and her associates, and finally via the Scientific Management Movement and Frederick Winslow Taylor.

Other related topics include the contributions of the quality movement, JIT designers, and the industrial engineering viewpoint of Shigeo Shingo. The cultural implications of successful TPS implementation compared with earlier industrial relation problems are also exemplified herein. An important adjunct is the positing of "contemporary" industrial engineering. This perspective is keenly shared by at least one Japanese author[①]. However, an American author apparently still anchored in the "traditional" IE more reminiscent of the inter-war years had a simple vision for TPS — the achievement of continuous material flow. We also examine the "systems" context of TPS operation which ensures the whole is greater than the sum of the constituent parts.

The references found helpful in providing the evidence supporting this paper are manifold. However, it may be useful to emphasize that they all fall into three major groups. First, there are the industrial historians. Second, the analysts and chroniclers. Third and finally, the "hands-on" industrial engineers. In some particular cases, the foregoing divisions are separated by flexible curtains, rather than brick walls. For example, several authors have at some time published under more than one category.

16.2 Continuous material flow

An early example of JIT is the 1851 design and construction of the UK Crystal Palace. Important contributions to the future of logistics and mass production were undoubtedly made in the execution of this massive project. The real innovation was in the process of producing the components, delivering them to the site, and putting them together. Wilkinson (2000) thus comments:

The exhibition hall was not built. It was assembled. The various parts (including cast-iron columns, wrought iron beams, wooden components, and glass) were made all over the UK and delivered directly to the exhibition site by train. They arrived more or less ready for use, and at the right time and were taken straight to the place where they were needed.

He continues:

There was very little stockpiling. There was also very little waste. A few panes of glass were broken, but not much else. The entire process, from Paxton's initial design to completion on the Hyde Park site took less than nine months. The feat (of covering a floor area 563m × 124m) is rarely matched, even today.

[①] J. Ishiwata. Industrial Engineering for the Shop Floor: Productivity Through Process Analysis [M]. Cambridge, MA: Productivity Press, 1991.

Clearly this was a massive "lean construction" achievement requiring design for manufacture and strict quality control superimposed on the developments of design for manufacture, transportation, and logistics which so impressed Wilkinson. In the sense of totality the 1851 Crystal Palace can be argued to be one comprehensive forerunner of this aspect of the TPS delivery capability.

In the UK, Burbidge retrospectively claimed that to his personal knowledge some Spitfire aircraft assembly lines operated during the Second World War in similar fashion hence needing relatively little work in progress. He also deplored the tendency, once hostilities ceased, for those same manufacturers to drift back into their "comfort zone" with high stock levels throughout the production system. The phenomenon was later confirmed via the industrial studies (1964). The significance of the work by Jay Forrester (1958) in attaining smooth material flow was well recognized by Burbidge (1984) who posited the Law of Industrial Dynamics. Broadly speaking, it suggests that "if there is any way in which demand might be amplified, then in practice it always will." Ohno's (1988) view of TPS extols the virtue of continuous workflow.

According to Ohno (1988), JIT production involved two components: kanban and level production. Consequently kanban and "pull production" controls became the hallmark of TPS. Statistical evidence has shown the powerful influence on smoothing production observed on many other Japanese companies mimicking Toyota. TPS was also frequently but wrongly referred to as simply just in time (i.e. nothing else required) to the point where many authors regarded JIT and TPS as synonymous. In reality there is much more to this system. Kanban was really just a convenient but powerful means to an end. Ohno famously described his inspiration for kanban when returning from a visit in the USA during the 1950s in which he was more impressed with supermarkets than with US manufacturing. The idea of having all goods available at all times was, to Ohno, rather novel and revolutionary. He said:

From the supermarket we got the idea of viewing the earlier process in a production line as a kind of store. The later process (customer) goes to the earlier process (supermarket) to acquire the needed parts (commodities) at the time and in the quantity needed. The earlier process immediately produces the quantity just taken (re-stocking the shelves).

To achieve this in Toyota, Ohno had to make many major changes to production operations. Because the supermarket logistics were designed to replenish only what had just been taken in a timely manner, lot sizes had to be drastically reduced. Hence, the Single-Minute Exchange of Dies (SMED) initiatives. To achieve the efficiencies needed, Ohno and his Toyota colleagues engineered many creative ways to reduce such changeovers. These beneficially impacted on the traditional problem of "boom-and-bust" alternately flooding then starving various workstations. Nevertheless, the researchers examining the Japanese Renaissance often rediscover American ideas! So it is not surprising to find "contemporary" industrial engineering (IE) exploits the appropriate combination of available

166 CHAPTER 16

procedures irrespective of age or place of origin.

16.3 Holistic view of TPS

In their seminal paper, Spear and Bowen (1999) argue that to unravel the DNA of TPS the key factor to understand is that the (surprisingly) rigid specification is the very thing that makes the flexibility and creativity possible. That conclusion was reached by Spear and Bowen (1999) based on an extensive four-year study of the Toyota Production System. They examined the inner workings of more than 40 plants in the USA, Europe, and Japan, some successfully operating the system, but others not. These authors studied the artefacts produced in both continuous process and discrete manufacturing companies. Products ranged from prefabricated housing, auto parts and final auto assembly, cell phones, and computer printers through to injection-moulded plastics and aluminium extrusions. They studied not only routine production work but also service functions such as equipment maintenance, workers' training and supervision, logistics and materials handling, and process design and redesign.

The output from the Spear and Bowen (1999) detailed research into TPS methodology is best illustrated using the concept of the four-level model, which summarizes the research output by Werr et al. (1997). It requires the "vision," "principles," "toolbox" and "learning organizations" characteristics of any existing (or proposed) methodology to be clearly identified. This concept has been tested by these authors and found to be both consistent and realistic when applied to the procedures actually adopted by leading internationally renowned management consultants (Werr et al., 1997). Figure 16-1 summarizes the output as a comprehensive prism model.

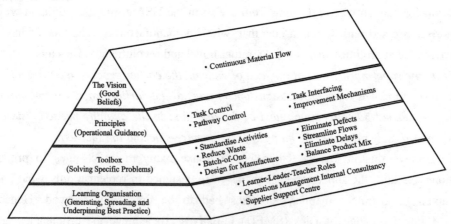

Figure 16-1 Prism model of the totality of the product delivery process within the Toyota production system

For the Spear and Bowen (1999) TPS DNA such an equivalent analysis outputs the following characteristics:

The "vision" of continuous material flow defines what the goal is.

- The "principles" of task control, pathway control, task interfacing, and improvement mechanisms to engineer (and update JIT).
- The "toolbox" includes the detailed defect elimination, delay elimination, waste reduction, engineering batch-of-one, design for manufacture, standardization of activities, balancing product mix, and steps to streamline (all) flows to enable how we achieve it.
- The "learning organization" comprising learner-leader-teacher roles operations management consultancy, and support centers such as educating suppliers emphasize the underpinning people contribution.
- In a nutshell, as Spear and Bowen (1999) identify as key operating features "Activities, connections, and production flows in a Toyota factory are as rigidly scripted as mass production, yet at the same time Toyota's operations are enormously flexible and adaptable. Tasks and processes are constantly being challenged and pushed to a higher level of performance, hence enabling the company to continually innovate and improve." From this perspective it is now apparent that the Gilbreth method study improvement of old now takes place within a much more comprehensive environment. This is confirmed by the practical manufacturing systems route via which the European analogue of TPS emerged. Indeed the critical necessity to organizationally connect management and workers with all processes from "beginning to end" had been identified even earlier when achieving continuous flow in UK automotive manufacture during the 1920s.

16.4 Ancient rite of waste elimination

Wrege (1983) was particularly clear in detailing the types of the activities engaging Frank Gilbreth. Typically the tasks were monitored via camera recordings with time intervals between frames as small as (1/1,000) second. The grids composed of $4''\times4''$ reference squares were marked on vertical walls to determine optimal movement trajectories and best equipment locations, etc. An estimate of three-dimensional movements was also made to ensure that there was no hidden snags facing motion re-design. This is, of course, a detailed description of the minute of Method Study as practiced at the start of the twentieth century. It does, however, illustrate the power of the Gilbreth approach, since the forgoing description leads naturally to the conceptual equation:

$$[\text{Method study}]=[\text{Time study}]+[\text{Motion study}] \quad (1)$$

But equation (1) also conveniently links directly to particular "good" present day practices. Typically eliminating "Waste time" and "Waste motion" features prominently in the modern methods developed for enabling effective processes change. Furthermore, it so happens that the best known of such approaches is the Toyota Production System (TPS). For example, Suzaki lists seven waste sources targeted for elimination under the TPS regimen. "Time" and "Motion" are specifically highlighted. But both Gilbreth "processing" and "transportation" waste elimination are clearly directly implied from equation (1).

Conceptually it is a small step to regard the remaining areas of "overproduction," "excess inventory," and "scrap" as the consequences of waste motion and time lost in its execution. It is therefore not surprising to find that Suzaki is quite open, that the individual activities carried out within TPS were not novel. It is their combination and execution that were innovative (and arduous) in the creation of comprehensive and effective production systems.

As an example Zipkin (1991) commented "JIT exalts simplicity. Do JIT writers (ever) explain that simple is hard?." As confirmation, consider that Ohno once remarked that full implementation in Toyota took some 20 years to accomplish. The detailed description of the engineering required suggests why this might be so. Yet Figure 15-1 suggests JIT is a major principle necessary for minimizing several sources of waste. If smooth material flow is the ultimate goal, then JIT is an essential part of the industrial engineering route to its achievement.

As a target, waste elimination is a well-established historical goal. Benjamin Franklin was a well-known protagonist. One of his major interests was in the promulgation of the movement for Daylight Saving Time. Even earlier was the case in 1690 of Bishop Huet who extensively multi-tasked by having a servant on hand to read aloud during mealtimes and other breaks. Any lingering doubt on the central focus of the Gilbreth's work is immediately removed by considering the title of one of Lillian's early books—"The psychology of management: the function of the mind in determining, teaching, and installing the methods of least waste." This prominent role for waste removal pre-dates the phrase "lean production" by three quarters of a century. This immediately raises a fundamental question this paper is designed to answer.

Q. What (if anything) did the Toyota industrial engineers and managers add to the original Gilbreth method study concept to transform it within TPS?

As we shall see, the answers are highly variable (from a lot to a little), depending on the "dimension" of enquiry. Developing the arguments requires not only considering how the Gilbreths worked, but also on the subsequent development of the industrial engineering discipline.

16.5 Three pathways

Historically there are three distinct pathways which link and influence TPS dating back to the factors originating from the Gilbreths. The first is the teaching route starting with Frank Gilbreth lecturing to Japanese shipyard engineers immediately after WWI. Robinson and Robinson (1994) have thoroughly researched these circumstances to good effect. They report that a Japanese admiral, aware of this Gilbreth US work on method study, much later became director of the Japanese Management Association (JMA) in the aftermath of WWII. Toyota worked closely with JMA in building up their post-war manufacturing activities. JMA also trained industrial engineers and the lectures being the copies of the original Frank Gilbreth notes! JMA also employed consultants to work with Toyota, and form an effective industrial engineering cadre with Ohno and Shingo.

The second pathway emanates from Lillian Gilbreth, who became an established management researcher in her own right. The link between the USA and Japan continued after the death of Frank, and Lillian was extremely prominent in a 1930 Tokyo Management Conference. Moreover, a powerful European advocate of method study was Anne Shaw. Trained in Manchester, UK by Lillian Gilbreth during the Second World War, Anne became a distinguished practitioner who was extremely influential in Great Britain. She extolled the virtue of the MOI^2 process chart shown in Table 16-1. As stemming from the original Gilbreth and Gilbreth (1917) definition and which will be detailed later. Lillian also travelled to Japan. The research by Robinson and Robinson (1994) establishes, and she was definitely only two handshakes (and maybe just one handshake) away from the Toyota innovators.

Table 16-1 The Gilbreth emphasis on modus operandi, information, and innovation — using MOI^2 process charting a century ago

Target status	Infrastructure supporting target status	Aid to advancement
Modus operandi for the process chart	The process chart is a device for visualizing a process prior to improving it. Every detail of a process is to some extent affected by every other detail. The entire process must be presented in such a form that it can be visualized in totality before some changes are made to any part of it. Any change made without due consideration of their impact on the total system will be found unsuited to the ultimate plan of operation.	Establishes where we are now.
Information stored on the process chart	The process chart is an adequate record of present activities. It is a simple, transparent display of the data studied ahead of any improvement in the existing conditions and methods. If the existing conditions are apparently satisfactory, the chart is still useful as an informative condensed benchmark.	Interprets present information.
Innovation via the process chart	The process chart serves as an indicator of profitable changes. It assists in preventing "inventing downwards," and stimulates the invention that is cumulative and of permanent value. It is not only the first step towards visualizing the "one best way to do work," but also useful in every stage of enabling it.	Suggests how we might improve.

The third pathway starts with the Scientific Management paradigm of Frederick Winslow Taylor. The latter argued that prior to meeting Taylor, Frank Gilbreth was not actually a time study advocate. Instead he exclusively concentrated on claiming expertise in improving motion study as his "intellectual property." Nevertheless, the evidence suggests that he (and Lillian) started to project the benefit of their proposed improvements partly in time saved, or its inverse, the throughput rate. An example is the very detailed studies Lillian did at Macey's Store. But according to Peterson (2002), Henry Ford quickly became an avid advocate of Just-in-Time (JIT) as part of his application of scientific management, and was clearly much influenced by Taylor. The latter also engaged in inter-plant comparisons, an exercise known many decades later as benchmarking.

Manifestly the Frank Gilbreth "handed-down" conceptual route as identified by Robinson and Robinson (1994) dominates the origins of some aspects of TPS. But clearly the other pathways influence what is actually done within the system. For example, as we have seen earlier, Ohno is said to have been impressed and hence implemented US JIT practice. So "learning from best practice" and then successfully transferring it to a new market sector was actually achieved, and not just talked about. This ties in with the innovative approach characterized by Lillian Gilbreth, but nowadays applied more widely to the complete system rather than individual tasks. The public outcome of all this professional development is the appearance of many useful handbooks on performance improvement.

16.6 The Gilbreths' "four step" approach

According to Currie (1977), "Frank Gilbreth first applied himself to his original work of bricklaying and evolved a method of laying bricks, which reduced the motions required from 18 to 5 and in one case down to 2. At the same time he was able to increase individual output from 120 to 350 bricks per hour. Later on, as a construction engineer, he was struck by the wasted effort and some of the illogical practices that were carried out and took positive steps to eliminate them. He then moved into the wider field of management consultancy eventually working in many industries. Hence, the motivation for the gradual evolution of the procedures, which we are more familiar with today. His four-step method was:

Step 1: To define the current situation noting anything that could have any possible effect on job and its performance.

Step 2: To analyze the job using the special equipment he had either invented or adapted for use for this purpose and supported by one of the several systems of analysis that he had also developed.

Step 3: To examine the results of these analyses, cutting out any part of the job he found unnecessary, combining different parts where possible and, if practicable, designing the equipment that would reduce still further the motions to do the job.

Step 4: Taking what was left of the job to synthesize this into a new job method which was, to him, the best way the job could be done in the given situation."

"Here surely is the genesis of the Method Study Basic Procedure. In addition, however, to the procedure that he devised Gilbreth's contribution probably lies in the practices and devices he invented or developed to enable this procedure to be carried out." This preceding statement is a succinct summary of the (Frank) Gilbreth methodology. In similar vein, Wren

(1994) highlighted the method study originators and their activities as follows:

The Gilbreths also devised process charts as a technique for charting the flow of work as it moved through the shop. The technique, and the symbols used to depict the various stages in the process, remain essentially unchanged in modern systems analysis. One should not confuse the techniques with (the totality of) what the Gilbreths were trying to build. Their search for efficiency and economy included flowcharts, of both products, and work, a three-position plan of promotion, and a notion of the impact of motion study on the worker. All their techniques were focused on eliminating waste in industry.

Wren (1994) then describes the employee position within the company via "The (lost on many Gilbreth successors) promotion plan was designed to prepare workers for advancement and as a morale and incentive booster. According to the plan, each worker held three positions in the organization: first, the position last occupied and for which the worker was now serving as a teacher to the successor; second, the present position; and third, preparing for the next higher position. The system required charting promotion paths and records for appraising performance and kept the worker from getting lodged in blind-alley jobs. The psychology of motion study was to impress on the worker the benefits of reducing fatigue and improving pay through motion study. Motion and fatigue study displayed management's interest and facilitated the elimination of monotony." How similar are these concepts to some aspects of TPS, such as preparing for job enhancement, or even actively producing a fatigue allowance, as exploited 80 years later by Monden (1983).

16.7 Origin of the MOI^2 process chart

The *modus operandi*, information and innovation (MOI^2) process chart already met and summarized in Table 16-1 is output from the description by Shaw (1952). Note that this book is dedicated to her teacher, Lillian Gilbreth. Anne Shaw examined Frank Gilbreth's ideas in great depth. She determined his process chart was designed for recording observations, data and procedural logging, visualization, and innovating an improved method of doing things, such as apparently tripling bricklaying throughput. Shaw poured scorn on the movement for standardizing excessively simplistic process charts, which blossomed during WWII. It reduced them to basically "ticking boxes" rather than encouraging for significant innovation. This creativity theme was carried on by Fields (1969) including the coverage of such topics as ergonomics, network synthesis and value analysis. Years ahead of his time, he interpreted the problem of electricity meter reading (then carried out by personal visitation) as a "black box" data transmission exercise.

Much more recently, Schonberger (2007) commented "A variation of process flow-charting is to map routings necessary to produce a family of products (remarkably similar to the Production Flow Analysis concept). Such maps may extend beyond a single entity to include links to suppliers and customers. Just as Taylor and Gilbreth-era flow charting featured "before charts" and "after charts" with wasted steps removed, value stream mapping includes present state and future state maps noting non-value adding elements to be removed (by innovative industrial engineering)". So the Gilbreth's might reasonably argue that little has changed over the last 100 years (as we shall see in the next section, much has indeed changed, but not necessarily this particular aspect).

As Aldag (1997) laments, there is often an unseemingly scrambling to "shovel" industrial data into support for current transient fads. In its place he emphasizes that any hoped for management paradigms need to be based on sound basic research and innovative theories. Fortunately an exemplar of jargon-free description of a successful application does occasionally emerge. Thus Gawande (2008) provides a clear picture of the role of IE in reducing hospital MRSA infection. Unsurprisingly Sprague (2007) purposely replicated a course of lectures given 30 years earlier (then entitled "Work simplification") to executive students (but subject now retitled "BPR"). The outcome, as expected, was that when applied to current business projects, these same ageless principles delivered considerable performance enhancement in the then modern age. In other words practical innovation and creativity tends to be cyclic in "discovery." The key factor is highly competent industrial engineering. It is definitely not in the misleadingly projected "Old Wine in New Bottles."

Spear and Bowen (1999) regularly emphasize that within the TPS regimen "work" is treated as an experiment. This builds on the quality movement started by Sir Ronald Fisher in 1925 and which rapidly spread into industrial engineering influencing Japanese and Western practitioners and eventually leading to such publications as Edward Deming (1986) *Out of the Crisis*. His Plan-Do-Check-Act (PDCA) experimental procedure became a prime activity visible not only in TPS but in the other major effective methodologies such as Management-by-Projects-MBP. Finally, the current direct involvement of TPS managers in pursuing industrial engineering objectives was established by Spear (2004). His study of the training of Toyota executives really did show that "the devil is in the detail." Hence process innovation is best achieved via shop floor studies designed around PDCA. In the procedure (P-D) is the pilot scheme: (C-A) includes de-briefings, updating, and further "fine tuning" for optimality.

16.8 Contemporary industrial engineering

The present day professional engineer has inevitably moved on since the days when the Gilbreths studied individual tasks. At university level the industrial engineering discipline, which dates back at least as far as Anderson (1928) has become very closely associated (especially in Europe) with production management, and (especially in US) with operations management. Perhaps the UK University of Birmingham was very close to the mark in originally calling the concerned Department "(The) Engineering (of) Production" which made the intent quite specific. Burbidge (1995) complained at the later quite unnecessary proliferation of new descriptors (i.e. the "Old wine in new bottles" syndrome described by Locock (2003). Production engineering (from his practical experiences in WWII) covered every task from initially receiving orders to final delivery to the customer. What need was there, he argued to present these activities in a new guise? None, it appears, except as a manifestation of the pressure to emphasize small differences as management consultancy scoring points against their rivals.

As to the dichotomy of views concerning industrial engineering, there were the "traditional" and the "contemporary." But there is much more to the dynamic than just this distinction. So how has old "traditional" method study based IE moved on? Figure 16-2 illustrates the three dimensions along which the transformation is posited to have taken place. Especially when exploiting IE within the TPS context, the "width" dimension includes not only product flows, but also information, capacity, and cash flows as well. This may well be seen as the major point of departure of TPS from basic IE. System optimization integrates the design and management of these flows to best advantage. Similarly the "breadth" dimensions seek to integrate and balance these flows end-to-end across tasks, processes, and complete businesses exactly as defined by the concept of a manufacturing system.

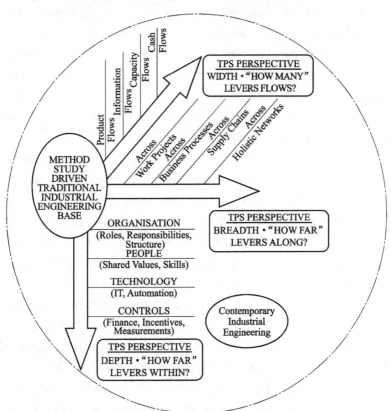

Figure 16-2 Width, breadth and depth dimensions inherent in contemporary industrial engineering

16.9 Shigeo Shingo and the JMA

In linking method study and TPS and hence understanding the essential industrial engineering therein, the contribution of Shigeo Shingo is particularly important. His work needs discussion here before the full extent is evident. In particular he is credited with much of the TPS detailed design work. This includes performing over 6,000 motion study experiments when planning the optimization of particular operations. It is hardly surprising that he should seek to do these, since as we have seen his professional education can be directly linked via the JMA right back to a lecture series given by Frank Gilbreth himself. The resultant notes formed the basis of the discipline of industrial engineering handed-down and taught to several generations of students by a succession of JMA teachers. Shingo was one celebrated student of many attending such courses.

Since then the work of Shingo has been well recognized by western engineers and educationalists. He was a consultant to many companies in Japan (not just Toyota, but including Matsushita, Hitachi, and Mitsubishi), also in Europe and the USA (especially advising on Single Minute Exchange Dies-SMED design procedures). During this period he also gave many lecture courses worldwide, and published books and reports. Some of these writings were translated into English. Most notable of these was an often-cited book on TPS. Is there anything unusual about it? Yes, unfortunately, it concerns the referencing style adopted by some subsequent authors. Generally these were eager to extol the virtues of TPS, and draw attention to their own subsequent contributions to the subject (however small). So what was missed in the citation? Only the remainder of the title, which in full reads *"A Study of the Toyota Production System from an Industrial Engineering Viewpoint."* This omission is one of the reasons why the true origin of TPS is effectively masked on superficial inspection. Instead, we have the current book-writing trend to hastily jump on the latest break-through bandwagon as soon as identified, whether this is real or imaginary.

Shingo (1989) argued the alleged secret of Toyota's success as alleged by others was generally considered to be only JIT coupled with the "kanban method." His view was predicated by the rapid proliferation of the books appearing with such titles as *The Secret of Toyota's High Profits*, and *Toyota-Secrets of the Kanban Method*. These books were often written by journalists, specializing in economics, not in engineering. Hence their style is normally not technical (Shingo's words). This was probably very annoying for him as the substantial and substantive industrial engineering input was inevitably much downplayed. Here was the outstanding life work of Shingo and his colleagues being discussed in a superficial manner. Although Ohno (1988) himself set out to dissuade this view, and emphasize the engineering innovation involved, it unfortunately had the limited impact among industrialists. This is unsurprising because the latter book is strong on principles but extremely weak in detail. Hence Shingo (1989) set himself the task of filling this particular publication gap. The result is a model textbook on the improvement of the production control system by detailing the attainment of smooth material flow.

16.10 Discussion

The first question to be answered is, if Frank Gilbreth were to be alive, what, if anything, would he regard as post-method study as encompassed in the "modern" IE model of Figure 16-2? From the behavioral description of Gilbreth, his forceful exuberant personality suggests he would argue that all three dimensions were "blindingly obvious" extensions of his declared intellectual property. However, there is little evidence to suggest that as an early twentieth century consultant Gilbreth worked with some companies to set up a supporting infrastructure regarded as so essential in TPS. Nor is there any inkling that he was especially concerned with anything much other than width flows as distinct from any other quantity along the work perspective of Figure 16-2. Nevertheless, there is evidence to suggest that Gilbreth was well aware of the importance of synchronizing activities between the sequential tasks performed by a succession of workers. It is therefore reasonable to conclude that the breadth dimension is a logical progression from elemental method study.

The historical overview and impact of method study on IE (and especially TPS) becomes more apparent on studying the Shaw (1952) version of the Gilbreth Process Chart shown in Table 16-1. Remembering the purpose of the investigation as *Modus Operandi*, Information, and Innovation (MOI^2), its relevance to task betterment becomes much more obvious. With the Deming PDCA experimental loop incorporated into the schema this procedure is starting to look very much like TPS characteristics at the individual worker level. Furthermore, Robinson and Robinson (1994) showed via tabletop experiments as originally demonstrated by Frank Gilbreth to Japanese industrial engineers that such trial-and-error investigation was indeed part of his repertoire. Although not noted for his "coaching" abilities (an essential part of TPS), his partner Lillian Gilbreth was nevertheless much involved at this level. Hence it is reasonable to conclude that at this particular level such a method study concept led to the industrial engineering contribution of Shingo to TPS.

What of the vision, principles, toolbox, and learning organization levels identified from the research of Spear and Bowen (1999)? Learning Organization is extremely difficult to trace back to the early nineteenth century. Although popularized more recently by Senge (1990) this does seem to be a real TPS industrial innovation, which is a key integral feature of successful implementation. The Toolbox has taken many years and many contributors to reach the present comprehensive stage. But working out how to actually reduce waste is manifestly traceable to Lillian Gilbreth (1914) and was also a fetish with Henry Ford. Standardized activities, streamline flow (within the process), and delay elimination (within the process) can all be readily attributed as far back as Frank Gilbreth.

The Principles start structuring TPS within an industrial engineering framework. Even at this level the Gilbreths output of task control and improvement mechanisms seem familiar and apparently embraced at Morris Motors UK. Vision depends on the marketplace, and is therefore a function of the era. Whereas Ohno (1988) rightly acknowledged some aspects of TPS as previously visible in the operation of US supermarkets, it took much innovation and tenacity to actually create a substantive production system to cope with the new industrial environment. In this sense Ohno was evidently the industrial engineering architect. But achieving the goal of Continuous Material Flow built on the contributions of many. Prominent among these were the Gilbreths and their contemporary Taylor followed by Ford (in the USA) and Woollard (in the UK) automotive industry.

16.11 Conclusions

Despite the evidence from Spear and Bowen (1999) on significant implementation failure rates, given the right environment and high standards of industrial engineering, TPS does travel well between industries, between market sectors, and between countries. It therefore passes that particular requirement to be considered as established management theory. Success specifically necessitates competence and innovation in industrial engineering applied within a system context. Given such ambition and resources, then the Vision, Principles, and Toolbox levels of TPS guide the implementation towards achieving continuous material flow. As major method study innovators, Frank Gilbreth and Lillian were early very high caliber industrial engineers. At the detailed level their influence on TPS many years later is readily identifiable. It is also directly traceable via the JMA, Lillian Gilbreth teaching, and Scientific Management routes. It can be confirmed indeed that much of TPS can be claimed to have been "invented in USA" early in the twentieth century.

But what of the importance of the learning organization? In MBP, great emphasis is placed on new knowledge generation, and its retention, and promulgation throughout the enterprise. Within Toyota, working closely with JMA consultants over an extended period of time, and developing "internal" experts enabled started this culture. MBP emphasizes that such an organization has to include the active involvement of everybody if it is to be a success. Certainly Toyota ensure that even their new executives (and especially those recruited from elsewhere in the automotive industry) are comprehensively exposed to "real" life style within the company.

Hence for a period of months it is customary for such newcomers to participate in a companywide acclimatization course. They work and actually solve problems (as distinct from merely watch) on a number of Toyota and associated factory floors. Hence a range of production challenges are experienced at first hand. Only in this way is it considered possible to properly absorb the TPS ethos. Similarly Frank Gilbreth had a generalized promotion path mapped out for shop-floor operators. But it would be a massive step to suggest that he might have thought of expanding it into a full-scale learning organization as associated with both

TPS and MBP.

So the answer to the question "how much influence (if any) did the Gilbreths have on present-day TPS?" is double edged. They undoubtedly had a major impact on the detailed industrial engineering inputs. Unfortunately, nowadays, such contributions are downplayed and masked in the constant claims of "Eureka" made when old ways of doing things are re-discovered, hence the "Old wine in new bottles" cliché. Learn-by-doing must be the mantra here. But it is in the learning organization aspect of TPS there is least to link it back to the Gilbreths.

What of Toyota? Making everything work is a fundamental axiom (fully implementing JIT took 20 years — because it has many practical steps). Understanding and creating a "system" embracing the whole enterprise and later embedding this within the learning organization are massive achievements behind TPS. This is our (and many industrialists) paradox. At the detailed level, Gilbreth type shop floor demonstrations are easy to arrange, impressive, and easily transferable. It is an essential step towards success, but only in the context of the full-blown system will real competitive advantage be obtained. An industrial engineering architect is indispensable in achieving this goal.

 Professional Vocabularies and Expressions

Toyota production system	丰田制造系统
continuous material flow	连续物料流
kanban	看板
level production	均衡生产
single-minute exchange of dies (SMED)	一分钟换模
method study	方法研究
motion and fatigue study	动作和疲劳研究
job enhancement	工作丰富化
process flow chart	工序流程图
value stream map	价值流图
plan-do-check-act (PDCA)	PDCA 循环
management-by-projects (MBP)	项目管理

 Notes

1. This is the remit of the industrial engineering discipline, which is the TPS area linked

(by just two handshakes at most) to Lillian Gilbreth.

工业工程学科需要重新思考的一个问题是丰田制造系统(的思想)与Lillian Gilbreth (的思想)密切相关。

2. In some particular cases, the foregoing divisions are separated by flexible curtains, rather than brick walls.

有些情况下，上述分类是柔性的，而不是刚性的。

3. These beneficially impacted on the traditional problem of "boom-and-bust" alternately flooding then starving various workstations.

这些举措（大野耐一与同事们在实施快速换模过程中所采取的诸多行之有效的方法和措施）使得（流水线上）各工作站（的在制品库存）时而"堆积如山"时而"捉襟见肘"的老问题得到有效解决。

Discussion Questions:

1. How much do you know about TPS?
2. From historical perspective, state your understanding of the relationships between TPS and traditional IE.
3. How can Chinese companies benefit from TPS?

编者注：

日本在第二次世界大战后经济的迅速崛起，原因有多个方面，其中的一个共识是丰田制造系统（Toyota Production System）在效率改善、质量提升、成本压缩、库存消减和浪费剔除等方面起到了举足轻重的作用，使得日本企业尤其是制造企业获得了前所未有的竞争优势。本文在翔实文献研究的基础上，从管理学发展的历史角度解读了TPS与传统工业工程、质量管理、项目管理等领域以及Gilbreths，Taylor，Deming等人管理思想的继承关系，并对TPS在管理理论上的贡献做了中肯的评价。

CHAPTER 17

Toyota's Practical Thinking Shared Among Its Employees

17.1 Introduction

Toyota's management system, more formally known as the Toyota Production System (TPS) is a modern technology aimed at reducing cost and eliminating waste. TPS which is more commonly known as lean manufacturing, initially originated on the production floor, where several tools such as 5S[①], visual control and standardized work were created. Over the last decade, lean has grown from a manufacturing philosophy to a business strategy. Currently, the companies all over the world are in a state of kaizen to modernize their accounting systems, design practices, maintenance areas and human resource functions to emulate their business systems like Toyota. While few researchers see gain in holding interest on a particular aspect of TPS, most consultants and authors actively seek new ways to apply lean in the uncharted areas of the business. This craze to upload lean into all aspects of the business has weakened organizations mainly because practitioners insist on applying the manufacturing tools of lean (i.e. visual control, 5S, standardized work) rather than applying the thinking of lean.

What is unique about Toyota's system is not particularly any single piece of TPS, but how the pieces are combined to bring out something new, different and very difficult to imitate. So much work has been completed in examining and dissecting the parts of the Toyota Production System that little has been done to examine how the parts work together! It is argued in this work that Toyota's management system is a richly interconnected set of parts and relationships that are more important than the nature of the parts themselves. This means that even if the parts themselves can be identified, their relations are often lost, which loses the meaning of the system. It is believed that research in TPS must follow the same type of systems thinking to discover how TPS emerges from the way the parts are organized in the system.

---

① 指整理（SEIRI）、整顿（SEITON）、清扫（SEISO）、清洁（SEIKETSU）、素养（SHITSUKE）等5个项目，因日语的罗马拼音均以"S"开头，所以简称为"5S"。开展以整理、整顿、清扫、清洁和素养为内容的活动，称为"5S"活动。

Holism, rather than reductionism can provide a more entire solution than a partial one.

Historically, practitioners have been concerned about what Toyota is doing now rather than what Toyota was doing when TPS did not exist. The pioneers like Taiichi Ohno, the father of TPS and one of his close friends, Sheigo Shingo, an industrial engineering consultant to Toyota during the time, are less received and noted for developing TPS. In very simple terms, not to make TPS any more complicated than what it needs to be, TPS is an old way of thinking. In Ohno's book, named the Toyota Production System, Ohno firmly believed that TPS is simply a form of industrial engineering (IE) aimed at reducing cost through systematic study. By treating everything as a process, Ohno and Shingo built the interconnections of TPS one by one, but more importantly passed on this industrial engineering way of thinking to future generations.

The purpose of this work is to evaluate and quantify some of Toyota's thinking styles as it relates to Ohno's traditional view of TPS. It is speculated that one of the ways Toyota is able to develop such a holistic approach to TPS is by passing down from generation to generation a type of thinking similar to industrial engineering. The managers throughout Toyota are believed to teach, share and develop this kaizen mind to encourage the systematic study and evaluation of business practices. The secondary goal of this work is apply a new form of management science, named dimensional reduction analysis to highlight and quantify managerial preferences. This work is expected to substantiate quantitatively many of Toyota's perceived industrial engineering practices, but also indicate the particular form. Most outsiders view lean as an extremely sophisticated form of industrial engineering mainly due to the influences of six sigma, lean sigma and now the popularized kaizen specialist. Due to these latest trends, one could dispute that the flavor of industrial engineering is very different from Ohno's more practical view of productivity improvement. This work is expected to bring insight and hopefully simplicity into understanding an old familiar way of thinking about problems from an industrial engineering viewpoint that acts as a catalyst for making the TPS system come alive. In this work the link between TPS and IE will be established and analyzed to determine which trend of IE practices is utilized to maintain the TPS structure.

17.2 Literature review

On August 15, 1945, Kiichiro Toyoda, then president of Toyota Motor Company, said: "Catch up with America in three years. Otherwise, the automobile industry of Japan will not survive." In Ohno's book, Taiichi went on to say: "To accomplish this mission, we had to know America and learn American ways."

Ohno believed that the quickest way to catch up with America was to import American production management techniques and business management practices. Toyota studied industrial engineering (IE) which by Ohno's accounts can best be compared with the Toyota Production System. That is, a company-wide system tied directly to management to systematically lower cost and raise productivity.

Shingo also viewed TPS as a way of thinking to address plant improvement. He believed that management should possess a set of fundamentals closely related to industrial engineering as a way to spread and teach the Toyota Production System. Shingo believed that TPS is a system made up of the principles that can be applied through practical implementation. If management cannot understand how to attack the rationalization of the current system, through scientific study, then it cannot be expected to improve or change.

17.2.1 Industrial engineering

An industrial engineer is one who is concerned with the design, installation and improvement of the integrated systems of people, material, information and equipment which utilizes specialized knowledge and skills in mathematical, physical and social sciences together with the principles and methods of engineering analysis. Over the years industrial engineering has drawn upon mechanical engineering, economics, labor psychology, philosophy, and accountancy in an effort to bring together people, machines, materials and information. If industrial engineers had to focus on one aspect of their field, it would be productivity or productivity improvement. That is the total elimination of waste by increasing efficiency through cost reduction.

Industrial engineering not only covers the technical aspects of systems, but also the systems relating to management. It is proposed that industrial engineering is one of the primary drivers for linking the needs of the employers to the needs of the employees. Employers want industrial peace, reduction of cost, higher efficiency and improvement in quality. Employees want steady work, higher wages, better personal relations with their supervisor and good working conditions. By utilizing industrial engineering techniques, management can develop, evaluate and improve the wants of both groups.

17.2.2 Scientific management

One of the earliest contributions to the field of industrial engineering and to the industrial efficiency movement in the early 1900s was by Frederick Taylor with his invention of scientific management. Scientific management is the saving of energy, materials and time, or in other words the elimination of waste through studying, recoding and analyzing work. The Gilbreths (Frank and Lillian) also were the advocates of scientific management and were concerned with how to properly raise productivity without the degradation of an employee's health and well-being. Scientific management was never a manner of how much a person can do under a short burst of speed but instead a safe and comfortable working speed that can be done day after day. Unfortunately, many charlatans attempting to break into the field of scientific study who had neither proper training nor interest except for the quick financial benefit portrayed scientific management incorrectly. Scientific management was intended to secure the maximum prosperity for the employer coupled with the maximum prosperity for the employee. The long term prosperity of the employer cannot exist unless it is accompanied by the prosperity of the employee. Scientific management included employees to some degree in decision making. In 1935 Mogensen[1] suggested that IEs (then referred to as efficiency experts) should solicit suggestions and ideas from those working directly with the operation. While it is assumed that workmen and foremen are incapable of such suggestions, some of the most valuable ideas have come from this source.

17.2.3 Skill sets of industrial engineers in the era of scientific management

Table 17-1 illustrates some of the basic efficiency tools and concepts used by industrial engineering during the era of scientific management. IEs were mostly concerned with defining processes, identifying problems and establishing standard operations. Some of the most practical techniques employed by IEs were the use of direct observation and work sampling. Combined with a questioning attitude, IEs could obtain facts to make productivity improvements simply and quickly. The industrial engineer also was proficient with the use of charting. By breaking down processes into smaller units, the IE could analyze work flow by examining process steps visually.

Table 17-1 Skill sets of industrial engineers in the era of scientific management

Importance of Direct Observation	Observation is carried out to ensure that all pertinent facts are collected and that each fact is checked for accuracy. Logic or deduction cannot enter the analysis until the observed facts are obtained.
Work Sampling, How to Study	Also known as the ratio delay technique. A small number of chance occurrences tend to follow the same distribution pattern as that in the entire population of occurrences. Excellent and inexpensive tools for making accurate studies and predictions in many areas of the business and industrial activity.
Questioning Attitude	Questioning attitudes develop the point of view that considers the good of the plant rather than that of the department or individual. Question low productivity areas: 1. Delays in routing work to and from the operators. 2. Excessive personal time (variation). 3. Lost time is setting up or in other work preparation. 4. Insufficient work to do (waiting). 5. Bottlenecks. 6. Obsolete methods (using the wrong work method). 7. Unbalanced work loading. 8. Defects in process.
Standardization	Standardization is one of the prime tools for the elimination of waste. 1. A standard is simply a carefully thought out method of performing a function. 2. The idea of perfection is not involved in standardization. The standard method is the best method that can be devised at the time the standard is drawn. Improvement in standards are wanted and adopted whenever and wherever they are found. 3. Safeguards protect standards form change for the sake of change, standardization practiced in this way is a constant invitation to experimentation and improvement.

---

[1] A. Mogensen. How to set up a program for motion economy? Factory Management and Maintenance Plant Operation Library, 1935, 93(11).

(Continued)

Standards Engineer	The standards engineer is the starting point for standardization. 1. The qualities of an effective standards engineer must be particularly strong in the ability to handle human relation problems and a good engineer. He must also be an able administrator. 2. The standards engineer must have the ability to understand people as individuals and in groups. Have the ability to cope and be patient with the common human characteristics of resistant to change and resentment of criticism. 3. The standards engineer should be encouraged to cut across organizational lines to make standardization company-wide and not departmentalized.
Systems Thinking	Basic system concepts traced back to the 1800s are: 1. The whole is more important than the sum of its parts. 2. The whole determines the nature of the parts. 3. The parts cannot be understood if considered in isolation from the whole.
The Process Flow Chart	Charts are the graphical representation of the work that has been broken down into basic components or units. First developed by Frank Gilbreth to record in detail operations which cannot be understood through direct human observation. After charting the process, ask: 1. Can the operation be eliminated? 2. Can it be combined? 3. Can we combine the sequence of operations? 4. Can it be simplified?
Work Distribution Charts	More formally known as line balance charts, they are used in the factory and in the office. Evaluate areas: 1. Tasks that consume most time. 2. People working on jobs below or above their skills. 3. People who are doing too many different things. 4. Tasks in which everyone has some part. 5. Employees who require overtime to complete their duties.
Time Study	The study is one of the most common methods for setting standards. Divide the operations into motion components or elements, time each element, set a representative time for each element, allow for such factors such as fatigue, personal needs.
Testing, Adaptive One Factor at a Time	To get results quickly as possible each test is run where last left off. 1. Experiments seek to optimize the response along the way allowing investigators to find out more rapidly whether a factor has any effect. 2. When performance improvement is the primary purpose of the experimental effort, one at a time plans will often be the best choice.

Lastly, the IE was concerned with running trials to test new productivity ideas. By testing factors one at a time and by sequentially changing those parameters based on previous trials, the IE could speed up decision making while focusing on improvement.

17.2.4 Industrial engineering today

Today, industrial engineering has become a more integral part of the organization. With the invention of the high speed computer in the 1960s industrial engineering has evolved into a hard discipline where data can be recalled at any time and decision making can be improved through the use of models and simulations. Computers have given industrial engineers the ability to analyze and optimize complex systems throughout the organization. The field has also become more specialized over the years much like mechanical engineering in the earlier twentieth century. Industrial engineering offers several sub specialties such as human factors, job design, labor psychology and systems engineering. Now it is not uncommon for IEs to work on planning systems, supply chains, accounting systems and organizational polices.

One of the most significant changes in the industrial engineering profession has been their role in change management. One of the main reasons why the IE function has become more of a driver for change is the growth of service functions within modern industry. Because IEs are skilled to analyze social-technical systems, they can help improve the fit between technology and the worker.

17.2.5 Skill sets of industrial engineers in the 21st century

The skill sets of the modern industrial engineer are much different compared with the days of scientific management. Most modern IE skill sets emphasize rapid organizational change instead of spending time stabilizing and documenting current operations (Table 17-2). The techniques such as Process Design and Re-engineering can result in radical change by focusing on end to end processes. PDR assumes a clean state change and suggests skipping documenting existing processes because it limits the vision of the design team with nothing to be gained.

Table 17-2 Skill sets of industrial engineers in the 21st century

Systems Engineering and Optimization	Systems are described mathematically by their properties such as continuous, discrete, lumped or distributed, linear or non-linear, constant or time varying, deterministic or structures and behaviors.
Process Design and Reengineering	A systematic discipline for achieving dramatic, measurable performance improvements by fundamentally reexamining, rethinking and redesigning the processes that an organization uses to carry out its mission.
	Reengineering processes are usually described in terms of the beginning and the end states, forces thoughts towards the activities taking place between the end points.
Experimental Design, Design of Experiments, Taguchi Methods	Experimental design enables industrial engineers to study the effects of several variables affecting the response or output of a process using statics.
	Taguchi's approach to DOE is based on orthogonal designs to simplify and accelerate testing.
	Replications and randomization are required for an estimate of error to determine the basis for decision making on the importance of factors contributing to the response variables.

	(Continued)
Six Sigma	IEs specializing in statistical improvement utilizing quality management processes such as: 1. Affinity diagrams. 2. Multivariate charts. 3. FMEA (failure mode and effects analysis). 4. DMAIC (define, measure, analyze, improve, and control). 5. Analysis of variance, ANOVA. 6. Regression analysis. 7. TRIZ.
Lean Sigma	A business improvement strategy based on combining the statistical tools of Six Sigma and the waste reduction methodologies of lean. Integrating the tools of six sigma and lean includes: 1. Chi-square analysis and 5S. 2. DOE and kanban. 3. FMEA and value stream mapping.

A popular tool to aid in the study of complex organizational factors in PDR is Experimental Designs (ED) and Design of Experiments (DOE) concepts. These techniques allow industrial engineers to understand the complexities of the business and interacting factors acting on and within the organization before leaping towards a new state. Today DOEs are packaged with structured initiatives for business improvement known as Six Sigma and Lean Sigma. Six Sigma is a systematic method for strategic process improvement that relies on statistical methods to make dramatic reduction in customer defect rates. Initially established by Motorola in 1987, Six Sigma has been extremely popularized as a new form of business management strategy. Six sigma often involves large masses of data and concerns itself with percentages and averages or the presentation of data in tables and charts.

Lean Sigma is another improvement methodology that is being employed by industrial engineers. Proponents suggest that by integrating statistical methods with the ideas of work simplification a common language can be developed to help organizations be responsive to changing markets while eliminating defects. It is suggested that the key to Lean Sigma is through integration. Six Sigma provides the detailed statistical study to optimize projects while lean is usually implemented through a series of short focused kaizen blitz.

17.2.6 Has lean followed the trends of industrial engineering?

The lean community has followed many of the same trends and skill sets as applied by the industrial engineering profession. While initially focused on more practical concepts in the days of scientific management, the experts working in lean are now expected to lead transformational change utilizing advance statistical tools and techniques.

The kaizen specialist is one of the main figure heads used by organizations in implementing lean. Similar to the master black belts in Six Sigma, kaizen specialists are charged with the developing solutions that aim to lower the cost and improve the efficiency of operations.

It is suggested that a kaizen specialist should be capable of performing value engineering in product design and development. Other work indicates that specialists should be capable of performing environmental scanning using complex engineering techniques such as the x-matrix, Porter's matrix and other sophisticated diagnostic tools. Lastly, there is work that suggests the kaizen specialist should be able to perform cellular manufacturing, production flow analysis and supply chain infrastructure design. In these contexts, the kaizen specialist is illustrated as a person that exists within an organization to advance lean concepts in highly specialized areas single handedly.

In other ways the kaizen specialist is also expected to work with the employees utilizing team-based worker participation activities often referred to as kaizen events. Compared with extreme Taylorism, where the IE function is responsible for telling workers what to do, kaizen specialists appear to be much nicer and softer. A successful kaizen event is one where the specialist can get employees to get involved and feel they have ownership. While workers are more involved compared with extreme Taylorism, the kaizen specialist is still responsible for the results and outcome. Kaizen events are popular because they have been used to accelerate productivity improvements in a short amount of time.

17.2.7 Is Toyota sheltered from modern industrial engineering?

IE handbooks today are emphasizing system optimization, advance computational mathematics and rapid overhaul within organizations. Interestingly, Toyota's approach to TPS appears to be highly shielded from modern trends in the industrial engineering profession and mainstream business improvement methodologies. In 1935, Sakichi Toyoda, the founder of Toyota, developed five basic teachings based on the Toyoda family work ethic. His teachings emphasized the importance of practicality, good study habits and healthy homelike work environment. In the 1950s, Taiichi Ohno initiated a new type of production system (i.e. TPS) with an emphasis on standardization, just-in-time, jidoka and kaizen. Ohno's shop floor focus and the idea of testing practical ideas immediately encouraged learning by getting employees to confirm failure with their own eyes. Ohno viewed that management should join with subordinates in experimentation and each supervisor must have the ability to teach. In 2001, Toyota continued this practical view of TPS when Fuijo Cho, then President of Toyota Motor Corporation, released the Toyota Way, a set of managerial values to strengthen the organizational thinking as it relates to work. The Way was based on five principles, one being genchi genbutsu which in Japanese means "go and see for yourself." Toyota's constant reinforcing of getting managers out of the office and on to the shop floor to see for themselves appears to be a reoccurring trend within Toyota. In 2005, Cho re-issued the company's 8-step problem solving process named Toyota Business Practice (TBP) as an effort to share a common way of thinking about problems in the workplace. Again, Toyota's emphasis to attract and recruit employees to follow one system, one voice, one image of TPS is a much different trend compared with most other mainstream business improvement methodologies where one individual is expected to accomplish the needs of the organization single handedly.

17.3 Research approach

The overall approach in this analysis is to analyze Toyota's organizational documents by applying statistical data mining. This work will use Latent Semantic Analysis (LSA) to study Toyota's industrial engineering techniques, systems and managerial practices. LSA is a theory and method for extracting and representing the contextual-usage and meaning of words and phrases by the statistical computation applied to text. LSA is based on Singular Value Decomposition (SVD) which is a mathematical matrix decomposition technique using factor analysis.

17.4 Conclusions

This work uses a new method for analyzing managerial practices. LSA was used to mathematically describe Toyota's approach towards industrial engineering. Various components and features of Toyota's management techniques were identified and described in a way that offers many unique insights. This technique has many other potential uses and can be accomplished with minimum resources in evaluating an organization's ideal strategy, image or management technique with less bias. The other goal in this work was to understand the similarities or differences of industrial engineering towards Toyota's management style. Early work indicates that Ohno and Shingo modeled much of their thinking towards the earlier versions of industrial engineering, namely scientific management. Up to this point, most work describes Toyota or lean methods as modern IE techniques. This research shows quantitatively that Toyota's managerial practices of today very much resemble the IE profession in the early 1900s. It is argued that Toyota has remained successful applying TPS because they have sheltered themselves from modern IE influences that seek to raise the competence of a single employee (i.e. industrial engineer) rather than the basic thinking skills of all employees. The findings of this work suggest that Toyota's managerial practices would rather deploy the simplified techniques that are easy to learn by all rather than to leave kaizen up to a single group (i.e. continuous improvement team) or an individual (i.e. kaizen specialist and master black belt).

These findings could suggest the following. True kaizen means small improvements add up to big results, which means the organization needs many ways to involve lots of people. The involvement techniques have to be practical, easy to apply and quick to implement. In this context, it makes sense why Toyota is pushing for skills such as direct observation, charting, standardization, and how to run simple tests to verify solutions. Surprisingly, modern IE approaches (at least from studying IE handbooks) do not emphasize teamwork, doing practical things first, or using techniques that relate to everyone. It could be argued that

Toyota is watering down IE thinking and should give up on the idea of trying to treat everyone as an engineer. Consider an organization that does not have a progressive human resource function. For some companies a small group of kaizen specialists or master black belts may be an optimal solution compared with fixing hiring processes and workplace incentives to learn. While not a competitive advantage, the modern IE approach could raise an organization's performance.

Lastly, this work illustrates that Toyota has been successful passing down scientific management practices from generation to generation. Results show that Toyota is not following mainstream practices but instead trying to maintain basic fundamentals and common sense practices. Interestingly, Toyota's drive to "get back to basics" continues and remains a constant force among managers to prepare future generations of Toyota employees.

 Professional Vocabularies and Expressions

Toyota production system	丰田制造系统
lean manufacturing	精益制造
5S	整理、整顿、清扫、清洁和素养
work sampling	工作抽样
standardization	标准化
standards engineer	标准工程师
systems thinking	系统思维
process flow chart	流程程序图
work distribution charts/line balance chart	流水线平衡图
time study	时间研究
process design and re-engineering	流程设计和再造
experimental designs (ED)	实验设计
design of experiments (DOE)	实验设计
six sigma	六西格玛
lean sigma	精益西格玛
kaizen blitz	持续快速改进行动
value engineering	价值工程
cellular manufacturing	单元化制造
production flow analysis	生产流程分析
supply chain infrastructure design	供应链基础设施设计
latent semantic analysis (LSA)	潜在语义分析
data mining	数据挖掘
singular value decomposition (SVD)	奇异值分解

Notes

1. This craze to upload lean into all aspects of the business has weakened organizations mainly because practitioners insist on applying the manufacturing tools of lean (i.e. visual control, 5S, standardized work) rather than applying the thinking of lean.

试图将精益制造应用到企业方方面面的时尚做法弱化了企业的竞争力,这主要是因为实践者拘泥于诸如图示化管理、5S 和标准化作业等精益制造工具的应用,而不是强调精益思维的运用。

2. In very simple terms, not to make TPS any more complicated than what it needs to be, TPS is an old way of thinking.

简言之,丰田制造系统是一套古老的思维模式,没必要将其搞得过于复杂。

3. PDR assumes a clean state change and suggests skipping documenting existing processes because it limits the vision of the design team with nothing to be gained.

流程设计与再造采取一种全新的变革方式并建议略过现有流程的建档过程,因为对现有流程的建档过程可能会束缚设计团队的视野且会徒劳无功①。

Discussion Questions:

1. To what degree have you mastered the techniques and skills mentioned in the traditional industrial engineering skill set?
2. Is the industrial engineering program in your university more traditional or more modern?
3. Why does Toyota shelter itself from modern industrial engineering practices?
4. Are there any approaches for modern industrial engineering skills to be integrated into Toyota's production system?

编者注:

本文取材于 2011 年发表在英文期刊《工业工程与管理》上的一篇文章。作者根据实践中所用到的技能将工业工程领域划分为传统工业工程和现代工业工程两个阶段,之后运用潜在语义分析的方法对丰田制造模式与传统工业工程和现代工业工程间的关系进行了量化研究。结果发现丰田制造模式的成功之处在于发动企业各层面的员工将传统的工业工程方法以持续快速改进的方式用于管理实践,强调全员参与以及从一线员工到企业高层管理理念的一致性,而不认可以单兵作战的方式对复杂的现代工业工程方法的

---

① 编者注:这里关于流程再造与现有流程建档关系的陈述有些偏激,在编者 10 余年的 IE 教学和科研工作中发现,即使是要对现有流程进行根本性的变革,也需要对现有流程和其背后的工作原理等予以充分尊重和理解,否则全新的流程尽管可能充分发挥了 IT 的使能作用,但可能与企业的传统文化和思维定式形成尖锐冲突而使变革无疾而终。

应用。编者在教学实践中将该文所归纳的两个关于基础和现代工业工程技能的表格用于学生对自身所掌握的工业工程技能的评估和检查，进而引导其发现需要完善和努力的方向，尤其强调相关技能所对应的各种软件和分析工具的学习，以提升学生的动手能力和应用能力。有鉴于此，文中关于潜在语义分析的内容没有被作为重点，因而予以省略。感兴趣的读者可以通过原文阅读而获取相关知识。

第五篇

工业工程前沿

CHAPTER 18

Total Quality Management

18.1 Introduction

Right from the dawn of history, people in all walks of life around the globe have been striving to survive in a highly competitive world. The industrial scenario is no different. Corporate executives have been working overtime to achieve business excellence by striving to find the solutions to those problems which have defeated their counterparts in other parts of the globe. The message is amply clear: The gospel of globalization has come to occupy center stage. The focus on price, which hitherto ruled the competition, has shifted to both price and quality. Today, customers are demanding quality in products, services and in life. They have become increasingly discerning and have started looking for options more in tune with their basic needs, requirements and self-esteem. In fact, they are prepared to pay a premium for a quality product or service. One of the approaches that seems to provide the solution to the aforesaid challenges is the management philosophy of total quality management (TQM).

TQM is an approach for continuously improving the quality of every aspect of business life, i.e. it is a never-ending process of improvement for individuals, groups of people and the whole organization. It is an integrated approach and set of practices that emphasizes *inter alia*, management commitment, continuous improvement, customer focus, long-range thinking, increased employee involvement and teamwork, employee empowerment, process management, competitive benchmarking, etc.

The origin of the TQM movement dates back to the early 20th century when Walter Shewart, in the early 1920s, first introduced the concept of statistical process control (SPC) to monitor quality in mass production manufacturing. This was followed by many quality management gurus and practitioners who all advocated various approaches to TQM. Crosby (1979, the four absolutes), Deming (1986, fourteen points), Feigenbaum (1993, total quality control), Ishikawa (1985, quality control circles), Juran et al. (1988, quality triology) and Taguchi (1986, loss function), have prescribed different techniques and organizational requirements for the effective implementation of TQM.

The evolution of the quality improvement movement is a conglomeration of various

Japanese and US philosophies, precepts, strategies and approaches. Even though the Japanese first took the lead in successfully applying the strategy later named TQM in the USA, it is also true that several Americans are recognized internationally as the drivers behind the concept. The genesis of modern management/administrative theory (let alone quality management) had its roots in the manufacturing milieu and blossomed under the auspices of the manufacturing stalwarts right from the early 20th century when Fredrick W. Taylor, in 1911, introduced the concept of scientific management. This development can be attributed to the fact that the entire industrial world was predominantly manufacturing oriented and undergoing a revolution with a prime focus on assembly lines, mass production manufacturing, supplier partnerships, just-in-time (JIT) production and cellular manufacturing, etc. Because of these factors, most of the techniques and strategies of administrative theory, and naturally quality management, were quantitative in nature and targeted to address the problems of the production line.

The management of service organizations and marketing of services has been a Cinderella among the organizational behavior and marketing literature in the past, in contrast to the management of manufacturing organizations and marketing of goods. But with the blossoming of the service sector in almost every economy, quality imperatives are no longer the sole concern and province of manufacturing. Of late, service providers are facing the same ground realities that confronted their manufacturing counterparts in the past.

The subject of quality management in manufacturing industry has been a matter of great interest and concern for business and academia alike. Several works have thoroughly investigated the various dimensions, techniques and organizational requirements for effective implementation of TQM. These dimensions include top management commitment and leadership, quality policy, training, product/service design, supplier quality management, process management, quality data and reporting, employee relations, workforce management, customer focus, customer involvement, benchmarking, SPC, employee empowerment, employee involvement, corporate quality culture and strategic quality management. These dimensions are, in essence, the tools of the intellect that were forged in the administrative theory, tempered in manufacturing quality management and therefore are naturally expected to be honed to cutting sharpness in service quality management. *Per contra*, though most of these dimensions and other techniques and strategies proposed by various theorists and practitioners, starting from the birth of the quality revolution, seems to provide a near-universal remedy to the problems of the manufacturing business, they are not a complete yardstick for service quality improvement. The reasoning here is that although from a logical point of view most of the dimensions of manufacturing quality management should naturally apply to services, the transferability of manufacturing quality management dimensions to services calls for some serious soul-searching as services differ from the manufacture of goods in a number of different ways: service intangibility, simultaneity of production, delivery and consumption, perishability, variability of expectations of the customers and the participatory role of customers in the service delivery.

Interestingly, the literature on TQM with respect to services, i.e. total quality service (TQS), seems to be bereft of an integrative framework that will include all the critical dimensions of TQS by addressing the issue of possible transferability of manufacturing quality management dimensions to services, and by focusing on those dimensions that are unique to service organizations. The present study attempts to develop a conceptual model of TQS by comparing and contrasting the criticality of the different dimensions of quality management in both manufacturing and service organizations.

18.2   The research problem

It is evident that the research literature on manufacturing TQM is quite extensive and exhaustive, covering all the aspects of TQM, viz.

(1) The critical dimensions of TQM.

(2) The relationships between quality management practices and organizational/ business performance.

(3) The soft issues (i.e. people oriented issues) of TQM.

(4) The influence of contextual factors on TQM.

(5) The relationships between product quality and customers' perceptions of product quality.

(6) The demarcation between TQM and non-TQM firms.

(7) The effect of TQM age on operational results, etc.

Concerning the literature on TQS, the various aspects of TQM in service organizations have also been independently subjected to extensive research, e.g.

(1) Customers' perceptions of service quality.

(2) The concept of "service culture."

(3) The critical role of the personnel and HRM function.

(4) The influence of operational, organizational and human resource factors on service quality.

(5) The effect of the "built environment."

(6) Customer satisfaction, loyalty and purchase intentions.

(7) Service switching, service encounters, critical incidents and recovery.

(8) Financial outcomes of service quality initiatives.

18.3   The critical dimensions of TQS

The present work, based on the thorough review of the prescriptive, conceptual, practitioner and empirical literature on TQM and TQS spanning over 100 articles, identifies 12 dimensions of quality management as critical for the institution of a TQM environment in service organizations. The dimensions that have been identified are as follows:

(1) Top management commitment and visionary leadership.

(2) Human resource management.

(3) Technical system.

(4) Information and analysis system.

(5) Benchmarking.

(6) Continuous improvement.

(7) Customer focus.

(8) Employee satisfaction.

(9) Union intervention.

(10) Social responsibility.

(11) Servicescapes.

(12) Service culture.

These dimensions can be broadly grouped under three categories as follows.

(1) Those dimensions of quality management that are generic to both manufacturing and service organizations, but which were initially practiced in the manufacturing set-up and later transferred to service milieu (These include the dimensions such as Top management commitment and visionary leadership, Human resource management, Design and management of processes, Information and analysis, Benchmarking, Continuous improvement, Employee satisfaction and Customer focus and satisfaction).

(2) Those dimensions that are seldom addressed in the literature but are, nevertheless, the key elements of TQM in both manufacturing and service organizations (e.g. Union intervention and Social responsibility).

(3) Finally, those factors that are unique to service organizations (namely, Service scapes — the man-made physical environment — and Service culture).

Table 18-1 briefly explains the 12 critical factors of TQS. Several works have underlined the importance of these dimensions. Given the fact that services have certain unique characteristics, the different roles that each of these dimensions plays and the various aspects that they bring into the picture (like skills, values, tools, techniques and other requirements) vary from manufacturing to service organizations. Table 18-2 compares and contrasts the significance and relevance of the various quality management dimensions in manufacturing and service organizations.

Table 18-1 The critical dimensions of TQS

No. of Critical Dimensions	Explanation of the critical dimensions
1. Top management commitment and visionary leadership	Top management commitment is a prerequisite for effective and successful TQS implementation. Although different researchers proclaim various theories on the organizational requirements for the effective implementation of TQS, all would agree that the impetus for any quality improvement effort should come from the top. Visionary leadership is the art of leading and espousing a mental, strategic and spiritual change in the organization by the formulation of a long-range vision for the development of the organization, propagating the vision throughout the organization, devising and developing a plan of action and finally stimulating the entire organization towards the accomplishment of the vision.

(Continued)

No. of Critical Dimensions	Explanation of the critical dimensions
2. Human resource management	This refers to the number of the organizational behavior issues (ranging from selection and recruitment, training and education, employee empowerment to employee involvement) that form the cornerstone upon which the corporate strategy is built. The moot point here is that only if the employers treat their employees as precious resources would the employees, in turn, treat their customers as valuable. Therefore, it is indispensable for service organizations to look upon HRM as a source of competitive advantage.
3. Technical system	The technical system includes design quality management and process management. Sound and reliable service design echoes an organization's strategic quality planning abilities and enables the organization to surmount customers' needs, expectations and desires, consequently resulting in improved business performance. Service process management essentially involves the procedures, systems and technology that are required to streamline the service delivery so that customers can receive the service without any hassles, i.e. it delineates the non-human element of service delivery, as opposed to human element which is captured in the dimension "service culture."
4. Information and analysis system	Services, unlike manufactured goods, cannot be inventoried and used in times of emergency or demand. Therefore, during rush or peak periods, unless organizations keep themselves prepared for any such eventualities, they may not be able to provide quality service to customers. This can only be achieved by equipping the employees with the information regarding the process and customers. The prompt, sufficient and pertinent data that are critical to the implementation and practice of TQM constitute information and analysis. In a TQS ambience people need to communicate across organizational levels, functions and locations to work out current problems, eschew new ones and implement change. Measures for proactive prevention rather than reactive correction are employed to monitor quality in order to sustain a true customer focus.
5. Benchmarking	Benchmarking is actually a comparison standard that consists of analyzing the best products/services and processes of the best organizations in the world and then analyzing and using that information to improve one's own products or services and processes. While in manufacturing, the standards such as product characteristics, process, cost, strategy, etc. are used as benchmarks, it is all the more difficult to benchmark services. Because of the very puzzling nature of services and the consequent organizational contingencies that it warrants for its design, production, delivery and consumption, organizations need to focus on benchmarking not only hard data, but also certain behavioral features such as customer satisfaction and employee satisfaction, apart from comparing the services and processes through which they are delivered. An organization can achieve a world-class tag if benchmarking is targeted at the key or critical business processes.
6. Continuous improvement	The quest for quality improvement is not a specific destination but a continuous journey that throws up more and more opportunities for improvement. Improvement should be viewed as an ongoing process in the sense once targets are met, new ones must be set, aiming for even higher levels of service efficiency. It is a race which has no finish line but has the sole objective of striving for continuous improvement, and looking for breakthroughs with revolutionary order of magnitude changes that will result in the transmogrification of the organization into a world-class one.

(Continued)

No. of Critical Dimensions	Explanation of the critical dimensions
7. Customer focus	Customer focus is the ultimate goal of any TQS program because organizations can outscore their competitors by effectively addressing customers' needs and demands and anticipating and responding to their evolving interests and wants. Focusing on customers' needs and wants enables organizations to have a better market orientation than ever before by providing a competitive edge over their rivals, thereby resulting in enhanced business performance. In service organizations, as customer expectations are highly dynamic and complex in nature, focusing only on customer-defined areas (specific customer needs) so as to satisfy the customers will not yield fruit. In today's world of intense competition, satisfying customers may not be enough. The competitive advantage in a quality revolution comes only from customer delight. Customer satisfaction is a short-term concept which may or may not lead to commitment. The management's responsibility is to ensure that satisfaction manifests itself as commitment in the long run.
8. Employee satisfaction	Employee satisfaction is a multi-dimensional concept, which is defined as the degree to which employees of an organization believe that their needs and wants are continuously satisfied by the organization. An organization must not only have a focus on service quality/customers, but also concentrate on employees' satisfaction, as research has shown much evidence of strong relationships between employee perceptions of employee well-being and customer perceptions of service quality and satisfaction.
9. Union intervention	With a major chunk of the workforce in both developed and developing nations working in service organizations, industrial relation issues are as crucial (if not more) as they are in manufacturing industries. As TQM is an organization-wide approach, its success is greatly influenced by its employee union. These employee relation issues affect the organizational system and consequently determine the nature and extent of TQM implementation. And, with the technological growth (in terms of computerization, networking, etc.) gripping the service sector, and the known aversions and apprehensions of the unions towards such advancements, it could be concluded that union attitudes play a critical role in any quality improvement effort.
10. Social responsibility	The concept of corporate citizenship should come to the fore if an organization has to be successful and progress towards achieving business excellence. No doubt, a business or industrial enterprise exists to make profits. This can be achieved by fulfilling its mission. At the same time, an organization must also grow and have a good image, i.e. it should meet its social and community obligations. At the end of the day, it is not just the profit or revenue that counts for an organization, but an indomitable belief in corporate responsibility to its society becomes indispensable. With the entire world undergoing an upheaval — a quality revolution — it is this attitude that will certainly give an organization a competitive edge in the long run over many others who vie for greater honors in terms of profits, return on investments (ROI), market share, etc. completely ignoring the fact that they are accountable to the society in which they thrive upon. This subtle, but none the less powerful dimension sends strong signals towards improving the organization's image and goodwill, and consequently effecting the customers' overall satisfaction with the services and their loyalty to the organization.
11. Service scapes	The tangible facets of the service facility, i.e. the man-made physical environment (such as equipment, machinery, signage and employee appearance — the service scape), strongly influence both employees and customers in physiological, psychological, emotional, sociological and cognitive ways, particularly as the core service becomes more intangible.

No. of Critical Dimensions	Explanation of the critical dimensions
12. Service culture	In service organizations the boundary separating the customers and employees is very frail and pervious, with the result that the physical and psychological propinquity between them is so intense that only a firm's culture that stresses service quality throughout the organization could establish the seamlessness in the service delivery. Service culture is actually the extent to which the employees at all levels realize that the real purpose of their existence is "service to customers." While customer focus is seen as a goal of the TQS movement, service culture is an organizational strategy that motivates the employees to have a service orientation in whatever they do. An organization characterized by such a service orientation is more likely to offer a reliable, responsive, empathetic service to customers and provide them with assurance in conveying trust and confidence that will result in improved quality in service delivery, which, in turn, will lead to higher perceived service quality from the customers' point of view. A strong internal culture helps an organization to effect and sustain an organizational change that will make the TQS approach more effective.

Table 18-2 Significance of the quality management dimensions in manufacturing and service settings

Function/dimension	Manufacturing	Service
Impetus	Top management commitment and visionary leadership	Top management commitment and visionary leadership
Organizational system HRM		
Recruitment and selection	Task-oriented skills, teamwork, technical skills and quality values	Interpersonal relations, teamwork and quality values
Training and education	Hard topics: Accounting, engineering, statistics, etc.	Soft topics: communication skills, interpersonal relations, teamwork, employee behavior and customer service
Employee empowerment	Supporting infrastructure such as required resource and technical assistance, increasing autonomy and responsibility; emphasis on shop-floor workers	Providing power, information, rewards and knowledge; protection of employees in times of their inadvertent and unforeseen behavior during customer service; emphasis on customer contact personnel
Employment involvement	Quality control circles, problem hit squads, quality improvement teams, suggestion schemes, brainstorming, Gordon technique, etc.	Quality control circles, problem hit squads, quality improvement teams, suggestion schemes, brainstorming, Gordon technique, etc.; greater emphasis on employee involvement in service organizations as they run the service operation, market the services and are equated with the service by the customers

(Continued)

Function/dimension	Manufacturing	Service
Technical system		
Design quality management	Quality function deployment, house of quality, Taguchi's design of experiments, error prevention and zero fault strategy, failure mode effect analysis, poke-yoke, etc.	Error prevention and zero fault strategy; gap analysis; critical incident technique
Process management	Statistical process control, statistical quality control, just-in-time production, cellular manufacturing, six sigma quality, 5S approach, seven old and new tools of quality, etc.	Systematization, standardization, simplification and streamlining of the service delivery processes; computerization; networking of operations; etc.
Information system	Data related to cost and financial accounting, sales, marketing, purchasing, etc.	Data related to customer satisfaction, service quality and employee satisfaction
Culture	Though the importance of culture is acknowledged even in the manufacturing literature, the emphasis has been more on technology.	Seamlessness in service delivery, moments of truth, critical incident and recovery
Tangibles	Not applicable	Ambient conditions such as temperature, ventilation, noise, odor, etc.; signs, symbols, advertisement boards, pamphlets, employee appearance and other artifacts in the organization; physical layout of premises and other furnishings
Social responsibility	Environmental management, ISO 14000, etc.	Corporate citizenship — to lead as a corporate citizen by promoting ethical conduct in everything the organization does
Industrial relations	Role played by the Union in establishing the policies, strategies and procedures of the organization; Union's influence in recruitment, selection and career development programs, and the extent of automation	Role played by the Union in establishing the policies, strategies and procedures of the organization; Union's influence in recruitment, selection and career development programs, and the extent of automation; Union's support and co-operation in the drive for customer focus, quality conscious culture and continuous improvement
Benchmarking	Product characteristics, processes, cost, strategy, etc.	Behavioral features such as customer satisfaction, employee satisfaction and service quality apart from the service product and processes through which they are delivered

(Continued)

Function/dimension	Manufacturing	Service
Goals		
Customer focus	Though customer satisfaction and employee satisfaction are acknowledged as vital elements of TQM, they are not seen as the goals of a TQM process. The focus is on product quality, elimination of defects, conformance to specifications, requirements, reliability, durability, fitness for use, etc.	Customer delight and loyalty, favorable purchase intentions, repeat business, etc.; customers are treated as productive human resources, substitutes for leadership and as organizational consultants
Employee satisfaction		Employee satisfaction and commitment — recognition for small as well as big quality contributions and achievements, better behavior, work values, ethics, etc.
Ambience	Continuous improvement	Continuous improvement

18.4 Summary

As firms aspire to spread their wings in the global market, TQM promises to provide a potential solution to many of their business-related problems. Though many corporations throughout the globe have already set out on this never-ending Odyssey and many others have started exploring what is required in order to embark on a TQM journey, the question of how to start a TQM program is still shrouded in uncertainty. As decision-makers become more involved in implementing TQM, questions are raised about which management practices should be accentuated. This scenario gains even more significance, especially in a service business where the very concept of quality itself is difficult to define.

Professional Vocabularies and Expressions

total quality management (TQM)	全面质量管理
management commitment	管理承诺
continuous improvement	持续改进
customer focus	以客户为中心
employee involvement	员工参与
teamwork	团队合作
employee empowerment	员工授权
process management	流程管理
benchmarking	标杆超越

statistical process control (SPC)	随机过程控制
quality control circle	质量控制圈
assembly line	装配线
mass production	大规模生产
supplier partnership	与供应商的伙伴关系
just-in-time (JIT)	准时生产
cellular manufacturing	单元制造
quality policy	质量政策
training	培训
product/service design	产品/服务设计
supplier quality management	供应商质量管理
employee relations	员工关系
customer involvement	顾客参与
corporate quality culture	企业质量文化
strategic quality management	战略质量管理
service intangibility	服务的无形性
simultaneity of production	生产的同时性
perishability	易逝性
total quality service (TQS)	全面质量服务

Notes

1. Right from the dawn of history, people in all walks of life around the globe have been striving to survive in a highly competitive world. The industrial scenario is no different.

有史以来，全世界所有的人就在这个高度竞争的世界中奋斗。工业界也同样如此。

2. The genesis of modern management/administrative theory (let alone quality management) had its roots in the manufacturing milieu and blossomed under the auspices of the manufacturing stalwarts right from the early 20th century when Fredrick W. Taylor, in 1911, introduced the concept of scientific management.

现代管理理论（更不用说质量管理理论）起源于制造环境，并以从20世纪早期（1911年）弗雷德里克·泰勒引入科学管理理念以来的制造业健康发展为前兆走向繁荣与发展。

3. *Per contra*, though most of these dimensions and other techniques and strategies proposed by various theorists and practitioners, starting from the birth of the quality revolution, seem to provide a near-universal remedy to the problems of the manufacturing business, they are not a complete yardstick for service quality improvement.

相反，尽管上述的由各种理论家和实践者从质量革命以来所倡导的大部分理论、相关技术和策略似乎可以提供解决制造领域（质量）问题的灵丹妙药，但它们并不能作为服务业质量改善的完全标准。

Discussion Questions:

1. Total quality management is quite popular in the manufacturing sector. Summarize the achievement of TQM having been gained so far and explain why it is so prevalent in manufacturing companies.
2. In your opinion, what are the fundamental differences between the quality management in manufacturing sector and service sector? What are your comments on the critical dimensions of total quality service proposed in the paper?

CHAPTER 19

Agile Manufacturing

19.1 Introduction

Businesses are restructuring and re-engineering themselves in response to the challenges and demands of the 21st century. The 21st century business will have to overcome the challenges of the customers seeking high-quality, low-cost products, and be responsive to customers' specific unique and rapidly changing needs. Agile enterprises represent a global industrial competition mode for 21st century manufacturing. "Agility" addresses the new ways of running companies to meet these challenges. In a changing competitive environment, there is a need to develop the organizations and facilities that are significantly more flexible and responsive than the existing ones.

Agility requires the capability to survive and prosper in a competitive environment of continuous and unpredictable change by reacting quickly and effectively to changing markets, driven by customer-designed products and services. The key enablers of agile manufacturing include: ① virtual enterprise formation tools/metrics; ② physically distributed manufacturing architecture and teams; ③ rapid partnership formation tools/metrics; ④ concurrent engineering; ⑤ integrated product/ production/business information system; ⑥ rapid prototyping; and ⑦ electronic commerce.

Agile manufacturing is a vision of the manufacturing that is a natural development from the original concept of "lean manufacturing." In lean manufacturing, the emphasis is on the elimination of waste. The requirement for organizations and facilities to become more flexible and responsive to customers led to the concept of "agile" manufacturing as a differentiation from the "lean" organization. This requirement for manufacturing to be able to respond to unique demands moves the balance back to the situation prior to the introduction of lean production, where manufacturing had to respond to whatever pressures were imposed upon it, with the risks to cost, speed and quality. Agility should be based on not only responsiveness and flexibility, but also the cost and quality of the goods and services that the customers are prepared to accept. It is, however, essential to link agile capabilities in manufacturing with product needs in the marketplace. Agility as a concept increases the emphasis on speed of response to new market opportunities. Thus, it is more relevant to a One-of-a-Kind Product (OKP) than it is to commodity products that compete primarily on price.

19.2 Agile manufacturing — definitions

In this section, we explore a variety of definitions and a range of concepts with the objective of developing a new and feasible concept of AM. The reason for analyzing the present conceptions and definitions of AM is to identify the gap between practice and theory in order to enhance the confidence of practitioners. The manufacturing processes based on agile manufacturing are characterized by customer integrated processes for designing, manufacturing, marketing, and support for all products and services; decision-making at functional knowledge points; stable unit costs; flexible manufacturing; easy access to integrated data; and modular production facilities. The focus is on the integration of critical functional areas with the help of the advanced design and manufacturing technologies, and alignment between strategies.

According to Gupta and Mittal (1996), AM is a business concept that integrates organizations, people and technology into a meaningful unit by deploying the advanced information technologies and flexible and nimble organization structures to support highly skilled, knowledgeable and motivated people. "Lean" implies high productivity and quality, but it does not necessarily imply being responsive. "Agile," on the other hand, stresses the importance of being highly responsive to meet the "total needs" of the customer, while simultaneously striving to be lean — a manufacturer whose primary goal is to be lean compromises responsiveness over cost-efficiencies. Agile manufacturers place equal importance on both cost and responsiveness. This is the main reason for incorporating cost and quality into agile competitive bases.

Agile manufacturing can be said to be a relatively new, post-mass-production concept for the creation and distribution of goods and services. It is the ability to thrive in a competitive environment of continuous and unanticipated change and to respond quickly to the rapidly changing markets driven by customer-based valuing of products and services. It includes rapid product realization, highly flexible manufacturing, and distributed enterprise integration. DeVor and Mills (1995) argue that technology alone does not make an agile enterprise. Companies should find the right combination of strategies, culture, business practices, and technology that are necessary to make it agile, taking into account the market characteristics.

As stated before, agile manufacturing is driven by the need to respond quickly to changing customer requirements. It demands a manufacturing system that is able to produce effectively a large variety of products and to be reconfigurable to accommodate changes in the product mix and product designs. Manufacturing system reconfigurability and product variety are the critical aspects of agile manufacturing. The concept of agility has an impact on the design of assemblies. To implement agile manufacturing, the methodologies for the design of agile manufacturing are needed. The design for agile assembly is accomplished by considering the operational issues of assembly systems at the early product design stage.

According to Tu (1997), the manufacturing industry, particularly the OKP (One-of-a-Kind Production) industry, tends to be lean, agile and global. This tendency leads to a new concept of a virtual company that consists of several subproduction units geographically dispersed in the world as branches, joint ventures and subcontractors. Many OKP companies, such as those in shipbuilding have become virtual companies. For these virtual companies, traditional production control and management systems, methods and theories do not satisfy their needs for production planning and control. For some companies, therefore, there is a need to be transformed into a virtual enterprise in order to become agile. However, selecting partners based on flexibility and responsiveness alone will not lead to a reduction in cost and an improvement in the quality of products and services. A much wider spectrum of factors needs to be taken into account.

Agile manufacturing is an expression that is used to represent the ability of a producer of goods and services. The changes needed for agile manufacturers to thrive in the face of continuous change can occur in markets, in technologies, in business relationships and in all facets of the business enterprise. Such changes, according to Kidd (1996), are not about small-scale continuous improvements, but an entirely different way of doing business. Agile manufacturing requires one to meet the changing market requirements by suitable alliances based on core-complementary competencies, organizing to manage change and uncertainty, and leveraging people and information.

The analyses of the various definitions and concepts of AM (See Table 19-1.) show that all these definitions are polarized in a similar direction. Most definitions and concepts seem to highlight flexibility and responsiveness as well as virtual enterprises and information technologies. However, the question is whether one can achieve agility with minimum investment in technologies and processes. Hence, there is a need to redefine the definition of agility within this context. Figure 19-1 presents the new model for explaining the agile manufacturing paradigm. The model takes into account the characteristics of the market, infrastructure, technologies and strategies. Its purpose is to highlight the new dimension of the definition of the agile manufacturing paradigm. The justifications for the need to redefine the agility are listed below.

Table 19-1 A summary of agile definitions and key concepts

Authors	Definition	Keywords
DeVor and Mills (1995)	Ability to thrive in a competitive environment of continuous and unanticipated change and to respond quickly to rapidly changing markets driven by customer-based valuing of products and services.	A new, post-mass production system for the creation and distribution of goods and services.

(Continued)

Authors	Definition	Keywords
Booth (1996), McGrath (1996)	More flexible and responsive.	Moving from lean to agile.
Adamides (1996)	Responsibility-based manufacturing (RBM).	Most adjustments for process and product variety to take place dynamically during production without *a priori* system reconfiguration.
Gupta and Mittal (1996)	Agile stresses the importance of being highly responsive to meet the "total needs" of the customer, while simultaneously striving to be lean. Agile places a higher priority on responsiveness than cost-efficiency while a manufacturer whose primary goal is to be lean compromises responsiveness over cost-efficiencies.	Integrates organizations, people, and technology into a meaningful unit by deploying the advanced information technologies and flexible and nimble organization structures to support highly skilled, knowledgeable and motivated people.
James-Moore (1996), Kidd (1996), Gould (1997)	More flexible and responsive than current.	New ways of running business, casting off old ways of doing things.
Hong et al. (1996)	Flexibility and rapid response to market demands.	Flexible technologies such as Rapid Prototyping, Robots, Internet, AGVs, CAD/CAE, CAPP and CIM, FMS.
Abair (1997)	Provides competitiveness.	Customer-integrated process for designing, manufacturing, marketing and support, flexible manufacturing, cooperation to enhance competitiveness, organizing to manage change and uncertainty and leveraging people and information.
Kusiak and He (1997)	Driven by the need to quickly respond to changing customer requirements.	Demands a manufacturing system to be able to produce efficiently a large variety of products and be reconfigurable to accommodate changes in the product mix and product designs. Design for assembly.
Gunasekaran	Capability to survive and prosper in a competitive environment of continuous and unpredictable change by reacting quickly and effectively to changing markets.	Virtual enterprise, E-commerce, strategic partnership formation, and rapid prototyping.
Cho et al., (1996), Gunasekaran (1999a), Yusuf et al. (1999)	Capability for surviving and prospering in a competitive environment of continuous and unpredictable change by reacting quickly and effectively to changing markets.	Standard exchange for product (STEP) models, concurrent engineering, virtual manufacturing.

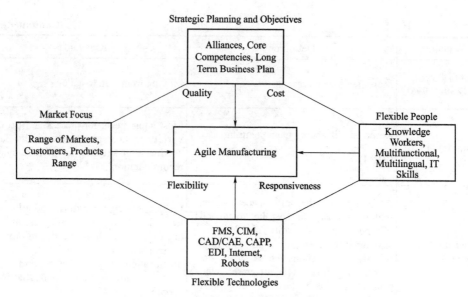

Figure 19-1 Agile manufacturing paradigm

(1) In some cases, flexibility and cost are not complementary. Yet, there is a need to consider the *cost* aspects of agility. Agility without cost effectiveness is not a real competitive strategy. Therefore, there is a need to consider cost in defining agility.

(2) The implications of technologies in achieving agility are paramount compared with partnership formation that is based on core competencies in a virtual enterprise. For certain businesses one needs to identify a set of technologies that are more important to the selected market segments, and to product and service requirements. Yet, the implications of integrating complementary core competencies are highly significant. A lack of focus on utilizing core competencies would not improve productivity and quality.

(3) The nature of a given market certainly defines the characteristics of agile organizations. No organizations can satisfy unlimited product/service requirements of different markets. The characteristics of markets may vary from industry to industry and from country to country.

(4) The implications of e-commerce have not been properly addressed in the development of agile manufacturing systems. Direct input from customers, the reduction in response time and the cost of identifying market requirements using Concurrent Engineering principles would certainly reduce the gap between marketing and production.

(5) Human resources play a significant role in the development of agile manufacturing systems. However, the issue of an agile workforce has not been well addressed. It is still not clear how the agility of the workforce and its characteristics can be defined with reference to changing market requirements and value-adding systems.

(6) Logistics plays an important role, especially in physically distributed virtual enterprises. Therefore, due attention should be paid to the effective management of logistics

and, in turn, to supporting agility in manufacturing.

Based on some of these observations, agility in manufacturing may be defined as: The capability of an organization, by proactively establishing virtual manufacturing with an efficient product development system, to ① meet the changing market requirements, ② maximize customer service level and ③ minimize the cost of goods, with an objective of being competitive in a global market and for an increased chance of long-term survival and profit potential. This must be supported by flexible people, processes and technologies.

19.3 Agile manufacturing strategies and technologies

Analyzing the overall characteristics of strategies and technologies, the literature available on AM can be grouped under the following themes: ① strategic planning, ② product design, ③ virtual enterprise, and ④ automation and Information Technology (IT). The details of the classification are illustrated in Figure 19-2. Achieving agility may require focusing on strategic planning, product design, virtual enterprise and automation and IT.

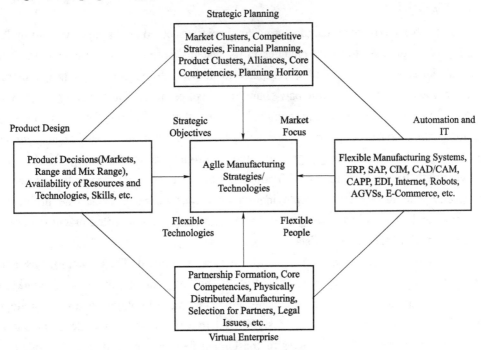

Figure 19-2 Agile manufacturing strategies/techniques

19.4 A framework for the development of agile manufacturing

The framework proposed here constitutes the following major strategies and technologies for achieving agile manufacturing:

(1) Partnership formation and supplier development.

(2) IT in manufacturing.

(3) Enterprise Integration and Management with the help of advanced IT/IS.

(4) Virtual reality tools and techniques in manufacturing.

(5) The application of most of the advanced manufacturing concepts and technologies, such as Computer-Integrated Manufacturing/Services, Manufacturing/Service Strategy, Enterprise Integration, Rapid Prototyping, CE, New Product Development, BPR, Systems Design and Operations and SCM.

(6) Global manufacturing/service perspectives (physically distributed manufacturing environments) with the help of IT, such as E-Commerce, ERP, SAP, Internet, WWW, CAD/CAM, Simulation, Multimedia and MRPII.

19.5 Summary and conclusions

In this paper, an attempt has been made to review the literature on AM with the aim of revising the outlook for agility in manufacturing and identifying the corresponding major strategies and technologies of AM. In addition, a framework has been offered in the paper to develop an AMS.

Two key characteristics of manufacturing companies discussed in this paper are "Agility" — the ability of a company to effect changes in its systems, structure and organization — and "Responsiveness" — the ability of a company to gather information from its commercial environment and to detect and anticipate changes, to recover from changes and to improve as a result of change. Manufacturing companies, even those operating in relatively stable conditions with good market positions, are facing fast and often unanticipated changes in their commercial environment. Being agile in such environments means being flexible, cost effective, productive and producing with consistent high quality. Each company will respond in a specific and different way deploying its own agile characteristics. The problem of identifying, analyzing and evaluating agility is that no commonly accepted practical frame of reference or analytical structure exists.

The literature available on an AM workforce is rather limited. The reason for this is that there is no clear-cut framework for identifying the implications of AM on workforce characteristics, and most of the literature deals with enabling technologies and some strategies of AM. However, human factors play a significant role in the successful development and implementation of AM. The key issues of the human factors that need to be considered in agile environment are knowledge workers, multilingual workforce, multinational workforce, incentive schemes, type and level of education and training, relation with unions, and pay award. Most of the available systems (control and information) are developed for traditional manufacturing environments where static market behavior and resources have been employed for producing goods and services. The support systems for AMS rely heavily on computer-based information systems such as EDI, Internet and Electronic Commerce. Therefore, a flexible architecture for systems to accommodate temporary alliances will help improve enterprise integration and hence agility in organizations.

The following is the summary of the issues that should be addressed in an attempt to fully embrace agile manufacturing: ① the implications of temporary alliances on the enterprise communication and coordination, ② the influence of a virtual enterprise and physically distributed manufacturing on human relations management, and ③ the technologies and human skills required for the information intensive manufacturing environment. Agile manufacturing/service requires multidisciplinary skills, which include manufacturing management, computer science, operational research, software engineering, systems design, sensors, mechatronics, robotics, systems integration, virtual manufacturing/services, enterprise integration and management and advanced information technologies. The major problems that need most attention in the development of AM are: ① modeling of evolutionary and concurrent product development and production under continuous customers' influence; ② real-time monitoring and control of the production progress in virtual OKP; ③ a flexible or dynamic company control structure to cope with uncertainties in the market; ④ an adaptive production scheduling structure and the algorithms to cope with the uncertainties of a production state in virtual OKP; ⑤ modeling of production states and a control system in virtual OKP; and ⑥ the reference architecture for a virtual OKP company.

Professional Vocabularies and Expressions

agile manufacturing	敏捷制造
agile enterprise	敏捷企业
virtual enterprise	虚拟企业
concurrent engineering	并行工程
rapid prototyping	快速原型
electronic commerce	电子商务
reconfigurability	可重组性，可重塑性
supplier development	供应商开发
virtual reality	虚拟现实
computer-integrated manufacturing/services	计算机集成制造/服务
manufacturing/service strategy	制造/服务战略
enterprise integration	企业集成
new product development	新产品开发
business process reengineering (BPR)	企业流程再造
systems design and operations	系统设计和运作
supply chain management (SCM)	供应链管理

enterprise resource planning (ERP)	企业资源规划
simulation	仿真
manufacturing management	制造管理
computer science	计算机科学
operational research	运筹学
software engineering	软件工程
systems design	系统设计
mechatronics	机械电子学
robotics	机器人学
systems integration	系统集成
virtual manufacturing/service	虚拟制造/服务
advanced information technology	先进信息技术

 Notes

1. Agile manufacturing is a vision of manufacturing that is a natural development from the original concept of "lean manufacturing."

敏捷制造是在精益制造原始概念基础上自然发展起来的一个对未来制造业的展望。

2. This requirement for manufacturing to be able to respond to unique demands moves the balance back to the situation prior to the introduction of lean production, where manufacturing had to respond to whatever pressures were imposed upon it, with the risks to cost, speed and quality.

对顾客独特需求迅速响应能力的要求，使得制造企业运作重点的权衡又回到了精益制造出现前的情形，即企业不得不在冒着成本、速度和质量等风险的情况下对其所面临的各种压力做出响应。

3. "Lean" implies high productivity and quality, but it does not necessarily imply being responsive.

"精益"意指高生产率和质量，但并不一定指迅速应变的能力。

Discussion Questions:

1. What is your definition of agility and agile manufacturing?
2. How is agile manufacturing different from Toyota production system?
3. What concepts of agile manufacturing are suitable for Chinese manufacturing companies? How can we benefit from them?

CHAPTER 20

Theory of Constraints

20.1 Introduction

Since The Goal first appeared in print (Goldratt and Cox 1984), the concepts introduced and collectively termed as "constraint management" or the "Theory of Constraints (TOC)" have drawn a wide range of responses from practitioners as well as from academicians. This has been particularly true in the academic world. There is a plethora of research published in the scientific literature that compares and contrasts constraints management ideas with existing production management tools and concepts such as linear programming, material requirements planning, just-in-time (JIT) and, lately, with lean manufacturing, supply chain management and six sigma.

Dr. Goldratt has long argued that production management has now become a science and that TOC research provides a scientific knowledge base. TOC has evolved from a manufacturing scheduling method to a management philosophy that can be used to understand and improve the performance of complex systems. Thus, he claimed that TOC is a theory of managing manufacturing organizations.

Judging by the large amount and wide range of the academic literature in the past few years, the TOC manufacturing management philosophy appears to be attracting an increasing amount of attention from both the academic and business communities. The number of researchers working in the area of TOC has increased quite dramatically as can be seen from the variety of scientific journals (e.g. International Journal of Production Research, Production and Operations Management Journal, International Journal of Operations and Production Management, Production and Inventory Management Journal) and conferences (e.g. The TOC World Conference organized by the Avraham Y. Goldratt Institute (AGI) and academic conferences organized by the Production and Operations Management Society, and Decision Sciences) where TOC research has been published and presented on a regular basis.

20.2 Historical background and basic concepts of TOC

The papers represent an addition to the large and growing body of TOC literature. The roots of TOC can be traced to the development of a commercial software product known as Optimized Production Technology (OPT) in the late 1970s. Since then, Goldratt and many other independent scholars have published a number of business novels and other books, operations management (OM) textbooks have begun to incorporate a complete chapter on TOC, suggesting that TOC is gaining acceptance and popularity among both academics and practitioners. A number of success stories have been reported and analyzed in the literature to suggest significant improvements. For example, Mabin and Balderstone (2000) concluded from their survey of over 100 published case studies in various industries such as automotive, semiconductor, furniture and apparel that, on average, inventories were reduced by 49%, production times measured in terms of lead times, cycle times or due date performance improved by over 60%, and financial performance improved by 60%. A significant number of journal articles have been written ① to trace the history of OPT as well as TOC, ② to review the basic concepts of TOC, ③ to categorize TOC concepts and terms, ④ to review TOC literature and ⑤ to demonstrate its applications in various areas such as supply chain management, enterprise resource planning, sales and marketing, and human resource management.

In summary, the TOC has two broad viewpoints: that of the business system and of an ongoing improvement process itself. Both perspectives of TOC use unique terminology to describe its basic concepts.

20.2.1 Business system perspective

As it applies to the business system, the TOC emphasizes change process implemented at three levels: the mindset of the organization, the measures that drive the organization and the methods employed within the organization.

One of the main assumptions of TOC theory is that every business has the primary goal of "making more money now as well as in the future" without violating certain necessary conditions. Two examples of such conditions are ① providing a satisfying work environment to employees and ② providing satisfaction to the market. This mindset stipulates that the organization should devote its energy to promote initiatives, e.g. exploring new markets and introducing new products (popularly termed as "throughput world thinking") by using the available resources instead of expending energy to reduce costs or save money, which invariably violates necessary condition(s). Further, this mindset emphasizes the management focus on high leverage points to ensure the financial success of the organization as a whole (i.e. synchronization of the flow among individual processes or functional areas).

The TOC measurement system was developed with an eye towards evaluating the effectiveness of decisions in helping to achieve the primary goal. The system consists of a set of global operational measures (i.e. throughput, inventory and operating expenses) to determine the extent to which the organization is accomplishing the goal. Table 20-1 has a brief description of these measures. These operational measures ① are financial in nature, i.e. they can be translated to conventional measures such as net profit, return-on-investment, ② are easy to apply at any level of an organization and ③ ensure that local decisions are aligned with the profit goal of an organization. Of the three measures, TOC views throughput as having the greatest effect on profitability. The emphasis on increasing throughput is referred to as "throughput world thinking," which usually stands in marked contrast to the "cost world thinking" which emphasizes reducing cost (via operating expenses or even inventory).

Table 20-1   Measure of the theory of constraints

1. Throughput (T) is defined as "the rate at which the system generates money through sales." More specifically, it is the selling price minus totally variable costs (i.e. the money not generated by the system, e.g. purchased parts and raw materials).
2. Inventory (I) is defined as "all the money invested in purchasing things the system intends to sell." More specifically, it is synonymous with investments such as machines, equipment, etc., and finished goods and work-in-process inventory are reported at the raw material costs, i.e. the value-added component is not recognized.
3. Operating expenses (OE) are defined as "all the money the system spends in turning inventory into throughput." More specifically, it includes wages, salaries, utility expenses, depreciation, etc.

Relationship to standard financial measures
- Net profit (NP)=T-OE.
- Return on investment (ROI)=(T-OE)/I.

Relationship to standard financial measures
- Inventory turns (IT)=T/I.
- Productivity ratio (PR)=T/OE.

With a mindset established and a measurement system in place to evaluate the impact of decisions on the goal, the third aspect is a decision-making methodology for continuously improving an organization. TOC states that every business system has at least one constraint (or at most very few). According to Umble and Srikanth (1997), "any specific area, aspect, or process that limits the business performance from a customer, competitive, or profit point of view is a constraint." Constraints can be physical, such as a machine center or lack of material, but they can also be managerial, such as a policy or procedure. Goldratt proposed a five focusing steps (FFS) process for managing constraints and continuously improving an organization. Table 20-2 briefly summarizes them. Inherent in this FFS process are the concepts of V-A-T process structure analysis, drum-buffer-rope and buffer management (described in Table 20-3), which are used to describe/analyze the process, develop the constraint's schedule and manage buffer inventories respectively within an organization.

Table 20-2   Five focusing steps of process improvement

1. IDENTIFY the system's constraint(s), whether physical or policy constraint.
2. Decide how to EXPLOIT the system's constraint(s), i.e. get the most possible from the limit of the current constraint(s); reduce the effects of the current constraint(s); and make everyone aware of the constraint(s) and its effects on the performance of the system.
3. SUBORDINATE everything else to the above decision, i.e. avoid keeping non-constraint resources busy doing unneeded work.
4. ELEVATE the system's constraint(s), i.e. off-load some demand or expand capability.
5. If in the previous steps a constraint has been broken, go back to Step 1, but do not allow INERTIA to cause a system constraint.

Table 20-3 Glossary of TOC-based operational terms

1. V-A-T analysis: a constraint management procedure for determining the general flow of parts and products from raw materials to finished products (logical product structure). A V logical structure starts with one or a few raw materials, and the product expands into a number of different products as it flows through its routings. The shape of an A logical structure is dominated by converging points. Many raw materials are fabricated and assembled into a few finished products. A T logical structure consists of numerous similar finished products assembled from common assemblies and subassemblies. Once the general parts flow is determined, the system control points (gating operations, convergent points, divergent points, constraints, and shipping points) can be identified and managed.
2. Drum-buffer-rope: the generalized technique used to manage resources to maximize throughput. The drum is the rate or pace of production set by the system's constraint. The buffers establish the protection against uncertainty so the system can maximize throughput. The rope is a communication process from the constraint to the gating operation that checks or limits the material released into the system to support the constraint. Buffers can be time or material and support throughput and/or due date performance. Buffers can be maintained at the constraint, convergent points (with a constraint part), divergent points and shipping points.
3. Buffer management: a process in which all expediting in a shop is driven by what is scheduled to be in the buffers (constraint, shipping and assembly buffers). By expediting this material into the buffers, the system helps avoid idleness at the constraint and missed customer due dates. In addition, the causes of the items missing from the buffer are identified, and the frequency of occurrences is used to prioritize improvement activities.

20.2.2 Ongoing improvement process perspective

From the perspective of an ongoing improvement process, TOC suggests that an organization must ask three fundamental questions concerning change to accelerate its improvement process: ① What to change, i.e. how do organizations identify the weakest link, i.e. the constraint(s)? ② To what to change, i.e. once the weakest link is identified, how should organizations strengthen it by developing practical and good solutions? ③ How to cause the change, i.e. how should organizations implement the solutions?

Though these three questions are not new, Goldratt and his associates have developed a set of techniques (Table 20-4) known as the thinking processes to address them. The process begins with an identification of a set of undesirable effects (UDEs), i.e. the symptoms of a system to be improved. A current reality tree (CRT) connects various UDEs systematically by following the effect-cause-effect diagramming principles and diagnoses what in the system needs to be changed, i.e. what the core problem is. The evaporating cloud (EC) verbalizes the inherent conflict, surfaces the assumptions and provides a mechanism to come up the ideas, which can be used to resolve the core problem. The future reality tree (FRT) takes the ideas from EC and ensures the new reality created would resolve the UDEs without creating any new UDEs. The prerequisite tree (PrT) identifies obstacles to the implementation of new ideas and determines intermediate objectives to overcome the obstacles. Finally, the transition tree (TrT) is used to create a step-by-step implementation plan. These tools of the thinking processes can be used as a set of integrated tools to address the specific phase of change management process or as stand-alone tools to address specific aspects of the problem.

Table 20-4 Tools of thinking processes

Thinking processes	Tools and diagnosis
What to change?	Current reality tree: Why is the system sick?
What to change to?	Evaporating cloud: What conflict is preventing the cure? Future reality tree: Will the injection lead to all desired effects without creating new undesirable effects?
How to cause change?	Prerequisite tree: What currently prevents the implementation of the injections? Transition tree: What actions does the initiator have to take to implement the cure effectively?

Recently, new and successful applications in the areas of distribution, sales/ marketing, project management and strategic planning have been demonstrated. Furthermore, the tools of thinking processes have been used to enhance the successful implementation of specific TOC applications.

20.3 Issues and research opportunities

20.3.1 Pedagogical perspective

Most of the standard OM textbooks discuss some concepts of TOC, specifically the scheduling of constraint resources. Recently, the OM textbooks have begun to incorporate a complete chapter on TOC summarizing the main concepts. However, if TOC has indeed evolved from a production scheduling technique into an OM philosophy, then its implications for the gamut of OM topics must be discussed and elaborated. Indeed, although the business novels The Goal (Goldratt and Cox 1984), It's Not Luck (Goldratt 1994), Critical Chain (Goldratt 1997) and Necessary But Not Sufficient (Goldratt 2000) provide excellent means to introduce TOC concepts and principles, it is still not clear how best to integrate TOC with conventional OM topics. Various questions still need to be addressed. Should TOC be taught as an important topic of OM (i.e. about 5%–20% of the time spent to cover TOC contents)? Should TOC be integrated throughout a typical OM course (i.e. about 20%–50% of the time spent to cover TOC contents)? Should TOC be taught as a stand-alone course in OM (i.e. about 50%–100% of the time spent to cover TOC contents)? Based on our experience and interaction with OM instructors at the Production and Operations Management Society and Decision Sciences Institute conferences, it appears that only a handful of universities are teaching a complete course with the title "Theory of Constraints" or "Constraints Management," although many are teaching TOC concepts in courses under the labels: "Operations Management" (to a great extent), "Total Quality Management" (to some extent) and "Supply Chain Management" (an evolving possibility). It appears that a more formal survey needs to be performed to identify the alternative ways to integrate TOC topics into core curricula. Regardless of the percentage of the time spent to cover TOC concepts in business (and engineering) schools, it appears that a framework to introduce TOC concepts/principles with relevance to OM needs to be developed, evaluated and published to create awareness among academicians.

20.3.2 Research perspective

A quick review of the literature reveals that two main sources of references exist: Rahman (1998) and Mabin and Balderstone (2000). Rahman (1998) is the only comprehensive TOC literature review article in a peer-reviewed journal that has attempted to classify the TOC literature and propose guidance for future research. The paper reviewed TOC publications in refereed and non-refereed journals, conference proceedings, and books between 1980 and 1995, and used a classification framework consisting of three categories: TOC philosophy, TOC application and TOC books. Rahman found that a large number of TOC articles were published in practitioner-oriented production journals (e.g. Production and Inventory Management Journal) and management accounting journals (e.g. Management Accounting, UK and USA), which primarily focused on the concepts and principles of TOC. He also found that several articles ① compared TOC with other production methods (e.g. MRP, JIT) and management accounting methods (e.g. ABC/M) and ② referred to the applications of TOC in actual business settings. The paper found very little TOC research done in the service sector. However, this study did not investigate the TOC literature to discuss implications for various production management decisions (e.g. product-process design, production planning and scheduling, inventory management, quality management and control, and continuous process improvement). Moreover, since 1995, a significant amount of research has appeared in refereed production management journals. This new research needs to be reviewed, classified and synthesized to provide researchers with guidance on directions.

The book by Mabin and Balderstone (2000) is probably the most comprehensive catalogue of TOC literature. The authors have provided keywords and a brief summary of each reference as well as various indices to facilitate searches for TOC literature by the author, subject, source (e.g. the journal, and magazine), industry and publisher. This study did not investigate the TOC literature to discuss implications from an OM point of view or suggest future directions for research.

Although a comprehensive literature review must be done to highlight the significant contributions made by specific articles, we would like to make few observations. First, TOC research stresses improvement in organizational performance instead of functional improvement and thus has implications across major functional areas such as accounting, marketing and strategy. Second, early TOC research focused on understanding and illustrating the production planning and scheduling principles of TOC that formed the basis for the TOC-based software referred to as OPT and subsequently explained as basic concepts of TOC in the popular novel, The Goal. Third, a vast amount of research effort has been expended to compare TOC with ① traditional management and total quality management, ② traditional management accounting and activity-based costing, ③ material requirement planning and

JIT systems and ④ linear programming. Fourth, TOC has the potential to be established as a useful production management theory by developing and testing important research questions. Unlike the other theories reported in the production management literature such as trade-off theory, the cumulative theory and the theory of production competence, the TOC is much more comprehensive and widely applicable across the production function. However, the theory of CM has not been empirically developed and tested, which is required if it is to be accepted as a general theory in production management.

Professional Vocabularies and Expressions

constraint management	约束管理
theory of constraints (TOC)	约束理论
optimized production technology (OPT)	最优生产技术
throughput	产销率
inventory	库存
operating expenses	运作费用
net profit	净利润
return-on-investment (ROI)	投资收益率
cash flow	现金流量
V-A-T process structure analysis	（企业的）VAT 流程结构分析
drum-buffer-rope (DBR)	鼓–缓冲器–绳子
buffer management	缓冲器管理
thinking process (TP)	思维流程
negative branches	负效应枝条
undesirable effects (UDEs)	不良效果
current reality tree (CRT)	当前现实树
evaporating cloud (EC)	消雾法
future reality tree (FRT)	未来现实树
prerequisite tree (PrT)	必备树
transition tree (TrT)	转变树

Notes

1. Since The Goal first appeared in print (Goldratt and Cox 1984)... from practitioners as well as from academicians.

《目标》是一本奇特而有趣的书。其作者高德拉特博士原本是物理学家，却以这本用小说体裁撰写的关于企业经营与管理密切关系的专著而闻名。该书已经销售 300 多万册并且被翻译为 23 种语言，同时使得瓶颈管理理念风行全球。

2. TOC has evolved from a manufacturing scheduling method to a management philosophy that can be used to understand and improve the performance of complex systems.

约束理论已经从一种制造调度方法发展成为可以用来理解和改善复杂系统绩效的管理哲学。

3. One of the main assumptions of TOC theory is that every business has the primary goal of "making more money now as well as in the future" without violating certain necessary conditions.

约束理论的重要假设之一是商业组织最主要的目标——在不违反某些必要约束情况下，在现在和将来赚更多的钱。

4. Throughput (T) is defined as "the rate at which the system generates money through sales."

产销率被定义为"系统通过销售来盈利的速度"。

5. Inventory (I) is defined as "all the money invested in purchasing things the system intends to sell."

库存被定义为"系统用于购买生产最终产品所需资源上的投资"。

6. Operating expenses (OE) is defined as "all the money the system spends in turning inventory into throughput."

运作费用被定义为"将库存转化为产销率过程中的所有花费"。

7. Indeed, although the business novels The Goal (Goldratt and Cox 1984), It's Not Luck (Goldratt 1994), Critical Chain (Goldratt 1997) and Necessary But Not Sufficient (Goldratt 2000) provide excellent means to introduce TOC concepts and principles, it is still not clear how best to integrate TOC with conventional OM topics.

句中提到高德拉特博士继《目标》之后的一系列作品，如《绝不是靠运气》《关键链》和《必要但不充分》等。本句可以翻译为：

确实，尽管高德拉特博士的诸如《目标》《绝不是靠运气》《关键链》和《必要但不充分》等小说体裁的著作对约束理论的概念和原理进行了很好的介绍，但如何很好地将约束理论有机地融入传统的运作管理主题仍然不是很清楚。

8. A quick review of the literature reveals that two main sources of... and propose guidance for future research.

句中提到的两个参考文献的详细信息如下：

Rahman, S.U. 1998. Theory of Constraints: A Review of the Philosophy and Its Applications. International Journal of Operations and Production Management, 18, 336-355.

Mabin, V. J. and Balderstone, S. J. 2000. The World of the Theory of Constraints: A Review of the International Literature (Boca Raton, FL: St Lucie).

Discussion Questions:

1. Comment on the argument that TOC is only common sense science.
2. What are the limitations of the cause-effect reasoning logic behind the theory of constraints?
3. What kind of companies are most suitable for the use of TOC?

CHAPTER 21

Experimental Economics and Supply Chain Management

21.1 Introduction

Supply chain management is enjoying the increased attention from operations practitioners looking for ways to compete in the global economy. Much of this attention focuses on leveraging recent advances in information technology to coordinate decision making across firms. Anticipated benefits include the decreased inventory costs, reduced flow times, and better matching of supply and demand. Companies as diverse as Boeing, Target, and Eastman Chemical are investing new initiatives to share information and better coordinate production and order decisions between supply-chain partners.

Academics from many fields, including marketing, operations management, and information management and technology, are developing methods to direct such initiatives and quantify their benefits. For example, over 50 percent of the presentations sponsored by the Manufacturing and Service Operations Management Society (MSOM) at the INFORMS 1998 and 1999 meetings were dedicated to supply-chain-related topics. Academics commonly use operations research tools, such as stochastic modeling, simulation, and math programming to study the dynamics of supply chain decisions. These models normally operate under the assumption that decision makers are rational and have commonly known objectives. In practice, these models break down when ① the objective function of a firm or of an individual inventory manager is not simple or clearly defined or ② the assumption of perfect rationality is violated. Individual preferences, attitudes towards risk, and cognitive abilities vary widely in practice. These realities are difficult to capture in analytic models.

Recently, there has been growing interest in using controlled human experiments to identify and better understand the behavioral factors that affect efforts to coordinate supply chains. Our goal in this paper is to illustrate the potential of experimental economics for better understanding decision making in this setting. We do this by reviewing recent experimental studies of the popular beer distribution game.

The beer distribution game mimics the ordering and production decisions of a four-level serial supply chain. Participants play the game over several hypothetical weeks. In each week, players decide how much product (cases of beer) to order from their immediate suppliers to maintain enough inventory to fill the orders from their immediate customers. This task is complicated by delays in order processing, production, and shipping.

Instructors use the beer distribution game in many introductory operations management courses to illustrate an important supply-chain phenomenon known as the bullwhip effect. Proctor and Gamble first coined the term bullwhip effect to describe the systematic ordering behavior witnessed between customers and suppliers of Pampers diapers. While diapers enjoy a fairly constant consumption rate, Proctor and Gamble found that wholesale orders fluctuated considerably over time. The firm also found that the orders it placed for raw materials with its suppliers fluctuated even more than these wholesale orders. Other companies have observed a similar tendency in their internal supply chains. Baganha and Cohen (1998) provide empirical evidence of these problems in industries with high order variation, while Kahn (1987) offers a macroeconomic view of the relationship between order volatility, inventory, and cost.

The effect itself is described by two regularities; oscillations of orders at each level of the supply chain and amplification of these oscillations as one moves farther up the chain. Both oscillation and amplification are costly to supply chains. Although the cause of the bullwhip effect is not completely understood, current research suggests a combination of rational (for example, operational) and behavioral factors.

On the operational side, Lee et al. describe four of the most common causes. The first is demand-signal processing, the process a rational decision maker goes through to translate current demand information into a forecast of future demand. For example, Chen et al. (1998) show that following a simple forecast formula, such as exponential smoothing or simple moving average, can lead to bullwhip behavior in certain supply-chain settings. A second operational cause is rationing, where suppliers allocate limited resources, such as inventory, across several customers. This practice encourages customers to game the system by inflating their orders to gain a bigger slice of the pie. Other causes include batching orders (ordering once a week or once a month rather than every day) and varying prices (which can encourage forward buying). The ways to alleviate these last three operational problems include schemes to improve capacity allocation, staggered batching of orders, and everyday low pricing.

While operational causes are important, they are not the whole story. Our review of current research demonstrates that the bullwhip phenomenon remains even in the idealized supply chains, such as that used in the experiments discussed here, in which normal operational causes are removed. This result leads researchers to investigate other behavioral factors. Because this field of research is still growing, this review is not meant as the last word, but rather an indication of the field's potential. These experiments represent a growing interest in the literature concerning the cognitive limitations of managers in business settings. Before providing more details on the beer distribution game and its associated stream of research, we offer our thoughts on why experiments are a particularly relevant tool for studying supply-chain behavior.

21.2 Why do we need an experiment?

Experiments are useful for investigating behavior in supply chains for a number of reasons. First, experiments allow us to gauge the extent to which behavioral factors cause empirical regularities, such as the bullwhip effect. In an experiment, we can control the environment each firm faces. In particular, we can design environments devoid of possible operational causes of the bullwhip effect. The beer distribution game provides such an environment.

The game assumes infinite capacity and no competing customers (avoiding inventory-allocation issues), zero setup times (avoiding order-batching problems), and constant retail prices (avoiding price fluctuations). We can also avoid the effects of processing demand signals (forecasting) by making all participants aware of the underlying demand distribution. Chen (1999) shows theoretically that a base-stock ordering policy minimizes the total supply-chain cost in such a system when the retail-demand distribution is stationary and commonly known. A base-stock policy implies that participants place orders equal to the orders they receive from their immediate customers. In other words, they pass through the orders they receive, implying no bullwhip effect. This policy was also shown to be optimal for serial systems without delays by Clark and Scarf (1960) and Federgruen and Zipkin (1984).

However, the participants in experiments do not simply pass through orders but instead order in ways consistent with the bullwhip effect. Observing the effect in such a controlled environment confirms that behavioral causes do exist and are an important cause of the effect in the lab.

Second, experiments can help us to understand the relative strength of multiple causes of the bullwhip in empirical data. For example, if we observe a threefold amplification of order oscillation in the field (where both behavioral and operational factors exist) and only a two-fold amplification in the lab (where we have eliminated the operational factors), we can estimate the fraction of the effect caused by behavioral factors and the fraction caused by operational factors.

Third, we can use experiments to test operations theory, much as we use them to test economic theory. For example, we can use experiments to compare the extent of the bullwhip effect when the supply-chain relationship is one to one (one supplier, one customer) or one to many (one supplier, many customers). We can compare the performance of supply chains with and without limited manufacturing capability, with and without setup costs, with and without inventory — allocation problems, and so forth. In this way, we can use experiments to put supply-chain-management theory to the test by investigating whether the outcome of a particular operational configuration is consistent with theoretical predictions. While this approach has not yet been taken in the literature, we think it is an important area for future supply-chain research.

Finally, we can use experiments to measure the impact of varying operational factors in the presence of behavioral factors. For example, we can examine the behavioral impact of reducing ordering and shipping delays, adding inventory-information-sharing systems, and adding point-of-sale (POS) data-sharing systems. Within the tightly controlled environment of the experiment, we can demonstrate and quantify the gains from these institutional innovations, holding all else constants, in the presence of behavioral and cognitive limitations. Experimental work is thus an important complement to theoretical work.

21.3 The beer distribution game

The beer distribution game mimics the mechanics of a decentralized, serial supply chain operating under a periodic-review order system. The underlying supply chain normally consists of four echelons. The game normally begins as participants enter a laboratory, are assigned randomly to roles, and face a game either on a computer screen or a physical board. Each participant controls one of the four echelons playing the role of a retailer, wholesaler, distributor, or manufacturer of beer. Each participant/firm places orders with its upstream supplier and fills the orders placed by its downstream customers over a series of weeks (Figure 21-1).

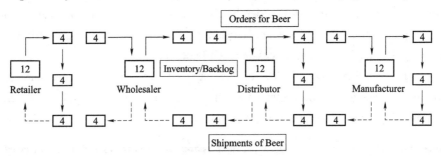

Figure 21-1 The game board in the noncomputerized experiments has four levels (retailer, wholesaler, distributor, and manufacturer). At each level is the number of units of inventory (or backlog if negative) currently in stock. Along the top of the figure are the boxes representing the ordering lags with the numbers indicating the units ordered in the previous two weeks. Along the bottom of the figure are the boxes representing the shipping lags with the numbers indicating the units shipped in the previous two weeks. The manufacturer faces a three-week production delay; the number in these boxes represents the units he has produced in the past three weeks. Each week the units in each position move one box and are incorporated into the inventory or backlog as appropriate. The numbers in the boxes represent the starting position in the game; each echelon member has 12 units in inventory and four units in each position ordering and shipping.

The game is complicated by order-processing and shipment delays between each supplier-customer pair. Once a firm specifies an order, some delay occurs (most commonly, two weeks) before the order actually arrives at the supply site. Similarly, once a firm fills an order, another delay occurs (Again, two weeks is common.) before the shipment arrives at the downstream customer's site. At the highest level (the manufacturer), orders represent production starts and therefore mean a slightly different type of delay (for example, three weeks for production, then two weeks for shipment to the distributor).

At the beginning of each week, shipments arrive from each firm's upstream suppliers. After the firm adds these shipments to its inventory, it processes new orders from its downstream customers (For the retailer, these orders are simply final consumer demand). Firms fill and ship orders from current inventory if possible and place excess demand in backlog. Firms earn revenue when they ship product and incur weekly inventory-holding costs and backlog costs. At the end of the week, each firm places an order with its upstream supplier. These orders are the decision variables of interest in the game.

As in most economics experiments, participants are typically paid according to their performance in order to induce preferences similar to those observed in the field. In some experiments, researchers run tournaments with the highest-earning supply chain winning a fixed prize. Others use a continuous incentive scheme in which more profitable chains earn more, either in an absolute sense or a relative sense.

This supply-chain setting eliminates three of the four operational causes of the bullwhip effect cited by Lee et al.: inventory allocation (since there are no competing customers and the manufacturing capacity is infinite), order batching (since setup times are zero), and price fluctuations (since retail prices are constant). Some experimenters control for the fourth operational cause (demand-signal processing) while others do not.

Table 21-1 provides an overview of the papers in our survey. These papers can be grouped into two categories: those that establish the existence of behavioral causes, and those that test methods for reducing the bullwhip effect.

Table 21-1 This table summarizes the parameters and results of the experiments reviewed in this paper. Demand functions can be stationary (with realizations drawn from the same distribution in each period) or nonstationary (with realizations drawn from different distributions in each period). They can also be known or unknown to the participants in the experiment.

Items	Number of echelons	Demand function	Incentives	Number of observations	Other roles	Key results
Sterman (1989)	4	Nonstationary and unknown (4-8 steps)	Tournament	11	Participants	Demonstrated bullwhip and underweighting
Kaminsky and Simchi-Levi (1998)	4	Stationary and unknown (N [6,2])	None	6:2 week lag 6:1 week lag	Computer simulated (s, S)	Shorter lead times yielded the same amplification but lower costs

(Continued)

Items	Number of echelons	Demand function	Incentives	Number of observations	Other roles	Key results
Gupta, Steckel, and Banerji (2001)	3	Nonstationary and unknown (4-8; S-shaped with and without noise)	Absolute performance	100 divided into 12 treatments	Participants	Shorter lead times yielded lower costs. Sharing POS data yielded equal or lower costs
Croson and Donohue (1999a)	4	Stationary and known (U[0,8])	Relative performance	5 without POS 5 with POS	Participants	Sharing POS data reduced bullwhip
Croson and Donohue (1999b)	4	Stationary and known (U[0,8])	Relative performance	5 without inventory information, 7 with inventory information	Participants	Sharing inventory information reduced bullwhip

21.4 Behavioral causes of the bullwhip effect

Sterman (1989) was the first to use the beer distribution game to rigorously test for the existence of the behavioral causes of the bullwhip effect. He ran the experiment using a game board similar to that shown in Figure 21-1. The players were organized into supply chains (teams) made up of one retailer, one wholesaler, one distributor, and one manufacturer. Each player started with four cases of beer on order and in shipment and 12 cases in inventory.

The incentive scheme used a tournament design. Each participant placed one dollar in a prize fund; the fund went to the team with the lowest supply-chain cost, with the winning team taking all. Sterman defined supply-chain cost as the sum of inventory holding cost and demand-backlog cost at each supply chain level over all weeks. Inventory-holding costs at each level were 50 cents per case of beer per week, while backlog costs were one dollar per case of beer per week.

Sterman used a simple, nonstationary retail-demand function (beginning at four units and jumping to eight units) that was unknown to chain members. In this sense, his experiments control for only three out of the four operational causes cited by Lee et al. Demand-signal processing remained as a possible operational cause because the demand distribution was both nonstationary and unknown.

Sterman reports results from 11 groups of four players each. His results duplicate the empirical observations of Procter and Gamble. Inventory levels varied widely over the course of the game, from an average maximum backlog of 46 cases to an average peak inventory of 50 cases of beer.

Sterman demonstrated both aspects of the bullwhip effect: oscillation and amplification of orders. First, he found significant oscillation of orders at all levels. For the 11 retailers, for example, average weekly orders were 15 cases of beer per week, but the average variance of those orders was 13 (For comparison the variance of customer orders was 1.6). Second, he found significant amplification of order variance. The variance of orders averaged 13 for retailers, 23 for wholesalers, 25 for distributors, and 72 for manufacturers.

Sterman went on to analyze individual ordering decisions in an attempt to identify the behavioral cause of the bullwhip effect. His data suggest that most players failed to account adequately for the supply line (that is, for outstanding orders and shipments in transit). Thus in responding to high demand, players increased their orders too much, leading to excess inventory and reduced orders in future weeks.

Sterman was the first to demonstrate that the bullwhip effect had behavioral as well as operational causes. Both aspects of the effect (oscillation and amplification) occurred in the controlled conditions with the most operational causes removed. Interestingly, when Sterman asked participants how they could have improved their performance, they called for the better forecasts of consumer demand. One could control for this operational concern by using a stationary demand distribution and announcing this distribution to all participants before the game begins. Chen and Samroengraja (1999) advocate this approach in a teaching note. They described running the beer distribution game in class with stationary and known demand (Demand was distributed normally, with a mean of 50 and a standard deviation of 20, discretized and truncated at zero), and they found that the amplification of the orders remained when this last operational cause was removed. However, they presented no statistical tests of their results.

21.5 Methods for reducing the bullwhip effect

Once biases in individual decision making have been identified, one can use experiments to test candidate institutions to counteract or ameliorate these biases. The remaining papers in our survey take this approach, demonstrating in the controlled settings the behavioral benefits of ① reducing lags, ② sharing inventory information, or ③ sharing point-of-sale (POS) data across the supply chain. Research suggests that only a subset of these institutions show promise for reducing the bullwhip effect.

Focusing first on the impact of order and delivery lags, Kaminsky and Simchi-Levi (1998) and Gupta et al. (2001) examine the impact of decreasing these lags under different supply-chain settings. Both use a computerized version of the beer distribution game. The version employed by Kaminsky and Simchi-Levi (1998) is unique in that the computer automates the decisions of all but one role within the supply chain. These automated decision makers order according to a simple (s, S) policy, in which orders are placed to replenish echelon stock to the level "S" whenever inventory falls below the threshold level "s." They compute "s" by continuously updating estimates of the demand mean and variance and fix "S" at 30.

Kaminsky and Simchi-Levi (1998) used a stationary demand function that was normally distributed ($\mu = 6$, $\sigma = 2$) and unknown to their subjects. No incentives were used. Each subject played the role of distributor in the game. In their baseline treatment, they used two week lags. In the reduced-lag treatment, they reduced order and delivery lags to one week. They report results from six subjects in each treatment (12 subjects overall).

In the baseline treatment, Kaminsky and Simchi-Levi again observed the bullwhip effect. Distributor-order oscillations were significant (The average standard deviation of distributor orders was 8.56) and were amplified over those of wholesaler-order oscillations. When they reduced lead times, distributor-order oscillations remained high (average standard deviation of 12.68), but the overall costs incurred by the supply chain dropped. The authors argue that this drop was caused by operational factors, particularly the reduced time items spent in the system, which reduced inventory costs. Evidence for behavioral improvement based on lag reduction is primarily anecdotal.

Gupta et al. (2001) also show that reduced delays lead to lower supply-chain costs. However, their setup is quite different. They use a three-echelon supply chain with live participants at each level of the supply chain interacting via a networked computer system. Once again, the participants were not informed about retail demand. Unlike other researchers in this area, the authors do not analyze the ordering patterns of participants (choosing instead to focus on supply chain cost) and thus do not report on the existence or reduction of the bullwhip effect. They use nonstationary demand distributions (unlike Kaminsky and Simchi-Levi, who focus on the normal distribution).

Gupta et al. examine 12 treatments, including ordering and shipping lags of one or two weeks, total or no access to POS data and varying consumer demand, including a step function (as in Sterman), an S-shaped function, and an S-shaped function with noise. The authors report data from 100 supply channels (300 subjects) divided across these 12 treatments, with five to 13 groups per treatment. Participants were paid in proportion to the total costs incurred by their channels.

Decreasing the lags in the system generally led to the reduced costs. With stepped demand and S-shaped demand with no noise, reducing the lags significantly reduced the costs at all three levels and thus over the entire supply chain (since supply-chain costs are simply the sum of the costs at each level). With S-shaped demand with error, reducing the lags significantly reduced costs for the retailer and the wholesaler but not for the manufacturer, resulting in no significant difference in channel costs overall. However, the authors do not provide an analysis of the variance of the orders placed. Thus it is unclear whether costs fell because of the reduced inventory costs inherent in shorter lags (as suggested by Kaminsky and Simchi-Levi) or because players can make better decisions in the reduced-lag environment. These results suggest that shorter lags translate into lower supply-chain costs under some conditions. However, the authors also identify conditions under which the efficiency gains may not be as great as anticipated.

Unfortunately, because the participants in both Kaminsky and Simchi-Levi (1998) and Gupta et al. (2001) did not know the demand functions facing the retailer, their results cannot be conclusively attributed to behavioral causes. It is difficult to quantify the inherent operational benefits of reducing delays when the retail-demand distribution is not commonly known. Theoretically, removing shipment lags reduces pipeline stock, while removing ordering lags reduces the need for safety stock at both supplier and customer sites. It would be interesting to quantify this theoretical savings and compare it with the actual savings achieved in these experiments, to separate out the behavioral effect. One could do this by running the beer distribution game (with and without lags) subject to a stationary retail-demand distribution that was announced to all players.

Moving on to the second institution, sharing point-of-sale (POS) data, we find that the impact of this intuitional change is again mixed. Gupta et al. (2001) and Croson and Donohue (1999a) provide different results.

Gupta et al. again focus on settings with a wide range of nonstationary demand distributions which are unknown to the participants. With step demand, sharing POS information significantly reduced the retailer's costs but had no significant effect on the wholesaler's and the manufacturer's costs. With S-shaped demand with no error, sharing POS data had no effect on the retailer's costs or on the wholesaler's costs, and it significantly raised the manufacturer's costs (That is, those costs moved opposite to the predicted direction). Finally, with S-shaped demand with error, sharing POS data significantly reduced the retailer's costs but had no significant effect on that of the wholesaler or the manufacturer. However, because the participants in the experiments did not know the demand functions and the authors did not analyze ordering behavior, these results cannot be conclusively attributed to behavioral causes.

In their study of POS-data sharing, Croson and Donohue (1999a) control for the remaining operational cause of the bullwhip effect by using a stationary and known distribution (uniform[0,8]). Their game is similar in spirit to the game advocated by Chen and Samroengraja (1999). They use the traditional four-level game with four human participants interacting via a computerized interface. They paid the participants in a continuous manner based on the cumulative chain profit (costs) of the chain relative to the highest — profit chain. This payment was designed to represent the benchmarked performance of an integrated supply chain.

Five groups of four firms played a baseline condition (without POS data) in which they were told only the distribution of consumer demand. Another five groups played in the POS-data-sharing treatment in which the players knew the demand distribution and the realized demand in each week.

The addition of POS-data transmission significantly reduced order oscillation at all levels of the supply chain, particularly at the distributor and manufacturer levels. This asymmetric benefit is consistent with intuition. The retailer gets no new information from POS data (since he sees customer orders anyway); thus we would not expect his behavior to change significantly. Upstream from the retail site, this information is more likely to affect order decisions. Because of this asymmetric reduction in oscillation, amplification of order variation significantly decreased when POS data were shared.

Croson and Donohue also replicate Sterman's result that players do not give enough weight to the supply line. They present a new analysis of individual behavior on the demand line; examining what information firms use when making their ordering decisions. They find, as predicted, that when POS data is available, participants incorporate it into their ordering decisions, supplementing the information contained in their downstream customers' orders.

This analysis suggests the mechanism by which POS data can affect performance in supply chains and helps to organize Gupta, Steckel, and Banerji's results. When demand is stationary and known, sharing POS data can help reduce the bullwhip effect and reduce supply chain costs (as Croson and Donohue show) by helping upstream suppliers better anticipate their customers' needs without biasing their estimates of future demand. In contrast, when the distribution of consumer demand is nonstationary and unknown, POS data can bias upstream participants' estimates of future demand, which can increase (rather than decrease) costs (as Gupta, Steckel, and Banerji argue). It remains unclear whether the cost increase in this case is caused by the bullwhip effect or by some other behavioral phenomena.

Turning to our final institutional change, Croson and Donohue (1999b) examine what impact sharing inventory information has on reducing the bullwhip effect. In this study, the participants knew the distribution of demand, which was stationary, and again faced a four-echelon, computerized supply chain. Five groups of four subjects participated in the baseline condition (without inventory-information sharing), and seven groups of four subjects participated in the inventory-sharing condition.

Their results suggest that making the inventory position of all supply-chain members known significantly reduced oscillation of orders at all levels of the supply chain, but particularly at higher levels (distributor and manufacturer). This additional information also reduced amplification, particularly between the distributor and wholesaler roles.

Croson and Donohue again replicate Sterman's results that players give too little weight to the supply line when they know the demand distribution and share inventory information. The persistence of this behavior when they shared inventory information makes one question the cause of performance improvement. After all, if the behavioral causes of the bullwhip effect, such as this underweighting, remain, why do oscillation and amplification decrease? Results suggest that although participants did not use inventory information to adjust their supply lines, they did use it to anticipate downstream members' orders. This anticipation of future orders from downstream customers allowed upstream players to adjust their own orders in advance (that is, in preparation for incoming orders). This use counteracted (but did not eliminate) their underweighting of the supply line and improved performance.

21.6 Conclusions and lessons for managers

The controlled experimental settings allow one to both demonstrate behavioral biases that cause empirically observed outcomes like the bullwhip effect and to identify the actions managers can take to reduce the impact of these biases. Such experiments can even offer insight into how best to implement institutional changes. For example, Croson and Donohue's results on the impact of inventory information suggest that when inventory information is shared across the supply chain, order oscillations decrease because upstream chain members have information about downstream members' inventory positions, rather than the other way around. The critical part of an inventory-sharing information system thus is not communicating the inventory position of the manufacturer to the retailer but instead communicating the inventory position of the retailer to the manufacturer. The biggest bang for the buck may lie in tracking and sharing downstream inventory information. Since the cost of tracking inventory is quite high, particularly at manufacturing sites, this result suggests that instituting tracking systems at the retail and wholesale levels will provide the greatest returns, with the returns diminishing for inventory sharing further up the supply chain. Similar implications can be inferred from the other experiments reviewed and (we hope) from future research in this field.

This survey suggests the types of the benefits that experimental research can bring to supply-chain management. We trust that future researchers will examine other important institutional changes that show promise for improving supply-chain performance. Examples include collaborative forecasting and planning systems in which supply-chain members work together to create a chain-level ordering strategy and other information-technology-enabled systems designed to improve efficiency. More work is also needed to understand the relationship between individual characteristics (such as patience, risk-neutrality, and abstract thinking) and the performance of supply-chain tasks. Finally, additional work is needed to discover the type of training managers need to improve their performance in these complex settings. We believe that experiments like these can illuminate the difficulties of managing supply chains and provide specific, behavioral suggestions for easing the task.

Professional Vocabularies and Expressions

supply chain management	供应链管理
supply chain partner	供应链合作伙伴
inventory cost	库存成本
operations management	运作管理

stochastic modeling	统计建模
simulation	仿真
math programming	数学规划
rational	理性的
objective function	目标函数，目标方程
individual preference	个人偏好
cognitive ability	认知能力
operational cause	运作因素
behavioral factor	行为参数，行为因素
experimental economics	实验经济学
beer distribution game	啤酒分销游戏
bullwhip effect	长鞭效应，牛鞭效应
exponential smoothing	指数平滑（预测方法）
simple moving average	简单移动平均（预测方法）
retailer	零售商
wholesaler	批发商
distributor	分销商
manufacturer	制造商
holding cost	库存成本
backlog cost	缺货成本
ordering cost	订购成本
setup cost	生产准备成本
inventory allocation	存货分配
infinite manufacturing capacity	无限制造能力，无限生产能力
order batching	批量订购
setup time	生产准备时间
price fluctuation	价格浮动
incentive scheme	激励机制
POS data	销售点数据
n-echelon	n 级，n 阶
subject	实验参加者，实验主体

Notes

1. For example, over 50 percent of the presentations sponsored by the Manufacturing and Service Operations Management Society (MSOM) at the INFORMS 1998 and 1999 meetings

were dedicated to supply-chain-related topics.

INFORMS 是运筹学与管理科学学会(The Institute for Operations Research and the Management Sciences)的简写。该学会旨在促进运筹学和管理科学(Operations Research and the Management Sciences，OR/MS)领域的发展和传播。其愿景是能够促进 OR/MS 的实践、研究和应用。详见 http://www.informs.org.

可翻译为：例如，在 1998 年和 1999 年的由制造和服务运作管理会赞助的 INFORMS 会议上，有超过一半的演讲主题是与供应链相关的。

2. The effect itself is described by two regularities: oscillations of orders at each level of the supply chain and amplification of these oscillations as one moves farther up the chain.

牛鞭效应本身可以用两个规则来描述：一是订货数量在供应链的各个阶段处于摆动状态；二是随着订单信息从供应链的下游向上游的传递，摆动的幅度逐渐增大。

3. A second operational cause is rationing, where suppliers allocate limited resources, such as inventory, across several customers. This practice encourages customers to game the system by inflating their orders to gain a bigger slice of the pie.

引起牛鞭效应的第二个运作原因是定量配给，即供应商将有限的资源，如存货等分配给几个客户。定量配给鼓励客户进行博弈，即试图通过扩充订单以期能从有限的蛋糕中分得较大的一块。

4. First, experiments allow us to gauge the extent to which behavioral factors cause empirical regularities, such as the bullwhip effect.

首先，通过实验可以确定行为因素引发经验规律，如牛鞭效应的程度。

5. The beer distribution game mimics the mechanics of a decentralized, serial supply chain operating under a periodic-review order system.

啤酒分销游戏模仿在定期盘点和订货方式下分散的串行供应链结构。

6. As in most economics experiments, participants are typically paid according to their performance in order to induce preferences similar to those observed in the field.

同多数的经济学实验类似，为了能够产生与现实生活中观察到的类似的偏好，实验参加者通常要根据其表现被给予一定的报酬。

7. Once biases in individual decision making have been identified, one can use experiments to test candidate institutions to counteract or ameliorate these biases.

一旦个体在指定决策时的偏好被识别出来，就可以通过实验来测试各种能够抵消或减轻这些偏好的游戏规则。

8. The biggest bang for the buck may lie in tracking and sharing downstream inventory information.

最大的收益也许能够通过跟踪和共享供应链下游的库存信息来得到。

Discussion Questions:

1. What is bullwhip effect? What are the contributing factors and what are the approaches that can be applied to reduce the bullwhip effect?

2. What are the benefits that experiment economics can bring to the field of supply chain management?
3. How can experiment economics benefit IE in general?

编者注：

实验经济学是研究人类行为的经济学。其价值不仅体现在实验方法的运用对传统经济学理论的验证上，更重要的是方法论上的意义。它将进一步加强经济学在行为研究层面上的发展与深化，赋予经济学"科学性"。实验经济学的发展有待于演进博弈论、社会经济学、经济心理学等学科的共同发展。实验经济学揭示了传统新古典经济学的缺陷，指出了以后经济学的前进方向。而弗农·史密斯因为通过实验测试和修正有关预测领域的经济学理论，创立实验经济学而获得了 2002 年诺贝尔经济学奖，成为继蒙代尔、斯彭斯之后的第三位诺贝尔经济学奖获得者，被誉为实验经济学之父。

2003 年 12 月 4 日，史密斯教授偕同夫人莅临华南理工大学工商管理学院，作了一场题为"如何将经济学和实验相结合"的专题学术报告。作为报告现场的同声翻译，编者不仅有幸和史密斯教授合作，而且亲身领略到了新世纪最前沿的经济学说的精髓，并感受到了世界经济学顶级大师的风采。

第六篇

工业工程展望

CHAPTER 22

The Evolution of Information Systems and Business Organization Structures[①]

22.1 Introduction

This article looks at the ways in which computerized information systems have impacted modern business organizations. While the influence of these systems on organizations in general has been both powerful and wide ranging, this article focuses primarily on how organization structures have specifically been impacted. To properly frame the various issues that are addressed, this article briefly traces early computers, and mentions their development by generations. Over the decades, both computer systems and organization structures have moved from a centralized to a decentralized design. This movement has had major implications in what organizations are capable of doing in the face of a turbulent environment by adopting organic and network like structures. These organizational metamorphoses have been possible, in large part, by the support provided by information technology that allowed autonomy and distribution of responsibility. A review of information system architecture and organizational form is made to underscore a natural compatibility or fit between information systems and organization structures. In conclusion, attention is drawn to the ways information systems are likely to create organizational interfaces between an organization's suppliers and customers, and how this may result in radically new structures.

22.2 Early developments

Modern computers, as we understand them, were essentially designed and developed in the USA around half a century ago. While punched card based unit record machines (URMs) were widely used for limited business data processing in the 1930s, the world's first fully automatic computer is considered to be the MARK I which was set in operation in 1944. This was followed by the ENIAC (1946), short for Electronic Numerical Integrator and Calculator,

---

① 本篇文章发表于 2002 年。

the EDSAC (1949), the Electronic Delayed Storage Automatic Computer, and by the EDVAC (1952), the Electronic Discrete Variable Automatic Computer. All these machines had been designed and built for military, scientific, or mathematical purposes. Von Neumann, an early pioneer, who developed the concept of the stored program, was convinced that computers could solve many important unsolved problems in applied mathematics.

Some time during the 1950s, the potential of computers in the realm of business was recognized, and a powerful impetus was now given to marry technology with commerce. The first commercial computer, a UNIVAC 1, manufactured by Rand Corporation, was delivered to the US Bureau of the Census in 1951, while the first non-government installation, also a UNIVAC 1, was installed at General Electric's appliance plant in Louisville, Kentucky. According to Lynch and Rice, the period from 1956 to 1958 saw three significant developments in computing. These were:

(1) the breakthroughs in increased core memories;

(2) the development of more standardized and higher level languages; and

(3) the development of a system for operating a computer or the operating system (OS).

22.3 Computers in business

22.3.1 Computer development by generations

The field of computers developed by what is now recognized as generations, starting with the first generation half a century ago onto the end of the fourth generation today. The concept of generations is both artificial and arbitrary, but is a useful framework for understanding developments in this field. Commonly, generations are associated with the levels of computer technology and processing speeds. The first generation computers, up to the mid-1950s, were associated with valves and electric relays. The second generation computers, developed in the late 1950s, used transistors instead of vacuum tubes. They occupied far less space than their predecessors, were faster in operation, required less maintenance, and were more reliable.

The third generation computers of the 1960s and early 1970s were characterized by large scale integration (LSI) of integrated circuits. Introduced with the third generation machines was the concept of the family of computers, and users could move upward adding computing power, storage capacity, and peripheral capability — without costly conversions. Each generation was characterized by a marked improvement in performance, capability, and a fall in prices. The fourth generation computers, from the early 1970s, were characterized by very large scale integration (VLSI), and the use of semiconductor memory and sophisticated software. Computers of this generation, apart from high speed and massive computing power, were characterized by the use of microprocessors, virtual memory, and highly developed communication and database facilities. They not only became powerful and fascinating, but their usage in business generally accelerated the possibilities and potentialities of growth.

22.3.2 Computer installations in business

The combination of increased computing power, powerful software, and continuously falling hardware prices became a very attractive proposition for business organizations, and from the mid-1960s onwards installations in businesses increased rapidly. From an installed base of ten computers in 1950 valued at $0.01 billion, a total of 138,000 computers valued at $53.0 billion were installed by 1980.

The transformation of the US economy took place in the 1950s when the information age overtook the industrial age. Sprague and McNurlin (1993) mention, "It was in 1957 that the USA passed from the industrial era to the information era. In that year, the number of employees in the country whose jobs were primarily handling information surpassed the number of industrial workers." This was important not only in the service or information industry, but also in the manufacturing industry owing to the dramatic effect of computers and information. Computers have been used to systematize and solve problems in diverse areas of business including planning, R&D, engineering, marketing, procurement, production, storage, distribution, operations and service, and management. Very simply, computers allowed the development of planning techniques hitherto too complex to develop, compute, or control. These included the development of systems planning like PERT/CPM models, planned program budgeting, and simulations, as well as developments in areas like production, automation, and other planning and control systems. Other contributions of computers were in the areas of high volume and repetitive computations, measures for operations control, and as an information and decision tool. There is no doubt that the contributions of computers are numerous and well-known, and US industry has, on the whole, been radically and beneficially affected by these contributions.

22.4 Growth of information systems and business organizations

Over the last three decades, computer-based information systems and business organizations developed in unique and special ways. As far as computers are concerned, the manner of hardware and software development resulted in unique architectures evolving over time. At the same time organization structures developed special forms to suit and fit their specific environmental and strategic requirements.

22.4.1 Development of information systems

Computer based information systems are categorized by their architecture or topology, which are a set of interconnections or nodes in a network. Categorizing information system architecturally is appealing since it is not idiosyncratic to particular settings, and further, these architectures are fairly well established and accepted. This section briefly discusses the four main types of information system architectures or typologies consisting of centralized, distributed, decentralized, and stand-alone systems.

The combination of hardware, software, data, and communication formed the core of information systems. As each of these dimensions developed and integrated, the concept, design, and capability of information systems underwent massive changes. The earliest systems were the classic centralized systems typically characterized by a mainframe host computer supported by an array of peripherals, including "dumb" terminals, which allowed interactive, information processing activities mostly of a transactional nature. These centralized systems were modest in size in the earlier generation computers, but grew from small, medium to large centralized mainframe systems over time. This was the trend up to the 1970s, and for the first 20 years the discussions on data and systems were about techniques to manage data in a centralized environment.

In the early 1960s, the main concern among hardware manufacturers and data processing managers was achieving machine efficiency. With increasing demands and the sophistication of the users of information, and with the availability of powerful personal computers (PCs), data processing activities became more distributed. This gradual shift from information availability in report form to information becoming available on demand, and forming a part of a decision support system (DSS), accelerated the trend from centralized to distributed systems, consisting of clusters of minicomputers networked through LANs, or local area networks at the intra-organizational level, and the later WANs or wide area networks at the inter-organizational level. The growth and importance of minicomputers, so fundamental to this trend, can be gauged from Table 22-1.

Table 22-1   Minicomputers installed in 1970–1980 and purchase prices

Year	Number/Minicomputers	Value/$ billions
1970	31,000	1.9
1975	202,000	6.0
1980	840,000	19.3

Source: Kanter (1982)

Distributed systems are defined as "peer-to-host systems," and are designed as "spokes" or terminals around a central processor or mainframe. Spokes might have their own processors, storage devices, and terminals that have their own computing facilities and databases. The distributed systems are now giving way to the decentralized information systems, and the role of the user is becoming paramount. This trend is continuing through the 1990s. The decentralized systems are referred to as "peer networks" and have no central processors through which communications must pass, and hence there are more degrees of freedom in communication, and communication constraints are substantially less than for distributed systems.

A fourth kind, though less common, are stand-alone systems, typically PCs, used in individual departments or as information systems in small organizations. Because of their limited capabilities and low cost, most large organizations do not plan for them, and their effect is on the work of individuals rather than on the organization as a whole.

22.4.2 Changes in organization structures

Businesses in the USA have changed in many different ways during the course of this century. The earlier trends were essentially the development of single businesses that preferred to retain overall control through vertical integration, and Chandler (1990) has observed that US organizations have invariably stressed the ascendancy and development of functional areas. In the 1960s, there were a spate of acquisitions and mergers primarily as a response to anti-trust laws. Companies went into unrelated businesses and formed huge conglomerates. In the 1980s, this trend changed through a process of readjustment, disinvestment, and restructuring, and the degree of unrelatedness was reduced somewhat, and large diversified businesses were formed. Many structural changes have taken place during the last 30 to 40 years, and the direction of these changes has been to move from centralized to decentralized organizations through various stages. These stages started with the earlier centralized single business organizations which were vertically integrated, and then moved onto the divisionalized structures used at Du Pont, and later at General Motors.

This basically was a movement away from functional control to divisionalized control. This was typical of the M-form of organizations where a division would be given complete autonomy and each division would have its functional areas under its control. The head or corporate office would have an essentially coordinating role, and each division would function with its divisional level corporate setup. These changes took place in order to handle changes more appropriately in the environment, and to have more effective responses to competition. Organizations found that a decentralized setup was in many cases better suited to cope with an environment marked with rapid changes. Perhaps the one key reason decentralization could meaningfully take place is by the support provided by information systems that allowed decentralized communication and control.

Decentralization has moved further, and later structures have been in the form of matrix, hybrid, and network organizations. Each of these structures has been found to be a more appropriate response to cope with increasing turbulence in the external environment. In modern business organizations, effectively handling a complex and turbulent environment has been the fundamental problem that top management and organizational administrators must cope with. Again, new structures to cope with new environmental realities have been possible in large part due to the possibilities of information and control provided by computers.

An important view of evolving organizations has been the five typological structures provided by Mintzberg (1979, 1981, 1983), and similar typologies have also been suggested by Daft (2001). These typologies are based in part on organizational life cycle, type of business, and the competitive environment. The five part typology of organization structures consists of the following:

(1) Simple structures. These are the characteristic of both young, start-up, entrepreneurial

organizations as well as well entrenched autocracies. They are usually small, operating in a market niche within a dynamic environment with few rules.

(2) Machine bureaucracies. These are characterized by standardization, functional structural design, and large size. These structures are generally differentiated both horizontally and vertically, and are normally associated with standardized, routine, mass production technologies in a stable environment.

(3) Professional bureaucracies. These rely on the standardization of skills as a basis for coordination, and have a high informational component. These organizations are decentralized down to the level of those professionals responsible for carrying out the organizations' tasks.

(4) Divisionalized forms. These are integrated sets of semi-autonomous entities loosely joined by an administrative framework. The semi-autonomous entities, often referred to as strategic business units (SBUs), determine the strategic portfolio of the organization. They may be decentralized from the perspective of the total organization, but can be centralized from within the division, or may exist in any other combination.

(5) Adhocracy. These can be construed as divisionalized forms, held together by a strong culture. These are usually small and have the characteristics of a young organization (without necessarily being young). Mutual coordination and cooperation are critical which cause these organizations to behave like project teams. They are essentially highly organic with little formalization.

22.5 Integrating computer architectures and organizational structures

It is interesting to note, based on the earlier discussion on computer systems and organizations, that evolving computer architectures and changing organization structures bore a similarity of form, in that both evolved from a centralized to a decentralized design. This shift in both cases can be understood as a distribution of power from one central node to a number of decentralized sources because of the many advantages that accrued from such a shift. In both computers and organizations, such a shift was characterized by a significant reduction in formality, or in computer terms, a reduction in "protocol."

In the computer or information system environment, such a shift from a centralized controller or "authority" had many implications. From a relatively rigid system of a single central processor servicing requirements of peripheral units, and handling requests on a rigid set of heuristic or algorithms, distributed systems distribute both data and processing to multiple machines and results are exchanged. While both centralized and distributed systems required varying degrees of central control and authority, distributed systems had far higher levels of communication and task accomplishment at relatively lower levels. With decentralized systems, there is no central controller, and both communication and task responsibilities have been devolved to independently be able to communicate and share resources with relatively high degrees of freedom. Although terminals or other systems communicate through bridges or gateways and require rules for connectivity, these constraints are substantially less than for distributed systems, and this flexibility gives the decentralized systems the capability to cope with a wide variety of information requirements. In other words, the power of the decentralized systems is maximum when protocol or rules are at a minimum. Electronic mail, local area networks, telecommunication systems, group decision-making systems, etc., allow messages to be sent through the network in an interactive mode which results in an increase in the quality, quantity, reliability, and capability of the system to process information.

Organizations, in the last half century, have undergone extensive structural changes, in a large part due to the changes in the operating environment, and also due to the advances in management and organization theory. To be highly efficient through a machine bureaucracy like structure was the requirement of an earlier age. Such a structure is still viable in an environment characterized by stability and reduced complexity. Such structures are relatively uncommon today as business organizations have moved from the criteria of efficiency to that of effectiveness, and such moves have seen machine bureaucracies evolving into more organic structures.

Many scholars, including Mintzberg (1983) and Daft (2001), have highlighted that different types of structures are more appropriate for different types of environments. Effectiveness was provided better by the divisionalized organizations operating in hybrid or matrix like structures, as is common today, compared with the earlier centralized structures. According to Snow et al. (1992), today's competitive pressures demand both efficiency and effectiveness, and firms must adapt with the increasing speed to market pressures and competitors' innovations, while simultaneously controlling or even lowering product or service costs. Under these conditions, they suggest that by using a network structure, a firm can operate an ongoing business both efficiently and innovatively, focusing on those things that it does well and contracting with other firms for the remaining resources.

It is quite clear from the above discussion that the move from centralized to decentralized information architectures, coupled with a similar move in organization structures, should be associated with each other because of the way both have such close similarities in their evolution. It must be remembered that both computers and organizations evolved and changed form for different reasons. Computers architectures evolved, at least in the earlier era, due to the pressure and impact of communication technology, while organization structures evolved as they were impacted by a multitude of forces, including the environment, competition, and technology. How is it possible to evaluate and separate this relationship, between computers and organizations, into cause and effect? This is hard to do except to understand that evolving computer architectures impacted and enabled newer organizational forms, and over time changing organizational requirements impacted the shape and design of computer systems and architectures.

Our discussion so far has been to examine the evolution of computer architectures and organization structures separately. In the following sections we combine the separate evolutions and discuss the impact of the relationship between computers and organizations in two ways.

22.6 The impact of computers on organizations

One of the earliest and more well known studies of the impact of computers on organizations was undertaken by Whisler in the late 1960s. In a study of 23 large insurance firms, the study revealed a number of interesting effects, some contrary to what were expected from computer-based information systems. Perhaps the kind of results highlighted in the study (Table 22-2) were due to the earlier stress on data processing as opposed to the later emphasis of using computers primarily as communication and decision support systems.

Table 22-2 Early impact of computers on organizations

Organization structure	Decision making	Authority and control	Job content
Decline in clerks and supervisors	Consolidation of separate decision systems	Centralization of control	Routinization at lower levels and broadening at upper levels
Increase in upper-level managers	Upward shift in decision making	Increase in machine control	Decline in interpersonal communication after computers
Decline in number of levels	Rational and quantified decision making	Control over individual behavior	Increase in communication during system development
Consolidation of departments	Rigidity and inflexibility in decision making	Blurring of traditional lines of authority and control	Decline of skill levels at lower and middle levels Increase in skill levels at upper levels

The study indicated a decline in the number of levels in the organization structure, greater consolidation and rigidity in decision making, the increased centralization of authority, and routinization in the content of lower level jobs. The impact of computers created shifts in power that were not anticipated before. In the initial stages of its introduction, the power of information was in the hands of the departments in which computers were installed, which was typically the accounting department. "Information is power" has become a maxim, and with it the realization that power devolves upon those who gather, process, disseminate, or simply possess information. According to them, the increasing value of information as a commodity brings with it the potential to change the bases of power and create new ones. Over the years, the availability of decentralized information systems allowed organizations to go ahead and attempt to decentralize their structures to more effectively cope with their environments. Organic structures such as hybrid, matrix, and network organizations were possible in a large part because of the distributed and decentralized decision-making powers made possible from new information architectures.

Mintzberg, (1983) has provided extremely compelling illustrations of how inadequacies in the machine bureaucracy structure led to the formations of more effective structures, and how management information system (MIS) capabilities were used to form new structures. He mentioned that as the environment remained stable, the machine bureaucracy had no great difficulty in adaptation. As environments changed, generating new non-routine problems, managers at the strategic apex quickly became overloaded due to the high degree of centralization inherent in such structures. One of the ways to overcome these information bottlenecks was to restructure, distribute authority, and decentralize management. A combination of environmental turbulence associated with information systems' capabilities provided a strong impetus and capability for organization structures to constantly reshape.

22.7 Phases of the computerization in organizations

In many organizations, computers were initially introduced as a part or a section in the accounting department, usually under the title of electronic data processing (EDP), and, for administrative purposes, was also under the control of the accounting department. At this stage, computers were generally centralized systems consisting of low capacity mainframes. As the need, usage, and capabilities of data processing increased, the data processing section in the accounting department became an independent department of its own, usually called the EDP and later the management information system (MIS) department. This department then serviced various departments in the entire organization, and became an information hub. This stage is still characterized by centralized computer systems, but they were generally high capacity mainframes that could take on the increased load. The current state of development in organizations is indicative of a situation where every department is networked into an information and communication system supported by the MIS/IS department. This is the stage of distributed and decentralized systems that are typical of a network environment. The three stages in the evolution of information systems are given in Figure 22-1.

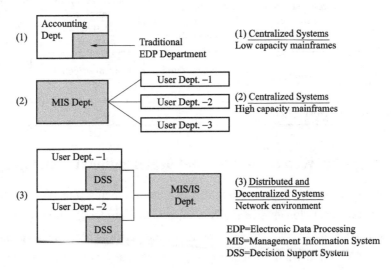

Figure 22-1 Three-part evolution of early information systems

The network environment presented in Figure 22-1 is suggestive of an information system that primarily operates as a decision support system (DSS). Here, users or user departments drive the system, communicate with each other, share the resources including databases, take greater responsibility for the data and the supporting information system, and use the MIS/IS department mainly for technical and software support. According to Wiseman (1985), over the years information system technologies have evolved from MIS to DSS, to strategic information systems (SIS), and now serve the purpose of combining with organization structures to serve as competitive weapons.

Another view of the growth, evolution, and impact of computers on organizations is given by Gibson and Nolan (1974). These researchers have provided an excellent four stage framework (Table 22-3), covering the evolution and growth of EDP departments as computers were introduced into the organization. These four stages were:

(1) initiation;

(2) expansion;

(3) formalization; and

(4) maturity.

At each stage they have looked at three specific dimensions, namely, the growth of applications, the growth of specialized personnel, and the management techniques applied.

Table 22-3 Four-stage growth of companies in organizations

Items	Initiation	Expansion	Formalization	Maturity
Applications	Cost reduction	Proliferation of applications	Emphasis on control	Database applications
Growth of personnel	Specialization for computer efficiency	Specialization to develop variety of programs	Specialization for control and effectiveness assurance	Specialization for database technology and tele-processing
Management techniques applied	Lax management	Sales-oriented management	Control-oriented management	Resource-oriented planning and control
Source: Gibson and Nolan (1974)				

22.8 Linkages between computers and organizational structures

While organizations evolve to adapt to their environments, the purpose behind such evolutions and transformation is essentially a question of strategy, which is to do with the organization's adaptation, survival, growth, and improved performance. Organization structures, therefore, serve a function which essentially suggests that an organization can function best when it assumes certain forms.

In a conceptual study by Leifer (1988), there were certain ideal matches between the four information architectures discussed earlier and the Mintzberg typologies. Leifer suggests that certain organization structures are more compatible with certain information architectures. A mismatch, according to him, would result in inferior performance, unless a change was effected onto either the architecture or the structure, or both.

It will be noticed from Table 22-4 that bureaucracies are matched with the centralized systems, while professional bureaucracies use both centralized and distributed systems. This is because such organizations need access to mainframe processing capabilities, as well as local processing linked to the specialized databases. The divisionalized organizations use the centralized, distributed, and decentralized systems because the divisionalized structures may take many forms. Some may be loosely coupled, while others may be tightly coupled. The coupling may be by way of formal controls, or through a strong culture. The division may have a centralized or decentralized relationship with its corporate office, and the structure within the division may be centralized or decentralized. Divisions, therefore, depending on the way they are organized, will have unique and different types of information architectures. Adhocracies, on the other hand, are linked with the decentralized systems as these are small autonomous structures that are highly organic and behave like project teams.

Table 22-4 Linkage between organization structure and information architecture

Types of organization structure	Types of information architecture
Simple structure	Stand-alone PCs
Machine bureaucracy	Centralized systems
Professional bureaucracy	Centralized and distributed systems
Divisionalized form	Centralized, distributed and decentralized systems
Adhocracy	Decentralized systems

Source: Leifer (1988)

22.9 Implications for emerging and future organizations

What are emerging and future organizations going to be like? And, what is the role of information systems in shaping future organizations? Many scholars have suggested that environmental factors, managerial attitudes, workforce sophistication, and numerous other factors are likely to affect the form, structure, and functioning of future organizations. According to Galbraith and Lawler (1993), emerging and future organizations are more likely to be characterized by the decentralization of decision making, and in order to facilitate this, they are likely to be designed as the distributed organizations. The newer structures are likely to have extremely close links, especially through computer based information systems, with their suppliers and customers. Enhanced coordination is likely to result, as is happening with the electronic data interchange (EDI) being increasingly used to integrate the operations of two or more organizations that do business with each other. Network organizations with their internal and external networks, high performance work teams, flexible work groups, centrality of customers, close coordination with suppliers and contractors, and the ability to respond quickly to changes are perhaps the shape of the organizations of the future.

22.10   Internet, stand-alone computers and small businesses

With the advent of the Internet, the greatest impact has been on the role and operations of small businesses. Traditionally, small businesses with simple structures (Mintzberg, 1983) used stand-alone computers. Small businesses were constrained to use the relatively simple off-the-shelf software packages that provided standardized solutions for typical business problems. Prior to the Internet, small businesses were neither networked nor capable of interorganizational communications using computers. However, the Internet has changed all that and has created completely new dynamics in the way small businesses can leverage the World Wide Web to overcome the disadvantage of size and accessibility.

A recent study (1999) indicated that consumers and businesses equipped with personal computers (PCs) and Internet access were poised to bypass paper transactions in favor of electronic information exchange. Studies have indicated that 60-67 per cent of small businesses were equipped with a computer and modem, were using online banking functions, and had their own web pages. Another survey revealed that about 61 per cent of small businesses operate some kind of computer network, and 20 per cent of those that do not plan to do so within the next 12 months, and nearly 40 per cent of the survey respondents plan to update their networks within a year (1999). An IBM survey in 1994 indicated that less than half of small business executives were aware of the Internet's existence, while in 1999 the Internet became an integral part of the daily business operations of small businesses. The next Internet growth spurt is expected to be among small- and mid-size businesses, and by about 2006, about 50 per cent of the US workforce will have jobs at Internet-related businesses.

What is of great interest is how small businesses with stand-alone computers can, on account of the Internet, have the same global reach and impact as the largest businesses. The potential for small businesses to take advantage of the web and leverage it for business purposes is enormous. In practical terms, the Internet is rapidly becoming a primary channel for conducting transactions known in business as purchasing, and in government primarily as procurement. The use of electronic procurement and purchasing, which was previously dominated by larger companies, is one that has been heavily impacted by the Internet and has been of great benefit to small businesses. As one can see, not only have computers impacted the structures in organizations over the years, but computer related developments have completely altered the commercial viability of small businesses and their usage of stand-alone computers.

Professional Vocabularies and Expressions

information system	信息系统
organization structure	组织结构
centralized design	集中式设计
decentralized design	分布式设计
punched card	穿孔卡片
unit record machines (URMs)	单元记录机
electronic numerical integrator and calculator	电子数字集成器和计算器
electronic delayed storage automatic computer	电子延迟储存自动计算机
electronic discrete variable automatic computer	电子离散变量自动计算机
stored program	存储程序
memory	内存
standardized language	标准计算机语言
higher level language	高级计算机语言
operating system (OS)	操作系统
valve	电子管
electric relay	电子继电器
transistor	晶体管
vacuum tube	真空管
large scale integration (LSI)	大型集成器
integrated circuit	集成电路
computing power	计算能力
storage capacity	存储能力
peripheral capability	外设（外部设备）能力
very large scale integration (VLSI)	超大规模集成器
semiconductor memory	半导体存储器
software	软件
microprocessor	微处理器
virtual memory	虚拟内存
communication facility	通信设备
database facility	数据库设备
information age/era	信息时代
industrial age/era	工业时代
program evaluation and review technique (PERT)	计划评审技术
critical path method (CPM)	关键路线法

centralized system	集中式系统
distributed system	分布式系统
decentralized system	分散式系统
stand-alone system	单机系统
mainframe host computer	大型主机
personal computers (PCs)	个人电脑
data processing	数据处理
decision support system (DSS)	决策支持系统
minicomputer	小型机
local area network (LAN)	局域网
wide area network (WAN)	广域网
processor	处理器
storage device	存储设备
terminal	终端
degree of unrelatedness	不相关度
centralized single business organization	集中式的单一企业组织
vertically integrated structure	纵向集成式结构
horizontally integrated structure	横向集成式结构
divisionalized structure	事业部式结构
matrix organization	矩阵式组织
hybrid organization	混合型组织
network organization	网络型组织
formality	形式化
protocol	协议
simple structure	简单结构
machine bureaucracies	机械官僚机构
professional bureaucracies	专业官僚机构
divisionalized form	事业部形式
strategic business unit (SBU)	战略业务单元
gateway	网关
organic structure	有机结构
electronic data processing (EDP)	电子数据处理
management information system (MIS)	管理信息系统
strategic information system (SIS)	战略信息系统
electronic data interchange (EDI)	电子数据交换

Notes

1. Very simply, computers allowed the development of planning techniques hitherto too complex to develop, compute, or control.

简言之，计算机使得人们能够开发那些在此之前由于太复杂而不能开发、计算和控制的规划技术。

2. Categorizing information systems architecturally is appealing since it is not idiosyncratic to particular settings, and further, these architectures are fairly well established and accepted.

根据信息系统的结构对其进行分类是有吸引力的，因为这种分类方法不因某些系统的特定设置（配置）而不同，并且根据这种分类方法所得到的各种系统结构很成熟并被广泛接受。

3. In the 1960s, there were a spate of acquisitions and mergers primarily as a response to anti-trust laws.

20世纪60年代，（美国企业）基本上针对反信任法而出现了收购和合并狂潮。

4. This is hard to do except to understand that evolving computer architectures impacted and enabled newer organizational forms, and over time changing organizational requirements impacted the shape and design of computer systems and architectures.

评价计算机和企业组织结构演化直接的因果关系是一件困难的事情，但二者之间的关系可以理解为：计算机结构的演化影响了企业的组织结构并使得企业能够尝试新的组织结构形式；随着时间的推移，不断变化的组织需求又反过来对计算机系统及其结构的设计产生影响。

Discussion Questions:

1. In this article, five typological structures are mentioned: simple structure, machine bureaucracies, professional bureaucracies, divisionalized forms and adhocracy. What might be the features of IE practices for each type of organizational structure?
2. How does the evolution of information systems affect the IE practices?

CHAPTER 23

The New IE: Information Technology and Business Process Redesign

23.1 Introduction

Those aspiring to improve the way work is done must begin to apply the capabilities of information technology to redesign business processes. Business process design and information technology are natural partners, yet industrial engineers have never fully exploited their relationship. The authors argue, in fact, that it has barely been exploited at all. But the organizations that have used IT to redesign boundary-crossing, customer-driven processes have benefited enormously.

At the turn of the century, Frederick Taylor revolutionized the workplace with his ideas on work organization, task decomposition, and job measurement. Taylor's basic aim was to increase organizational productivity by applying to human labor the same engineering principles that had proven so successful in solving the technical problems in the work environment. The same approaches that had transformed mechanical activity could also be used to structure jobs performed by people. Taylor came to symbolize the practical realizations in industry that we now call industrial engineering (IE), or the scientific school of management. In fact, though work design remains a contemporary IE concern, no subsequent concept or tool has rivaled the power of Taylor's mechanizing vision.

As we enter the 1990s, however, two newer tools are transforming organizations to the degree that Taylorism once did. These are information technology — the capabilities offered by computers, software applications, and telecommunications — and business process redesign — the analysis and design of work flows and processes within and between organizations. Working together, these tools have the potential to create a new type of industrial engineering, changing the way the discipline is practiced and the skills necessary to practice it.

23.2 IT in business process redesign

The importance of both information technology and business process redesign is well known to industrial engineers, albeit as largely separate tools for use in specific and limited environments. IT is used in industrial engineering as an analysis and modeling tool, and IEs have often taken the lead in applying information technology to manufacturing environments. Well-known uses of IT in manufacturing include process modeling, production scheduling and control, materials management information systems, and logistics. In most cases where IT has been used to redesign work, the redesign has most likely been in the manufacturing function, and industrial engineers are the most likely individuals to have carried it out.

IEs have begun to analyze work activities in non-manufacturing environments, but their penetration into offices has been far less than in factories. IT has certainly penetrated the office and services environments — in 1987 Business Week reported that almost 40 percent of all U.S. capital spending went to information systems, some $97 billion a year — but IT has been used in most cases to hasten office work rather than to transform it. With few exceptions, IT's role in the redesign of nonmanufacturing work has been disappointing; few firms have achieved major productivity gains. Aggregate productivity figures for the United States have shown no increase since 1973.

Given the growing dominance of service industries and office work in the Western economies, this type of work is as much in need of analysis and redesign as the manufacturing environments to which IT has already been applied. Many firms have found that this analysis requires taking a broader view of both IT and business activity, and of the relationships between them. Information technology should be viewed as more than an automating or mechanizing force; it can fundamentally reshape the way business is done. Business activities should be viewed as more than a collection of individual or even functional tasks; they should be broken down into the processes that can be designed for maximum effectiveness, in both manufacturing and service environments.

Our research suggests that IT can be more than a useful tool in business process redesign. In leading edge practice, information technology and BPR have a recursive relationship. Each is the key to thinking about the other. Thinking about information technology should be in terms of how it supports new or redesigned business processes, rather than business functions or other organizational entities. And business processes and process improvements should be considered in terms of the capabilities information technology can provide. We refer to this broadened, recursive view of IT and BPR as the new industrial engineering.

Taylor could focus on workplace rationalization and individual task efficiency because he confronted a largely stable business environment; today's corporations do not have the luxury of such stability. Individual tasks and jobs change faster than they can be redesigned. Today, responsibility for an outcome is more often spread over a group, rather than assigned to an individual as in the past. Companies increasingly find it necessary to develop more flexible, team-oriented, coordinative, and communication-based work capability. In short, rather than maximizing the performance of particular individuals or business functions, companies must maximize interdependent activities within and across the entire organization. Such business processes are a new approach to coordination across the firm; information technology's promise — and perhaps its ultimate impact — is to be the most powerful tool in the twentieth century for reducing the costs of this coordination.

23.3 Redesigning business processes with IT: five steps

Assuming that a company has decided its processes are inefficient or ineffective, and therefore in need of redesign, how should it proceed? This is a straightforward activity, but five major steps are involved: develop the business vision and process objectives, identify the processes to be redesigned, understand and measure the existing process, identify IT levers, and design and build a prototype of the new process. We observed most or all of these steps being performed in the companies that were succeeding with BPR. Each step is described in greater detail below.

23.3.1 Developing business vision and process objectives

In the past, process redesign was typically intended simply to "rationalize" the process, in other words, to eliminate obvious bottlenecks and inefficiencies. It did not involve any particular business vision or context. This was the approach of the "work simplification" aspect of industrial engineering, an important legacy of Taylorism.

Our research suggests strongly that rationalization is not an end in itself, and is thus insufficient as a process redesign objective. Furthermore, the rationalization of highly decomposed tasks may lead to a less efficient overall process. Instead of task rationalization, the redesign of entire processes should be undertaken with a specific business vision and related objectives in mind.

In the most successful redesign examples we studied, the company's senior management had developed a broad strategic vision into which the process redesign activity fitted. The most likely objectives are the following:

(1) **Cost Reduction.** This objective was implicit in the "rationalization" approach. Cost is an important redesign objective in combination with others, but insufficient in itself. Excessive attention to cost reduction results in the tradeoffs that are usually unacceptable to process stakeholders. While optimizing on other objectives seems to bring costs into line, optimizing on cost rarely brings about other objectives.

(2) **Time Reduction.** Time reduction has been only a secondary objective of traditional industrial engineering. Increasing numbers of companies, however, are beginning to compete on the basis of time. Processes, as we have defined them, are the ideal unit for a focused time reduction analysis. One common approach to cutting time from product design is to make the steps begin simultaneously, rather than sequentially, using IT to coordinate design directions among the various functional participants. This approach has been taken in the design of computers, telephone equipment, automobiles, and copiers.

(3) **Output Quality.** All processes have outputs, be they physical — such as in manufacturing a tangible product — or informational — such as in adding data to a customer file. Output quality is frequently the focus of process improvement in manufacturing environments; it is just as important in service industries. The specific measure of output quality may be uniformity, variability, or freedom from defects; this should be defined by the customer of the process.

(4) **Quality of Worklife (QWL)/Learning/Empowerment.** IT can lead either to the greater empowerment of individuals, or to the greater control over their output. Zuboff points out that IT-intensive processes are often simply automated, and that the "informating" or learning potential of IT in processes is often ignored. Moreover, Schein notes that organizations often do not provide a supportive context for individuals to introduce or innovate with IT. Of course, it is rarely possible to optimize all objectives simultaneously, and in most firms, the strongest pressures are to produce tangible benefits. Yet managers who ignore this dimension risk failure of redesigned processes for organizational and motivational factors.

Some firms have been able to achieve multiple objectives in redesigning processes with IT. Finally, all firms found it was important to set specific objectives, even to the point of quantification. Though it is difficult to know how much improvement is possible in advance of a redesign, "reach should exceed grasp." Setting the goals that will stretch the organization will also provide inspiration and stimulate creative thinking.

23.3.2 Identifying processes to be redesigned

Most organizations could benefit from IT-enabled redesign of critical (if not all) business processes. However, the amount of effort involved creates practical limitations. Even when total redesign was the ultimate objective, the companies we studied selected a few key processes for initial efforts. Moreover, when there was insufficient commitment to total redesign, a few successful examples of IT-enhanced processes became a powerful selling tool.

The means by which the processes to be redesigned are identified and prioritized is a key issue. This is often difficult because most managers do not think about their business operations in terms of processes. There are two major approaches. The exhaustive approach attempts to identify all processes within an organization and then prioritize them in order of redesign urgency. The high-impact approach attempts to identify only the most important processes or those most in conflict with the business vision and process objectives.

The exhaustive approach is often associated with "information engineering," in which an organization's use of data dictates the processes to be redesigned. The alternative is to focus quickly on high-impact processes. Most organizations have some sense of which business areas or processes are most crucial to their success, and those most "broken" or inconsistent with the business vision. If not, these can normally be identified using senior management workshops, or through extensive interviewing.

The companies that employed the high-impact approach generally considered it sufficient. The companies taking the exhaustive approach, on the other hand, have not had the resources to address all the identified processes; why do we identify them if they cannot be addressed? As a rough rule of thumb, most companies we studied were unable to redesign and support more than ten to fifteen major processes per year (i.e., one to three per major business unit); there was simply not enough management attention to do more. And some organizations have abandoned the exhaustive approach.

Whichever approach is used, companies have found it useful to classify each redesigned process in terms of beginning and end points, interfaces, and organization units (functions or departments) involved, particularly including the customer unit. Thinking in these terms usually broadens the perceived scope of the process.

23.3.3 Understanding and measuring the existing processes

There are two primary reasons for understanding and measuring processes before redesigning them. First, problems must be understood so that they are not repeated. Second, accurate measurement can serve as a baseline for future improvements. If the objective is to cut time and cost, the time and cost consumed by the untouched process must be measured accurately. Westinghouse Productivity and Quality Center consultants found that simply graphing the incremental cost and time consumed by process tasks can often suggest initial areas for redesign. These graphs look like "step functions" showing the incremental contribution of each major task.

This step can easily be overemphasized, however. In several firms, the "stretch" goal was less to eliminate problems or bottlenecks than to create radical improvements. Designers should be informed by past process problems and errors, but they should work with a clean slate. Similarly, the process should not be measured for measurement's sake. Only the specific objectives of the redesign should be measured. As with the high-impact process identification approach, an 80-20 philosophy is usually appropriate.

23.3.4 Identifying IT levers

Until recently, even the most sophisticated industrial engineering approaches did not consider IT capabilities until after a process had been designed. The conventional wisdom in IT usage has always been to first determine the business requirements of a function, process, or other business entity, and then to develop a system. The problem is that the awareness of IT capabilities can — and should — influence process design. Knowing that product development teams can exchange computer-aided designs over large distances, for example, might affect the structure of a product development process. The role of IT in a process should be considered in the early stages of its redesign.

Several firms accomplished this using brainstorming sessions, with the process redesign objectives and existing process measures in hand. It was also useful to have a list of IT's generic capabilities in improving business processes. In the broadest sense, all of IT's capabilities involve improving coordination and information access across organizational units, thereby allowing for more effective management of task interdependence.

23.3.5 Designing and building a prototype of the process

For most firms, the final step is to design the process. This is usually done by the same team that performed the previous steps, getting input from constituencies and using brainstorming workshops. A key point is that the actual design is not the end of the process. Rather, it should be viewed as a prototype, with the successive iterations expected and managed. Key factors and tactics to consider in process design and prototype creation include using IT as a design tool, understanding generic design criteria, and creating organizational prototypes.

(1) **IT as a Design Tool.** Designing a business process is largely a matter of diligence and creativity. The emerging IT technologies, however, are beginning to facilitate the "process" of process design. Some computer-aided systems engineering (CASE) products are designed primarily to draw process models. The ability to draw models rapidly and make changes suggested by process owners speeds redesign and facilitates owner buy-in. Some CASE products can actually generate computer code for the information systems' applications that will support a modeled business process.

(2) **Generic Design Criteria.** Companies used various criteria for evaluating alternative designs. Most important, of course, is the likelihood that a design will satisfy the chosen design objectives. Others mentioned in interviews included the simplicity of the design, the lack of buffers or intermediaries, the degree of control by a single individual or department (or an effective, decentralized coordinative mechanism), the balance of process resources, and the generalization of process tasks (so that they can be performed by more than one person).

(3) **Organizational Prototypes.** Mutual Benefit Life's (MBL) redesign of its individual life insurance underwriting process illustrates a final, important point about process design. At MBL, underwriting a life insurance policy involved 40 steps with over 100 people in 12 functional areas and 80 separate jobs. To streamline this lengthy and complex process, MBL undertook a pilot project with the goal of improving productivity by 40 percent. To integrate the process, MBL created a new role, the case manager. This role was designed to perform and coordinate all underwriting tasks centrally, utilizing a workstation-based computer system capable of pulling data from all over the company. After a brief start-up period, the firm learned that two additional roles were necessary in some underwriting cases: specialists such as lawyers or medical directors in knowledge-intensive fields, and clerical assistance. With the new role and redesigned process, senior managers at MBL are confident of reaching the 40 percent goal in a few months. This example illustrates the value of creating organizational prototypes in IT-driven process redesign.

23.4 Defining process types

The five steps described above are sufficiently general to apply to most organizations and processes. Yet the specifics of redesign vary considerably according to the type of process under examination. Different types require the different levels of management attention and ownership, need the different forms of IT support, and have different business consequences. In this section, we present three different dimensions within which processes vary.

Three major dimensions can be used to define processes. These are the organizational entities or subunits involved in the process, the types of the objects manipulated, and the types of the activities taking place. We describe each dimension and resulting process type below.

23.4.1 Defining process entities

Processes take place between the types of organizational entities. Each type has different implications for IT benefits.

Interorganizational processes are those taking place between two or more business organizations. Increasingly, companies are concerned with the coordinating activities that extend into the next (or previous) company along the value-added chain. Several U.S. retail, apparel, and textile companies, for example, have linked their business processes to speed up the reordering of apparel. When Dillard's (department store) inventory of a particular pants style falls below a specified level, Haggar (apparel manufacturer) is notified electronically. If Haggar does not have the cloth to manufacture the pants, Burlington Industries (textile manufacturer) is notified electronically. As this example of electronic data interchange (EDI) illustrates, information technology is the major vehicle by which this interorganizational linkage is executed.

A second major type of business process is *interfunctional*. These processes exist within the organization, but cross several functional or divisional boundaries. Interfunctional processes achieve major operational objectives, such as new product realization, asset management, or production scheduling. Most management processes — for example, planning, budgeting, and human resource management — are interfunctional.

A major problem in redesigning interfunctional processes is that most information systems of the past were built to automate the specific functional areas or parts of functions. Few third-party application software packages have been developed to support a full business process. Very few organizations have modeled existing interfunctional processes or redesigned them, and companies will run into substantial problems in building interfunctional systems without such models.

Interpersonal processes involve tasks within and across small work groups, typically within a function or department. Examples include a commercial loan group approving a loan, or an airline flight crew preparing for takeoff. This type of process is becoming more important as companies shift to self-managing teams as the lowest unit of organization.

Information technology is increasingly capable of supporting interpersonal processes; hardware and communications companies have developed new networking-oriented products, and software companies have begun to flesh out the concept of "groupware" (e.g., local area network-based mail, conferencing, and brainstorming tools).

23.4.2 Defining process objects

Processes can also be categorized by the types of the objects manipulated. The two primary object types are physical and informational. In physical object processes, real and tangible things are either created or manipulated; manufacturing is the obvious example. Informational object processes create or manipulate information. Processes for making a decision, preparing a marketing plan, or designing a new product are examples.

Many processes involve the combination of physical and informational objects. Indeed, adding information to a physical object as it moves through a process is a common way of adding value. Most logistical activities, for example, combine the movement of physical objects with the manipulation of the information concerning their whereabouts. The success in the logistics industry is often dependent on the close integration of physical and informational outcomes; both UPS and Federal Express, for example, track package movement closely.

The potential for using IT to improve physical processes is well known. It allows the greater flexibility and variety of outcomes, more precise control of the process itself, reductions in throughput time, and elimination of human labor. These benefits have been pursued for the past three decades. Still, manufacturing process flows are often the result of historical circumstance and should usually be redesigned before further automation is applied. This is particularly true in low volume, job shop manufacturing environments. Redesigners of physical processes should also consider the role of IT in providing information to improve processes.

Strangely, the proportion of informational processes already transformed by IT is probably lower than that of physical processes. True, the legions of clerks have become unemployed because of computers. But the majority of the information processes to which IT has been applied are those involving high volume and low complexity. Now that these processes are well known even if not fully conquered, the emphasis needs to shift to the processes that incorporate semistructured and unstructured tasks and are performed by high-skill knowledge workers. Relevant IT capabilities include the storage and retrieval of unstructured and multimedia information, the capturing and routinizing of decision logic, and the application of far-flung and complex data resources. A computer vendor's advertising videotape, for example, illustrates how artificial intelligence and hypertext; or mixed-media databases, combine to lead a manager through the process of developing a departmental budget. The IT capabilities in the video are available today, but they are rarely applied to such information-intensive yet unstructured processes.

23.4.3 Defining process activities

Our examples of business processes have involved two types of activities: operational and managerial. Operational processes involve the day-to-day carrying out of the organization's basic business purpose. Managerial processes help to control, plan, or provide resources for operational processes. The past uses of IT to improve processes, limited as they are, have been largely operational. We will therefore focus almost entirely on managerial processes in this section.

Applying IT to management tasks is not a new idea. The potential of decision support systems, executive support systems, and other managerial tools has been discussed for over twenty years. We believe, however, that the benefits have not been realized because of the absence of systematic process thinking. Few companies have rigorously analyzed managerial activities as processes subject to redesign. Even the notion of managerial activities involving defined outcomes (a central aspect of our definition of business processes) is somewhat foreign. How would such managerial processes as deciding on an acquisition or developing the agenda for the quarterly board meeting be improved if they were treated as processes — in other words, measured, brainstormed, and redesigned with IT capabilities?

The generic capabilities of IT for reshaping management processes include improving analytic accuracy, enabling broader management participation across wider geographical boundaries, generating feedback on the actions taken (the managerial version of "informating" a process), and streamlining the time and resources a specific process consumes.

23.5 Management issues in IT-enabled redesign

Companies have found that once a process has been redesigned, several key issues remain. These include the management role in redesigned activity, implications for organization structure, new skill requirements, creating a function to perform IT-enabled BPR, the proper direction for the IT infrastructure, and the need for continuous process improvement. We discuss each below.

23.5.1 Management roles

Perhaps the greatest difficulty in IT-driven redesign is getting and keeping management commitment. Because processes cut across various pans of the organization, a process redesign effort driven by a single business function or unit will probably encounter the resistance from the other pans of the organization. Both high-level and broad support for change are necessary.

To perform the five redesign steps described above, several companies created a cross-functional task force headed by a senior executive. These task forces included the representatives from key staff and line groups likely to be affected by the changes, including IT and human resources. It was particularly important that the customer of the process be represented on the team, even when the customer was external. The team composition was ideal if some members had some record of process or operations innovation involving IT.

As the redesign teams selected processes and developed objectives, they needed to work closely with the managers and staff of the affected units. Managing process change is similar to managing other types of change, except that its cross-functional nature increases the number of stakeholders, thereby increasing the complexity of the effort.

It was also important to have strong, visible commitment from senior management. The employees throughout the organization needed to understand that redesign was critical, that the differences of opinions would be resolved in favor of the customer of a process, and that IT would play an important role. In many cases, the CEO communicated any structural implication of the redesign effort.

23.5.2 Process redesign and organizational structure

A second key issue is the relationship between process orientation and organizational structure. Certainly someone must be in charge of implementing a process change, and of managing the redesigned process thereafter. But process responsibilities are likely to cut across the existing organizational structures. How can process organization and traditional functional organization be reconciled?

One possible solution is to create a new organization structure along process lines, in effect abandoning altogether other structural dimensions, such as function, product, or geography. This approach presents risks, however; as business needs change, new processes will be created that cut across the previous process-based organization. This does not mean that a process-based structure cannot be useful, but only that it will have to be changed frequently.

While no firm we studied has converted wholly to a process-based structure, a few organizations have moved in this direction. For example, Apple Computer recently moved away from a functional structure to what executives describe as an IT-oriented, process-based, customer satisfaction-driven structure called "New Enterprise." The company relishes its lack of formal hierarchy; Apple managers describe their roles as highly diffuse, and team and project based.

A more conservative approach would be to create a matrix of functional and process responsibilities. However, because of the cross-functional nature of most processes, the functional manager who should have responsibility for a given process is not always easy to identify. The company may also wish to avoid traditional functional thinking, in assigning process responsibilities. For example, it may be wiser to give responsibility for redesigning supplies acquisition to a manager who uses those supplies (i.e., the customer of the process), rather than to the head of purchasing.

23.5.3 New skill requirements

For process management to succeed, managers must develop facilitation and influence skills. The traditional sources of authority may be of little use when process changes cut across organizational units. Managers will find themselves trying to change the behavior of the employees who do not work for them. In these cases, they must learn to persuade rather than to instruct, to convince rather than to dictate. Of course, these recommendations are consistent with many other organizational maxims of the past several years; they just happen to be useful in process management as well.

Several organizations that are moving toward IT-driven process management are conducting the programs intended to develop facilitation skills. These programs encourage less reliance on hierarchy, more cross-functional communication and cooperation, and more decision making by middle- and lower-level managers. Such a program at American Airlines is being used to build an organizational infrastructure at the same time a new IT infrastructure is being built.

23.5.4 An ongoing organization

The organizations that redesign key processes must oversee continuing redesign and organizational "tuning," as well as ensure that information systems support process flows. In most companies, the appropriate analytical skills are most likely to be found in the IT function. However, these individuals will also require a high degree of interpersonal skills to be successful as the "new industrial engineers." The ideal group would represent multiple functional areas, for example, information systems, industrial engineering, quality, process control, finance, and human resources.

23.5.5 Process redesign and the IT organization

Just as information technology is a powerful force in redesigning business processes, process thinking has important implications for the IT organization and for the technology infrastructure it builds. Though few IT groups have the power and influence to spearhead process redesign, they can play several important roles. First of all, the IT group may need to play a behind-the-scenes advocacy role, convincing senior management of the power offered by information technology and process redesign. Second, as demand builds for process redesign expertise, the IT group can begin to incorporate the IE-oriented skills of process measurement, analysis, and redesign, perhaps merging with the IE function if there is one. It can also develop an approach or methodology for IT-enabled redesign, perhaps using the five steps described above as a starting point.

What must information systems' function do technologically to prepare for process redesign? IT professionals must recognize that they will have to build most systems needed to support (or enable) processes, rather than buy them from software package vendors, because most application packages are designed with particular functions in mind. IT professionals will need to build robust technology platforms on which process-specific applications can be quickly constructed. This implies a standardized architecture with extensive communications capability between computing nodes, and the development of shared databases. However, like the organizational strategies for process management described above, these are appropriate technology strategies for most companies, whether or not they are redesigning processes with IT.

23.5.6 Continuous process improvement

The concept of process improvement, which developed in the quality movement, requires first that the existing process be stabilized. It then becomes predictable, and its capabilities become accessible to analysis and improvement. Continuous process improvement occurs when the cycle of stabilizing, assessing, and improving a given process becomes institutionalized.

IT-enabled business process redesign must generally be dynamic. Those responsible for a process should constantly investigate whether new information technologies make it possible to carry out a process in new ways. IT is continuing to evolve, and forthcoming technologies will have a substantial impact on the processes of the next decade. The IT infrastructure must be robust enough to support the new applications appropriate to a particular process.

23.6 Summary

We believe that the industrial engineers of the future, regardless of their formal title or the organizational unit that employs them, will focus increasingly on the IT-enabled redesign of business processes. We have only begun to explore the implications and implementation of this concept, and only a few companies have ventured into the area. Many companies that have used IT to redesign particular business processes have done so without any conscious approach or philosophy. In short, the actual experience base with IT-enabled process redesign is limited.

Yet managing by customer-driven processes that cross organizational boundaries is an intuitively appealing idea that has worked well in the companies that have experimented with it. And few would question that information technology is a powerful tool for reshaping business processes. The individuals and companies that can master redesigning processes around IT will be well equipped to succeed in the new decade and the new century.

Professional Vocabularies and Expressions

work organization	工作组织
task decomposition	任务分解
job measurement	作业测量
information technology	信息技术
business process redesign	业务流程再造
process modeling	过程建模

production scheduling and control	生产调度和控制
materials management information system	物料管理信息系统
logistics	物流
workplace rationalization	工作现场的合理化
accounts payable	应付账款
accounts receivable	应收账款
cross-functional analysis	交叉职能分析
80-20 Philosophy	80/20 哲学，80/20 原则
computer-aided systems engineering (CASE)	计算机辅助系统工程
underwriting	保险业
value-added chain	增值链
electronic data interchange (EDI)	电子数据交换
local area network (LAN)	局域网
invoice	发票
bills of materials	物料清单
asset management	资产管理
production scheduling	生产计划，生产调度
human resource management	人力资源管理
continuous process improvement	持续流程改进

Notes

1. At the turn of the century, Frederick Taylor revolutionized the workplace with his ideas on work organization, task decomposition, and job measurement.

泰勒（1856—1915）：发展了工作研究（Work Study）、方法研究及工作评量（Method study and work measurement）。从 1898 年到 1901 年服务于伯利恒钢铁公司（The Bethlehem Steel Company）期间，除了顾问的工作外，泰勒还发展了各种新的制造程序，并且获得上百件专利。泰勒著名的论文有《A Piece Rate System (1895)》，《Shop Management (1903)》，《On the Art of Cutting Metals (1906)》。之后他汇集经验及思考，于 1911 年出版了其著作《The Principles of Scientific Management》，说明科学管理的 4 项原则：

（1）将每一个人的工作、每一单元均以科学方法加以分析，取代以往尝试错误所得的经验法则。

（2）选择最适当的作业员，而且要训练作业员，以经过研究的方法来改善。

（3）在管理员与作业员之间发展出合作的精神。

（4）在管理者和作业员之间，将工作责任公平地划分出来，使各方均能尽其所长。

泰勒倡导科学管理最早，因此大家公认他是"科学管理之父"、"工业工程之父"、"时间研究之父"。

该句可翻译为：20世纪初，弗雷德里克·泰勒利用工作组织、任务分解和作业测量对工作现场进行了革命性变革。

2. The importance of both information technology and business process redesign is well known to industrial engineers, albeit as largely separate tools for use in specific and limited environments.

尽管工业工程师对信息技术和业务流程再造的重要性有很深入的了解，但它们通常被作为不同的工具在特定的、有限的范围内使用。

3. Our research suggests strongly that rationalization is not an end in itself, and is thus insufficient as a process redesign objective.

我们的研究明确地表明流程的合理化本身并不是流程再造的最终目的,因此将其作为流程再造的目标是不充分的。

4. While optimizing on other objectives seems to bring costs into line, optimizing on cost rarely brings about other objectives.

尽管在优化其他目标时成本也似乎得到了优化，但对成本的优化很少能使得其他目标顺便得到优化。

5. Designers should be informed by past process problems and errors, but they should work with a clean slate.

尽管应该被告知过去发现的关于流程的问题和错误，但设计人员还是应该从零做起。

6. Information technology is increasingly capable of supporting interpersonal processes; hardware and communications companies have developed new networking-oriented products, and software companies have begun to flesh out the concept of "groupware" (e.g., local area network-based mail, conferencing, and brainstorming tools).

信息技术对处理人与人之间关系的流程的支持能力越来越强：硬件和通信公司已经开发出新的网络产品，软件公司已经逐步形成"组件"（例如基于局域网的电子邮件、网络会议和头脑风暴工具）的概念。

Discussion Questions:

1. Comment on the argument that the industrial engineers of the future will focus increasingly on the IT-enabled redesign of business processes.
2. Many scholars argue that IE should precede ERP for manufacturing enterprises. What are your comments about this argument?

CHAPTER 24

Post Industrial Engineering

24.1 Introduction

If any discipline is rightfully the child of the second industrial revolution and the changes it wrought in the nature of work, that discipline is industrial engineering. Forged in mills and on shopfloors at the turn of the 20th century, industrial engineering sought to tame the social and economic turmoil that emerged as productive activity shifted from fields to cities, from hand tools to dedicated machines and from steam to electrical power. Whereas other thinkers of the day hoped to solve industry's problems by "Americanizing" an immigrant workforce and by peddling the notions of leadership and self-reliance to the captains of industry, industrial engineers recognized that the key to industrial order lay in the design of work systems and practices. They understood that adapting to the new economic regime would require the philosophies and methods tailored to the forms of work that defined the new mode of production.

For the first half of the 20th century, industrial engineers articulated a philosophy of management and developed techniques for improving production systems by increasing the efficiency of work practices. Beyond developing methods for studying motion and time, for which they are widely known, industrial engineers organized and streamlined procurement, inventory, quality and accounting systems. They redesigned machine tools to increase accuracy and efficiency. They also experimented with incentive plans, which they believed would enhance motivation and yield workers a fairer wage. For the most part, these early industrial engineers focused on factories and clerical bureaucracies where tasks were largely manual and repetitive and where output was tangible.

After World War II the study of work began to slip slowly into the background as industrial engineers turned their attention to more quantitative and analytical endeavors. Some engineers, still concerned with the factory, began to develop the general models of efficient production and distribution. Others developed the mathematics of optimization in search of less contextualized models that they could apply not only to production but also to health care, transportation and military operations. Still other industrial engineers created the fields of risk and decision analysis in the hope of devising tools that any decision-maker could use. Engineering studies of work migrated toward controls, displays and human-machine interfaces: the topics that could be investigated more rigorously in a laboratory than on the factory floor.

At about the same time, the nature of work began to change. Initially, the rate of change was sufficiently slow that it was not unreasonable for industrial engineers to assume that the concepts and techniques developed for factories remained adequate for most other work settings. There is evidence, however, that the work in contemporary society has now changed sufficiently to render such an assumption suspect. The occupational structure of the US has changed dramatically over the last 50 years. Blue-collar employment has fallen steadily whereas white-collar work has expanded. The employment in services now outranks the employment in manufacturing. Professional and technical occupations employ more Americans today than any other occupational sector monitored by the Bureau of Labor Statistics (http://www.bls.gov/).

The dynamics of work are changing within occupational groups as well. Stable employment is declining and contingent work is on the rise, even among professionals and managers. Computers and other digital technologies have eliminated some types of work, created others, and transformed a significant portion of what remains. The work that formerly required direct operations on materials can increasingly be performed remotely. The ability to collaborate in distributed teams is more important than in the past. Under team systems, even factory workers may require interpersonal and analytical skills previously reserved for managers and engineers.

For these reasons, industrial engineering once again faces great challenges and opportunities. Like the field's founders, who confronted the transformation associated with the rise of the modern factory, we face a shift in the nature of work occasioned by a changing technical infrastructure. This shift is marked by the spread of information technologies, microelectronic controls and biotechnological tools that are every bit as revolutionary as were dedicated machines and electric motors 100 years ago. Industrial engineers' varied attempts to grapple with these changes have been hampered by the limited images of work and the workplace.

For example, ergonomics has changed considerably over the last several decades. Whereas in the 1950s most human factors research concerned "knobs and dials," today many ergonomists study the perceptual and cognitive loads that complex information systems create for white-collar, professional and military occupations. However, despite this change in focus, ergonomics' underlying model remains the relationship between a single individual and his or her machine. The model of the individual user has enabled ergonomists to champion many important modifications in design that have been crucial to the development of safer airplane cockpits, better computers and less taxing work spaces. However, focusing on human-machine interfaces and on the problems that can be studied in the lab has left ergonomists with little to say about how technologies fit into and modify work processes outside of the highly controlled and easily simulated environments. Focusing on the user as a biophysical perceiver has also directed attention away from the interactions among individuals and their joint use of technology. Yet, the studies by sociologists, anthropologists and computer scientists indicate that taking social dynamics into account is essential for successfully designing and deploying information technologies.

This paper begins by tracking the decline of work studies in industrial engineering over the past century. It explores the question of why industrial engineering lost its concern for work and, ultimately, its ability to speak to the kinds of social and economic changes that it was created to address. Our reading of historical documents and our analysis of data collected from nine industrial engineering departments reveal that the changes in industrial engineering were tied to social trends, to the shifts in the sources of funding, and to the field's concern with its own status. We follow the analysis of how and why industrial engineering distanced itself from work with a discussion of how work has changed in the past 50 years to show that industrial engineering is now ill-positioned to address the issues of modern work system design. We explain why the time has come for the field to rekindle its interest in the nature of work and the particulars of the workplace and suggest several paths for proceeding in this direction.

24.2 Methods

Because the question of what happened to the study of work in industrial engineering is a matter of history, its answer requires historical methods. Accordingly, we base our analysis on documents, on the oral histories that we collected from long-tenured Industrial Engineering (IE) faculty and on data on course offerings from IE departments. Although course bulletins do not document the research that IE faculty may have actually conducted, they do provide a credible record of topics and approaches that the field saw as legitimate during particular historical eras. Moreover, though faculty may have done research on the topics that had not yet entered the curriculum, it is reasonable to assume that when topics disappeared from the curriculum, faculty had ceased researching them.

We chose to study nine research-oriented IE departments whose foundings span the first and second halves of the 20th century. The four departments founded prior to World War II were Pennsylvania State University (1909), Columbia University (1921), University of Michigan (1924), and Ohio State University (1925). (These dates represent the first year that each department listed courses in its school's catalogue. In some instances, founding precedes listing by a year or two.) Those founded after the war were University of Southern California (1945), Georgia Institute of Technology (1946), Stanford University (1950), University of California, Berkeley (1955) and Purdue University (1956). This group includes the first IE department ever established (Penn State), the founder of the Institute of Industrial Engineers (Ohio State) and the founder of IIE Transactions (Georgia Tech).

The first step in developing our database on IE courses was to visit each of the nine campuses to photocopy the relevant sections of yearly course catalogues. These photocopies contained course titles and descriptions for every undergraduate and the graduate course offered by each department from its founding to the present day: a total of 26,000 courses spanning 92 years. We did so because our concern is not with the courses deemed necessary for a complete education of an industrial engineer (One might as easily include calculus and physics), but rather with the courses whose inclusion in the curricula implies their centrality to the department's image and focus. The second step in preparing our analysis was to develop a set of codes for categorizing the subject matter of these courses. Following the accepted practices for qualitative data analysis, we developed an initial set of codes for the courses offered by one IE department and wrote the short descriptions defining each code. We then employed a research assistant, who was unfamiliar with the study's purpose, to code a second department's courses using the categories and descriptions that we developed. This procedure allowed us to assess the adequacy of our codes and to refine them without incurring the risk of the informed bias. All three researchers discussed and resolved the differences in interpretation. The assistant then used the refined set of categories to code the remaining departments' courses.

Fourteen content categories emerged from this process: ① shop practices and factory methods; ② production systems; ③ motion and time studies and work measurement; ④ ergonomics; ⑤ job design; ⑥ organizations and management; ⑦ computers and information systems; ⑧ accounting, finance and engineering economics; ⑨ quality control; ⑩ optimization; ⑪ simulation and stochastic processes; ⑫ decision and risk analysis; ⑬ probability and statistics; and ⑭ miscellaneous courses (e.g., directed research, independent study, senior design projects and other courses with no specified content). On the basis of our coding we built an electronic database consisting of the tables that recorded the annual number of the courses taught by each department in each of these 14 areas.

We collected oral histories from senior faculty in eight of the nine departments. We identified the faculty from department web sites and by asking younger faculty to refer us to the colleagues whom they believed would be best positioned to speak on the history of work studies in their department. The interviews were structured around a small number of open-ended questions designed to elicit the informant's memories of events and attitudes that shaped the fate of work studies in his department.

We began the interviews by defining work studies for informants. We used the following definition: "Research and teaching that takes as its primary focus how humans work in organizations. We include in this term the following areas: motion and time studies, human factors, job design, ergonomics, and efficiency studies." The following were among the questions that we subsequently asked: how has the area of work studies developed over time at your school? What role did computerization and information play in the history of work studies? What were the research questions of interest among the work studies faculty and how or why did they change over time? We used the informants' responses to help us interpret trends in the course data.

24.3 The history of work studies in IE

Work studies encompass four of our coding categories: ① shop practices and factory methods; ② motion and time studies and work measurement; ③ ergonomics; and ④ job design. The history of work studies in IE can be divided into two periods roughly separated by World War II. The first period, beginning shortly after the turn of the century, was defined by an almost exclusive focus on actual shop practices. The post-war period saw a rise in the founding of IE departments, a decline of shopfloor studies, and the emergence of ergonomics and job design. Work studies dominated the curricula of IE departments in the first period, but in the second, it competed with and was quickly overshadowed by a move to more abstract mathematical and quantitative analyses.

24.3.1 The pre-war era

(1) The Birth of IE. In the 1880s engineers became increasingly interested in organizing the chaos of factory systems. The mechanical engineers in that era were responsible for maintaining physical plant, overseeing production processes and designing equipment. Because these engineers were enmeshed in the everyday operation of the factory, some began to experiment with what we would today call organization design. During the last two decades of the 19th century, mechanical engineers wrote a number of books and papers outlining schemes for improving management's coordination and control. Known as "systematic management," these schemes were of three types: ① cost accounting systems; ② production control systems; and ③ wage payment plans. In 1886 Henry Towne, president of the American Society of Mechanical Engineers, argued that because no management associations existed, the ASME should fill such a role. Towne's call was not heeded despite systematic management's growing influence in the engineering literature.

Finding little support within their own discipline, the mechanical engineers with managerial interests formed the first IE departments. They brought with them a craftoriented expertise in machine design, plant layout, tooling and shop processes such as grinding, milling, polishing and welding. The earliest courses reflected this blend of interests. For example, when Penn State founded the first IE department in 1909, it offered the courses entitled "Shop Methods," "Pattern Shop and Foundry Tools and Methods," "Manufacturing Accounts," "Shop Economics," "Factory Planning," "Shop Systems," "Accounting and Cost Keeping," and "Shop Time Study." To the degree that economics, accounting and management were taught, they were integrated with the study of physical processes, as the following description of "Shop Economics" shows:

"Economic theory of factory location and of general arrangement of buildings and departments. Equipment of various shop departments and economical arrangements and operation of same. Power, light, heat, ventilation, sanitation, and transportation arrangements. General organization and management. Departments and departmental reports. Cost, time-study, labor-efficiency, wage-systems, and welfare methods." (Pennsylvania State College Bulletin, 1909–1910, p. 169)

Between 1910 and 1912 a series of events transformed the systematic management movement almost overnight from the preoccupation of a handful of mechanical engineers into what became the first American business fad. In 1910, the Eastern Railroad requested a rate increase from the Interstate Commerce Commission (ICC). On behalf of the industrialists who felt that rates were already too high, Louis Brandeis argued before the ICC that had the railroad been managed more efficiently, it could have met its costs without raising prices. The testimonies that Brandeis solicited from Frederick Taylor and other efficiency experts became the centerpiece of the hearings and the term "scientific management" was coined during the hearings. Taylor used the Eastern Railroad rate case to popularize his views and, shortly thereafter, wrote his most famous tract, "The Principles of Scientific Management." Harrington Emerson, a self-proclaimed spokesman for the movement, published two even more popular books lauding the benefits of efficiency. These and other developments occasioned a public mania, known among historians as the "efficiency craze."

Scientific management's ideas and rhetoric immediately filtered into the curricula at Penn State. In 1912 Penn State began a course entitled "Principles of Industrial Engineering." The original description read: "The fundamental considerations as to materials, machines, and management which enter into the work of the Industrial Engineer." One year later, the description was amended to reflect Taylor's influence: *"The field and methods of the science of management and* the fundamental considerations as to men, materials, machines, methods, *and organization* which enter into the work of the *'efficiency'* or industrial engineer" (italics added). The text was Frank Gilbreth's "Primer of Scientific Management" whose preface was written by Brandeis. In the same year Penn State began a course entitled, "Scientific Management" for which the texts were Taylor's "Shop Management" and Frederic Parkhurst's "Applied Methods of Scientific Management."

(2) Scientific Management's Limited Role. Many people associate early IE with the study of work because they tie the field to Taylorism. But, in fact, scientific management had limited influence on IE's curricula beyond Penn State. The other departments in our sample founded in the pre-war era showed almost no interest in scientific management aside from motion and time studies. Ohio State's curriculum was nearly devoid of scientific management's rhetoric. Although Ohio State offered courses in "Work Analysis" and "Standardization and Simplification," the first course focused on machine speeds and

fabrication and the second made no mention of efficiency, motion or time. Instead, "Standardization and Simplification" emphasized tools and equipment and defined standards as the universal systems of measurement. The course description read:

"The importance of standards of design, of processing, of performance, of tools and of equipment. The work of the national engineering societies, government bureaus, and progressive plants in standardization and simplification." (Ohio State University Bulletin, 1926–1927, p. 97)

Ohio State did not launch a course in "Time and Motion Study" until 1935. The University of Michigan followed a similar pattern. In 1924 it began a course entitled "Standardization of Labor," whose description read, "The course treats on [sic] the employment of labor, wage payment in relation to standardized conditions and the position of labor in manufacture." Conspicuously absent were references to efficiency, motion or time. Moreover, the course was dropped in 1928 leaving behind only courses in shop practice.

At Columbia the story was more complex. Although founded and chaired for 30 years by Walter Rautenstrauch, a self-proclaimed Taylorite, the department offered no courses that reflected Taylor's rhetoric. Four of the six courses that Columbia offered in 1921 had "manufacturing" in their title. One was an internship, one was about production planning and two covered shop practices. The description of "Manufacturing Processes" left no doubt about its shopfloor orientation:

"Analysis of the operations performed in the cutting, sawing, stamping, milling, grinding, forging, moulding, and otherwise forming of metal products. Analysis of the characteristics of machines commonly employed in metal working plants."

The other two courses revolved around finance and accounting. For example, "Specifications of Productive Methods" was an early course in engineering economics despite its title. The course was "intended to develop the methods of analysis by which the machinery and equipment are selected for manufacturing a selected commodity at a given yearly rate as well as the preparation of a financial budget to cover its operations." Compared with the similar courses at other schools, Columbia's language was unique: It couched shopfloor issues in the terminology of finance and economics. What it did not do was employ the rhetoric of scientific management. In fact, Columbia joined the Department of Sociology in teaching a course on "Contemporary Social Problems" before it launched its first course in motion and time studies in 1939.

The question that begs answering is why scientific management had so little influence on IE departments other than Penn State. The easy answer is that Taylor was personally involved in Penn State's development. In 1907 Taylor recommended Hugo Diemer for the chair of Penn State's mechanical engineering department. Diemer had taught the first IE course in the nation at University of Kansas and founded Penn State's IE department a year after his arrival. Nevertheless, because Taylor's ideas were widely known, one would think that his influence would have extended beyond Penn State. To explain why it did not, we need to situate the founding of IE departments with respect to the intellectual history of the day.

By the end of World War II, enthusiasm for efficiency had cooled. Industry had resisted the majority of Taylor's ideas with the exception of motion and time study. Industrialists saw Taylor's notion that engineers were the proper designers of organizations as an attack on ownership's prerogatives. Meanwhile, the attempts to install motion and time studies had precipitated a number of labor strikes that attracted national attention, and several widely publicized studies had discredited Taylor's notions of systemic change. Scientific management's inability to substantially reduce waste and lower costs, doubt about its ability to uncover the laws of production, as well as its more obvious failure to bring about an industrial utopia, led many advocates to modify their stance. Even before World War I, a number of Taylor's devotees, including Lillian Gilbreth and Henry Gantt, had begun to admit that scientific management was no panacea for industry's ills.

This was the social and intellectual climate into which most early IE departments were born. One must remember that only four IE departments were founded before 1920. Aside from Penn State and Columbia, which we have discussed, departments existed at New York University and University of Kansas. The latter had disbanded by the late 1930s. In short, scientific management was on the wane before most IE departments began. In general, motion and time studies and methods analysis were the only parts of scientific management that IE departments adopted, largely because they were popular in industry and because employers expected graduates to understand their use.

(3) The Reign of the Shop. Notwithstanding scientific management's minimal influence, pre-war IE is rightfully regarded as a field centered on the study of work, especially the grounded study of work practices. Shop courses taught actual techniques for converting raw materials into products: forging, welding, cutting, stamping, sawing, milling, grinding, polishing, pulverizing, pattern making, jig making and so on. To study such processes was to study work. Figure 24-1 shows that the situated study of shop work continuously overshadowed scientific management's more analytic approach to work systems throughout the last century: Even today shop courses still outnumber courses on motion, time, work measurement and other topics associated with scientific management. [Figure 24-1 displays the percentages of the total number of the courses taught in all departments (rather than an average of departmental percentages) to avoid single departments skewing the data. The same is true for Figures 24-4, 24-6, and 24-7].

Figure 24-1 also leaves no doubt that work studies defined IE as a discipline in the pre-war era. Until 1932 work studies courses accounted for more than 50% of the curricula of the departments in our sample. Afterward, they hovered around 40% until the end of World War II. For the evidence that the industrial engineers of the day saw themselves primarily as the students of shop work, one needed to look no further than the names of departments. From

1925 to 1935 University of Michigan called its IE department the Department of Shop Practice. In 1934 the name changed to Metal Processing. It was not until 1952 that Michigan introduced "industrial engineering" into the department's title. Like-wise Ohio State's program was initially called "Shopwork." Today, Ohio State's Department of Industrial, Welding and Systems Engineering still acknowledges its shopfloor roots.

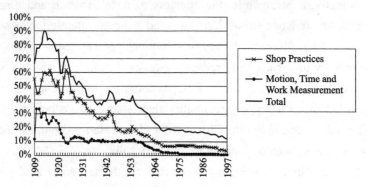

Figure 24-1 Percent of IE courses on shop practices and on motion, time and work measurement

Although work studies and a shop culture clearly characterized IE in the pre-war years, Figure 24-1 shows that shop courses steadily declined over the century as a percentage of the total courses taught and that the decline began before World War II. Figure 24-2 sheds light on what happened. As Figure 24-2 shows, shop courses accounted for almost all IE courses until 1922. After that, the number of other courses exploded. Meanwhile, the number of shop courses remained roughly the same.

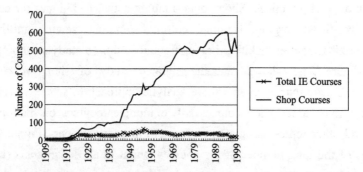

Figure 24-2 Number of IE and shop courses taught annually

24.3.2 The post-war era

(1) The Changing Face of IE. Stinchcombe argued that the organizations born in different eras exhibited different organizational structures. This was certainly true for IE departments. Figure 24-3 plots the average number of shop courses taught since 1909 in the departments founded before and after World War II. The graph shows that the departments founded after

the war taught, and continue to teach, far fewer courses on shop work. Purdue and Berkeley initially taught a number of shop courses and accounted for the post-war peaks in 1956 and 1963 respectively. Berkeley eliminated these courses from its curriculum in 1966. One year after its founding Purdue moved all of its shop courses to a program intended primarily for supervisors and foremen. Interestingly enough, Columbia had done the same in 1947. In fact, Columbia and Michigan had eliminated almost all shop courses by the 1970s, leaving Penn State and Ohio State as the only schools in our sample that remain significantly invested in teaching shopfloor knowledge.

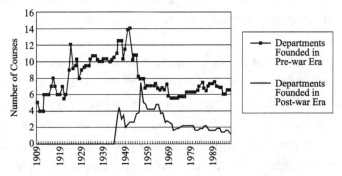

Figure 24-3 **Average number of shop courses taught by the departments founded before and after world War II**

Although the interest in shop practices declined after the war, the interest in work did not disappear. Instead, the nature of the interest changed and evolved along two paths. The first path was job design and the second was ergonomics. As Figure 24-4 indicates, job design began earlier and peaked soon thereafter, whereas ergonomics grew until 1975 when it began to plateau. The impetus behind IE's interest in job design lay in the rise of the human relations movement and attempts to institutionalize collective bargaining following the war. Ergonomics grew out of the military's wartime discovery that well-designed man-machine interfaces were crucial to a person's ability to operate complex technologies.

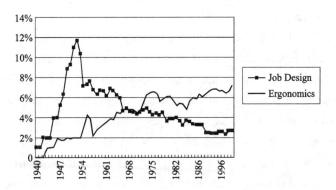

Figure 24-4 **Percent of IE courses on job design and ergonomics**

(2) Job Design. Although the human relations movement began in the late 1920s and 1930s with the Hawthorne studies, it did not gain widespread support until after World War II, when the corporate experimentation with techniques for enhancing the loyalty, motivation and satisfaction blossomed almost overnight. Researchers and managers alike were convinced that improving morale and treating workers more fairly could enhance productivity. Shopfloor interventions included innovative compensation systems, schemes for participatory decision-making and job enrichment. The philosophy of the human relations movement informed state and federal policies whose intent was to reduce the hostility between labor and management and, hence, the odds of strikes. In the late 1940s a number of states founded the schools of industrial and labor relations that were charged with institutionalizing the system of collective bargaining.

The tone of the human relations era quickly pervaded IE departments. Not only did industrial engineers become interested in designing work systems that enhanced morale and participation, but also they began to teach the courses on industrial and labor relations. Louis Davis, who taught at Berkeley in the 1950s, became a well-known advocate of job design. For a period of time, IE departments seemed to believe that their students needed to understand the role of labor in industry and the mechanics of collective bargaining. For example, Purdue's department was founded in 1955, just as the human relations movement was burgeoning. Tellingly, its new curriculum contained a course on "Industrial Relations" as well as a course on "Labor Relations." Although these courses were dropped a year later, the topics were taught in a number of other courses until 1963. Georgia Tech taught graduate courses in "Collective Bargaining" and "Job Evaluation." Among the schools in our sample, none was more heavily influenced by human relations than Columbia. In 1952 alone, it offered 11 courses in this area, including "Industrial Personnel and Labor Relations," "Industrial Relations for Engineers," "Job Evaluation," "Selection and Training," "Personnel Factors in the Design of Productive Operations," and "Personnel Techniques." Although the courses in job design accounted for just over 10% of IE courses in the early 1950s (See Figure 24-4.), by the mid 1960s industrial engineers' interest in human relations waned and the number of courses steadily declined.

(3) Ergonomics. More in tune with IE's identity was its embracing of ergonomics. At least philosophically, ergonomics was consistent with IE's interest in shop methods and motion. Like the students of motion and time, ergonomists approached work as a biophysical process and focused on how humans interacted with machines. But whereas Taylorites attempted to change the worker's behavior, ergonomists redesigned tools and technologies. Moreover, ergonomics departed from early IE's worship of efficiency by championing effective use and human safety. Finally, whereas scientific management was field-based, ergonomics was situated in laboratories and often required sophisticated instruments.

In general, industrial engineers perceived ergonomics to be more "scientific" than scientific management. The informants at all schools told us that during the 1960s IE became increasingly concerned with its status as a technical discipline. "The issue," explained a USC professor, "was what constituted good engineering studies. How could IE be a 'basic' engineering field?" The emphasis was on becoming "academically respectable." Despite its name, scientific management could not provide the technical legitimacy that industrial engineers sought:

"Taylor emphasized science because that was a big movement in those days. But what he labeled "science" is not what we would consider science. His studies were, at best, crude. What he was doing was a more systematic job at collecting data. Gilbreth's therbligs were an attempt to use the science model. It was great work in improving efficiency, but it certainly wasn't "scientific" as we use the term today. Time and motion became less important because there wasn't going to be much scientific progress in what was a subjective field." (USC professor)

A professor at Purdue added, "People perceived that work methods and measurement didn't have a scientific base and didn't provide the prestige that academics were looking for." A Penn State professor concurred:

"Work measurement used field studies and was not mathematically sophisticated. In traditional work measurement they didn't get into modeling. They used numbers, but this is not the same thing as building models or trying to understand human behavior."

Ergonomics also brought industrial engineers new opportunities for funding. By the 1950s neither industry nor government was interested in the research on motion, time or work methods, but both were anxious to fund the research on human-machine interfaces and operator safety. The availability of funding facilitated the shift away from motion and time studies. A professor at Michigan explained, "We were picking up research grants in the area of ergonomics and we required faculty. The whole idea of safety, ergonomics, was heavily supported by the government. They didn't care about productivity. They cared about how long it took to learn things." Additionally, unlike motion and time studies, ergonomics garnered moral, and even financial, support from unions because it promised to make jobs safer and easier.

The shift to ergonomics changed the flavor of work studies in IE. Although job design bolstered IE's pre-war interest in studying work *in situ*, ergonomics encouraged industrial engineers to leave the field for the laboratory. As a result, work studies became increasingly distant from the actual work that people perform. Ergonomics also had the side effect of defining work primarily as the individual's relationship with tools and machines. Gone from the picture were the notion of a work system and an appreciation for the fact that work is embedded in a social context marked by dependencies and interactions.

Although the shift to ergonomics partially represented a changing epistemological paradigm, the move also reflected pragmatic concerns. As "publish or perish" became the watchword in

American universities, industrial engineers could less easily afford fieldwork. In comparison with laboratory work, fieldwork yielded far fewer publications and at a slower pace. A professor at Purdue explained the problem:

"Twenty years ago I had a large NSF grant: A million dollars. We monitored 60 workers eight hours a day. In the end, we got only two publications. I could do it because I was a full professor. If you do fieldwork, you can't produce the type of things you need to do to get promoted. It just doesn't seem to work. I had another one, an NIOSH study. I got one publication!"

Although all IE departments in our sample have, at one time or another, offered the courses in job design and ergonomics, work studies never again dominated IE curricula as it did before World War II. Stanford and Berkeley eventually dropped ergonomics, albeit for different reasons. In Stanford's case, the cost of running an ergonomics program was simply too high for it to compete with other departments. When Stanford lost its last professor of ergonomics in the late 1970s the faculty

"... had a long discussion about what to do. Should we replace [him] with someone who could do ergonomics and time and motion? I was convinced that we should not, but that we should hire an organizations person because other departments had ergonomics covered. Michigan, Purdue, and Virginia Tech would have about five people working in that area. They had labs. We didn't have a lab and we saw no hope of getting one." (Stanford professor)

At Berkeley the move from ergonomics led to an emphasis on robotics. A Berkeley professor explained, "We had the discussions of critical mass. We didn't think we'd be able to support [ergonomics] in a small department. We chose robotics because manual labor is a steadily decreasing proportion of GNP. Robotics brings ties to EE's and ME's. This is good for us."

Ergonomics' incomplete diffusion partially accounts for the diminished role of work studies in IE after the war, but the larger reason for its decline lay in a fundamental change of the field's intellectual orientation. As Figure 24-5 shows, the percentage of work studies courses plateaued between 1936 and 1956. After this period an explosion of courses in other areas quickly dwarfed work studies of all kinds. Figure 24-6 reveals that this explosion occurred primarily because of a geometric increase in the number of courses relying on some form of mathematical analysis. Economics, finance and accounting, which had long been the quantitative staple of IE's curricula, actually declined during this period as did the courses on organization and management. The field of computers and information systems entered IE after the war, but has never accounted for more than 5% of IE's total offerings. Figure 24-7 clearly shows that the courses in optimization, production, simulation and stochastic processes drove the quantification of IE. As with ergonomics, the growth in these areas was tied to the events of World War II.

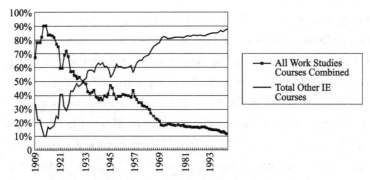

Figure 24-5 The relative balance of work and non-work courses in IE curricula

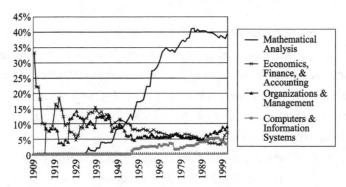

Figure 24-6 Other IE domains as a percentage of total courses

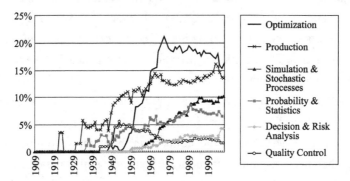

Figure 24-7 Mathematical analysis courses as a percentage of total IE course by type

During the war, the British and American military employed the teams of mathematicians, physicists, and statisticians to devise methods for solving logistical problems. Working with early computers, these "operations research teams" were so successful that after the war each of the services established its own operations research unit. Operations research quickly spread from the military to industry in the early 1950s. Hertz estimated that by 1954 at least 25 firms had established formal operations research groups and that as many as 300 analysts worked in industry. By the mid-1960s queuing theory, decision analysis, network analysis, simulation techniques, and theories of linear and dynamic programming were sufficiently well developed to be used by large corporations, and a number of universities had already established the programs leading to doctoral degrees in operations research.

IE embraced mathematically-oriented forms of analysis for much the same reasons that it turned to ergonomics. First, funding for optimization, production, decision analysis and similar fields became plentiful after the war. Not only were industry and the military willing to invest large amounts of money in the development of mathematical models and other tools for decision-making, but the National Science Foundation also made mathematical analysis a target of growth in the 1960s and 1970s. Second, like ergonomics, mathematical analysis played to the industrial engineers' desire for scientific legitimacy. In fact, having a vibrant operations research program quickly came to define what it meant to be a cutting edge department of IE:

"When Lehrer came back as director of school of IE (after 1965), he put in a program that came out of operations research. He didn't bring in more people so much as people changed their area of research. More math. More operations research. Probability theory. Game theory. The new things that were coming out then. This was the trend in the country. To be a progressive school you had to do this. Work studies was important, but never dominant (in the post war era.)" (Georgia Tech professor)

What Lehrer took to be a progressive department was explicitly defined in 1967 by the influential "Roy Report," an examination of IE curricula commissioned by the American Society for Engineering Education and the National Science Foundation. The committee consisted of Lehrer and the representatives of five other major universities (Cornell, Stanford, Purdue, Oklahoma State, and Johns Hopkins). The report outlined an ideal curriculum matched to "current trends in education and professional practice." The committee strongly recommended that industrial engineers be exposed to the social sciences. Moreover, they advised IE departments to "develop special programs, focused more specifically upon behavior at the technological-sociological interface." But as we have seen, few departments heeded the call. What IE departments did notice was the committee's strong advocacy for mathematics, probability, statistics, numerical analysis and operations research. The committee also noted that motion and time study, wage incentives, job evaluation, and tool design were among the topics that had long epitomized IE, but argued that they no longer defined the field:

"These skills no longer comprise... the frontiers of Industrial Engineering knowledge... Most work of this kind today is... in the hands of technicians, and the technical institutes seem best fitted to impart instruction in these important areas... We believe knowledge of these areas to be important to the professional Industrial Engineers of tomorrow (but that it) can be acquired by minimal exposure to courses with much greater emphasis upon engagement with unstructured, open-end design problems... (These techniques) deserve a place in Industrial Engineering but they no longer are Industrial Engineering.

In short, the Roy Report marginalized all forms of work studies in favor of quantitative methods. The committee suggested that it was acceptable for instruction in human factors and ergonomics to be outsourced to psychologists. They relegated job design and motion and time studies to the background of design courses and they deemed shop courses to be no longer "appropriate in the programs directed toward the education of professionals."

Together, the post-war trends that we have been discussing led to the current state of affairs in IE. Although most IE departments still offer some work studies courses, these courses represent a small percentage of every department's curriculum. Moreover, as we saw in Figure 24-4, ergonomics today comprises most of IE's work studies curricula. Ergonomics' contributions have been critical to improve the design of technologies and workspaces, and ergonomists have bettered the lives of large numbers of workers. Yet, of all the approaches to work studies that we have discussed, ergonomics is the most distant from work itself. This distancing is especially problematic because work has changed considerably over the last 50 years.

24.4 The changing nature of work

Although IE's retreat from the study of work and work systems undoubtedly helped the field build and sustain legitimacy in schools of engineering, what was a reasonable strategy in the 1960s and 1970s has today become an Achilles' heel. As Table 24-1 shows, over the last half-century changes in technology and the nature of the economy have slowly transformed the work that people do. Traditional factory jobs, as they were understood at mid-century, began to decline in the 1950s, just as industrial engineers began to jettison the field-based studies of work. Operatives and laborers fell from 26% of the workforce in 1950 to 13% in 1998. Moreover, many remaining production jobs have become more analytic and abstract as new technologies have transformed factory control systems. During the same period, professional and technical jobs expanded dramatically and now account for the largest percentage of all employed Americans. Their share of the labor force increased from 8% in 1950 to 18% in 1998. Since 1950 service jobs have increased by 5%, sales workers by 4% and managerial workers by 2%. As a result of these changes, our concepts for thinking about work are out of date: Our systems for classifying occupations are obsolete; our cultural dichotomies for distinguishing types of work are antiquated and our occupational archetypes are outdated.

Table 24-1 Occupational categories as a percentage of the labor force: 1900–1991

Category	Percentage in											Net change /%
	1900	1910	1920	1930	1940	1950	1960	1970	1980	1988	1998	
Farmworkers	38	31	27	21	17	12	6	3	3	4	3	−35
Professional/technical	4	5	5	7	8	8	10	14	15	16	18	14
Craft and kindred	11	12	13	13	12	14	14	14	12	11	11	0

(Continued)

Category	Percentage in											Net change /%
	1900	1910	1920	1930	1940	1950	1960	1970	1980	1988	1998	
Operatives/laborers	25	27	27	27	28	26	24	23	18	14	13	−12
Clerical and kindred	3	5	8	9	10	12	15	18	17	19	17	14
Service	9	10	8	10	12	11	12	13	13	16	16	7
Managerial/administrative	6	7	7	7	7	9	8	8	10	10	11	5
Sales workers	5	5	5	6	7	7	7	7	11	10	11	6

Note: Percentage employment by occupational category from 1900 to 1970 was calculated from employment data presented in Anon (1976, p.139). Data for 1980 were taken from Klein (1984) and data for 1988 and 1998 are taken from Braddock (1999).

24.4.1 Occupational classifications

Occupational sociologists generally agree that the detailed categories by which the US government classifies jobs are outdated (Attewell, 1990). For instance, since 1939 the Department of Labor has only incrementally revised The Dictionary of Occupational Titles (DOT), which still presents the best source of data on the content of jobs in the US economy. As a result, analysts can make much finer distinctions among blue-collar work than among managerial, clerical, service, sales, professional or technical work. For example, even though software development is divided into a large number of specialties, we have but one word for describing such work, computer programming. Cain and Treiman (1981) report that 76% of the listings in the most recent edition of the DOT (Anon, 1977) cover blue-collar jobs. Yet, only 26% of all employed Americans are blue-collar workers (a decline of 14% since 1940). Seventy-two percent are employed in some form of white-collar or service work (an increase of 28% since 1940). Thus, our most systematic image of what work is like is based on the categories developed for an economy that existed somewhere between a quarter and a half a century ago.

24.4.2 Cultural dichotomies

Our everyday concepts for talking about work are also the relics of the industrial revolution. Dichotomies such as blue-collar and white-collar, mental and manual, and exempt and non-exempt are the legacy of a world in which one's standing rested, in large measure, on whether one's hands were clean or dirty at the end of the day. Although these distinctions are still important, their utility wanes with each passing year. For example, low-skilled service jobs may be just as unappealing and as routine as factory work, but they cannot be easily classified as blue-collar or even manual in the traditional sense of the term. The distinction between managers and workers also less adequately signals the nature of a person's work and status than it once did. Workers today are as likely to be engineers or programmers as they are machinists; managers and administrators are as likely to have no employees as they are hundreds. These changes fundamentally undermine the traditional notion that productivity gains are to be made primarily on the shopfloor. In fact, they challenge the traditional notions of productivity altogether. For example, industrial engineers readily recognize that the length of the product development cycle directly affects market share. Yet, we know almost nothing about the actual work processes of product developers. As a result we are restricted to the use of metrics such as "on time and under budget" to evaluate a complex process of innovation and creativity.

24.5 Bringing work back into IE

The historical and interview data provide a springboard for critiquing the current situation in IE and for proposing directions for reintegrating the study of work into the field. We argue that the study of work would benefit from the attention of industrial engineers and that the discipline, in turn, could gain by studying work. We conclude with ideas for how industrial engineers could equip themselves to be the students of work in a post-industrial economy.

24.5.1 Why does the study of work need industrial engineers?

At present, most research on work is conducted by social scientists: typically, the students of industrial relations, sociologists of work, industrial psychologists and a handful of renegade anthropologists. In comparison with engineers, the researchers in these disciplines have greater expertise in the social dynamics of work ranging from power and politics to group behavior as well as the assessment of skills and social relationships. However, because most social scientists are not technically trained, they are less likely than engineers to understand the material properties of technologies and the complexities of modern production processes and to incorporate them into their analyses. It is here that industrial engineers can make an important contribution. Industrial engineers are trained in the physical sciences, computer science and engineering disciplines such as electrical engineering. They are also trained in the formalized problem solving and model building, which teaches them, among other things, how to model system dynamics and how to break down system complexities via simplifying the assumptions and modularization of system components. As a result, industrial engineers are well positioned to develop the grounded assessments of the technological aspects of work practices.

24.5.2 What could industrial engineers gain from studying work?

Because industrial engineers gradually distanced themselves from the study of work just as work dramatically changed, they now routinely find themselves addressing the problems of the post-industrial workplace with outdated theories and methods. For example, cellular and lean manufacturing initiatives often espouse the use of teams among production operators. Yet, our models of work teams derive primarily from the sociotechnical systems research conducted in coal mines in the 1950s, where autonomous teams made use of miners' deeply engrained craft knowledge as new technologies were introduced. Today, many production systems are so complex that relevant knowledge has become differentiated and distributed across the organization. Under these conditions, advocating worker autonomy may cause unanticipated problems while not necessarily achieving productivity gains, as Bailey (1998) discovered among team programs in semiconductor manufacturing. She found that as production operators took on preventative maintenance and gained greater autonomy, they threatened the job security of equipment technicians. Engineers also became concerned when teams' statistical process control activities were at odds with their own improvement goals. Furthermore, in asserting their independence, teams also sometimes interfered with kanban systems, circumvented electronic monitoring and attempted to control lot processing. As this example illustrates, designers of modern work systems cannot apply generic work solutions, but rather must work from an intimate knowledge of specific practices, processes, technologies and workplace dynamics.

Thus, the field needs new theories and methods tailored to a highly educated workforce and to a variety of sophisticated workplaces. Engineers are unlikely to develop these tools unless they return to study work *in situ*. By doing so, industrial engineers should be able to speak more knowledgably about work systems whose products are knowledge and information as well as tangible goods, allowing the field to reclaim its legacy as the discipline that specializes in the design of work systems.

The spillover from studying work could also have a broad revitalizing effect within IE as a whole. It is worth remembering that the shopfloor culture that pervaded IE at midcentury provided operations researchers with an empirical understanding of work and production processes, which, in turn, served as a contextual background that informed their models. Operations researchers have noted that, to its detriment, the field subsequently distanced itself from real-world applications. Re-emphasizing the close knowledge of work practices and processes could enhance the study of production systems, information systems, decisions, risk and other topics in IE in at least two ways.

First, the knowledge of work practices can help researchers better specify their models. Consider, for example, the analysis of risk in complex technological systems. Although every craftsman knows that techniques affect quality, few risk analysts take work practices into account when making the probabilistic estimates of failure. The value of doing so is nicely illustrated by Elisabeth Pate-Cornell's work on the risk of heat shielding tiles separated from space shuttles when they reenter the atmosphere. Unable to devise a satisfactory model on the basis of historical data and expert opinion, Pate-Cornell decided to observe the technicians who install the tiles at the Kennedy Space Flight Center. During her field visit, she discovered a technician who admitted to spitting in the glue to quicken the curing process as he installed tiles. The technician explained that the technique had been devised to help comply with management's relentless pressure for efficiency. Although the practice saved time, it had the unfortunate side effect of altering the glue's tensile strength. Taking spit and other work factors into account (e.g., that there was no notion of priority for applying and inspecting tiles in the most critical areas), Pate-Cornell's new models improved NASA's management of the orbiters' heat shield.

Second, with the knowledge of work practices, industrial engineers could blend qualitative and quantitative approaches to yield exciting new approaches and insights. The work of Nelson Repenning at MIT is exemplary in this regard. Repenning routinely draws on fieldwork to build the mathematical models that express the social dynamics of workplace systems. Typically, these models sharpen the findings of field research, point to the underlying processes whose complexities are difficult to observe, and extend theory in the directions that would otherwise prove difficult. For example, Rudolph and Repenning (2002) use prior studies of the Tenerife air disaster and the U.S.S. Vincennes incident to build a model that shows how routine interruptions can build to the point where a self-regulating resilient system is transformed into a fragile, self-escalating one. Repenning (2001) draws on his fieldwork in the R & D division of a major manufacturer to build a model that shows how "fire-fighting" becomes a self-reinforcing phenomenon, especially in a multi-project environment. This paper calls into question the sufficiency of many current methods of resource and product portfolio planning.

Delving into the material aspects of technology and work may also forge stronger links between IE and other engineering disciplines. The knowledge of work and work practices is becoming increasingly important to mechanical engineers, computers scientists and others who design products and processes for users. Because designers generally know little about work systems, industrial engineers could well serve as content experts for the design process. Additionally, one cannot study complex technologies and production processes without learning something about the engineering and science on which they are based. As a result, the industrial engineers who study work are likely to become more knowledgeable about the substantive domains of their engineering colleagues. Such knowledge should position them to engage in multi-disciplinary discourse and research. If industrial engineers could prove their ability to translate between work practices and the design of complex technologies, their credibility with the members of other engineering disciplines can only grow.

24.5.3 What does IE have to do to return to work?

To recover the study of work, industrial engineers will need to make a number of changes. First and foremost, they will need to return to the field. This, in turn, will require them to recognize that empiricism is a scientific activity. As we have seen, IE turned to mathematical analyses and laboratory studies to assert its claim to scientific rigor. Ironically, however, no matter how important mathematics may be to scientific practice, by itself it is insufficient: All sciences are rooted in empirical observation. In fact, in advanced sciences empiricism usually complements and supports mathematical modeling. We contend that the same is true for IE. The strongest mathematical models of systems are based on a substantive understanding of the phenomena being modeled.

To take work seriously, industrial engineers must also become more knowledgeable about social science. Doing so will enable industrial engineers to serve as better bridges between the technical and the social. Embracing the social does not mean that industrial engineers need to be social scientists. However, it does mean that social science needs to be part of the industrial engineer's toolkit, just as that toolkit currently contains skills in simulation, computer programming, probability, database design and so on.

Achieving these objectives will require IE departments to reconfigure their degree requirements to train the next generation of researchers and practitioners. A single course in organizational behavior or industrial psychology is unlikely to provide the depth of knowledge that industrial engineers will require to study work. Rather, they will need broad exposure to relevant theories and methods drawn from sociology, psychology and anthropology. The courses that cover social and political processes in organizations, social networks, social interaction and group processes, organizational sociology, social conflict, technology and society, social psychology, social structure, organization theory, organizational culture, the division of labor, power and status, interpersonal relations, cognitive psychology, social influence and persuasion, and technology and law are indicative of the kind of exposure industrial engineers should gain.

Taking work studies seriously will also require transforming the study of work as it currently appears in IE's own curriculum. As many schools have recognized, motion and time studies are less important for a knowledge-based economy. Shop courses also offer little leverage for understanding and designing most modern work systems. Even a course on human-computer interaction does not, by itself, suffice. To cover the full range of changes in the workplace, IE departments must accept the challenge of developing new courses on the topics that include knowledge work, service work, technical work, R & D management, and the relationship between technology and work across the entire occupational spectrum. The courses in human factors and information systems design should borrow significantly from research in computer-supported collaborative work, where an understanding of the social embeddedness of technologies and the inherent social relationships that shape and constrain technology use are considered crucial to effective system design. Finally, because field research will be crucial for gathering the data on work systems, departments must also offer the courses on observation, interviewing and qualitative data analysis tailored to the study of work.

To teach these courses and to further research in modern work systems, IE departments need to hire new faculty skilled in these domains. Granted, significant institutional barriers exist that may make hiring and promoting such individuals a daunting task at many engineering schools. Interest on the part of industry may prove helpful in convincing the deans and department chairs of the benefits of this direction. Such interest can be found, for example, in the growing worldwide application of new human resources practices brought to light in MIT's lean manufacturing auto industry study and in the growing corporate recognition, especially among software development firms, that distributed work teams pose unique management and organizational challenges.

In making these changes, however, IE departments must not abandon their technical roots. The changes in the nature of work over the past several decades clearly indicate that a broad education in the physical sciences and engineering is essential for designing work systems in high-technology environments. Ultimately, the educators in IE should strive to integrate an understanding of social dynamics with the substantive knowledge of engineering to produce the students who can design more effective work systems. By doing so IE may not only recover its heritage, but it should also be better positioned to assist society in adjusting to a post-industrial economy.

Notes

1. If any discipline is rightfully the child of the second industrial revolution and the changes it wrought in the nature of work, that discipline is industrial engineering.

如果说哪个学科是第二次工业革命的唯一产物且对工作的本质产生了根本变化的话，这个学科就是工业工程。

2. There is evidence, however, that work in contemporary society has now changed sufficiently to render such an assumption suspect.

然而，有事实表明，现代社会中工作的变化之快足以对这样的假设（起初认为工作变化的速度会很慢）产生怀疑。

3. Like the field's founders, who confronted the transformation associated with the rise of the modern factory, we face a shift in the nature of work occasioned by a changing technical infrastructure.

与当初面对现代化的工厂所带来的转变的工业工程领域的奠基者相似，我们（当代的工业工程从业人员）面对的是由于技术基础设施的变化所引起的工作性质的转变。

4. Towne's call was not heeded despite systematic management's growing influence in the engineering literature.

尽管系统管理在工程领域的影响正在日益增强，但 Towne 的呼吁并没有受到重视。

5. Between 1910 and 1912 a series of events transformed the systematic management movement almost overnight from the preoccupation of a handful of mechanical engineers into what became the first American business fad.

在 1910—1912 年发生的一系列事件几乎在一夜之间使得系统管理从少数机械工程师的偏好成为美国商业界的流行风。

6. The philosophy of the human relations movement informed state and federal policies whose intent was to reduce the hostility between labor and management and, hence, the odds of strikes.

人事关系运动的哲理触动了那些旨在缓解劳工与管理者之间的敌意进而减少罢工的州和联邦立法人员。

7. Although job design bolstered IE's pre-war interest in studying work *in situ*, ergonomics encouraged industrial engineers to leave the field for the laboratory.

尽管作业设计支持了战前工业工程师在工作现场对作业的研究,但工效学则促进了工业工程师将研究场所从现场到实验室的转移。

8. Engineers also became concerned when teams' statistical process control activities were at odds with their own improvement goals.

当小组的统计过程控制活动与他们自己的改进目标不一致时,工程师们也很担心。

Discussion Questions:

1. Under what circumstances is the concept of post industrial engineering proposed? What is your understanding of post IE?
2. In pre-war era, why did scientific management have limited influence on IE's curricula in America?
3. Why did work studies and shop courses steadily decline as a percentage of the total courses taught before World War II?
4. Summarize the development process of human relations, job design and ergonomics respectively after World War II.
5. How has the nature of work been changing in the past several decades?
6. Why should IE go back to work studies? What might be the possible effects and challenges?
7. How should IE's in China benefit from the ideas proposed in this article?

专业词汇汇总表
Summary of Professional Vocabularies and Expressions

A

5S	整理、整顿、清扫、清洁和素养
80-20 philosophy	80/20 哲学，80/20 原则
accident proneness	事故倾向性
accounts payable	应付账款
accounts receivable	应收账款
activity/work sampling	活动/工作抽样
activity-based costing (ABC)	基于活动的成本分析
activity-cycle diagram (ACD)	活动循环图
advanced information technologies	先进信息技术
agent-based simulation	基于主体的仿真
aggregate level simulation protocol (ALSP)	聚合级仿真协议
agile enterprise	敏捷企业
agile layout	敏捷布局
agile manufacturing	敏捷制造
algebra	代数学
algorithmic language (ALGOL)	Algol 算法语言
American standard code for information interchange (ASCII)	用于信息交换的美国标准编码
analog computer	模拟计算机
analysis methodology	分析方法
analytic solution	解析解，分析解
anthropometry	人体测量学
appraisal cost	估价成本
apprentice position	见习职位，实习岗位
artificial intelligence (AI)	人工智能
artificial sampling	人工抽样
assembly language	汇编语言
assembly line	装配线

asset management	资产管理
auditory sense	听觉
automated guided vehicle (AGV)	自动导航设备
automated storage and retrieval system (AS/RS)	自动存取系统
automated test equipment (ATE)	自动检测设备
automation	自动化
autonomation (ADW)	员工自治（有决定停线的权利）

B

backlog cost	缺货成本
batch mode	批处理模式
bayesian statistics	贝氏统计
beer distribution game	啤酒分销游戏
behavioral factor	行为参数，行为因素
benchmarking	标杆超越
bill of materials (BOM)	物料清单
biomechanics	生物力学
bootstrap sampling	自助法抽样
bound	界限
breaking of administrative barriers (BAB)	打破管理界线
breaking of physical barriers (BPB)	打破物理分隔
buffer management	缓冲器管理
bullwhip effect	长鞭效应，牛鞭效应
business planning and development	商业规划与开发
business process redesign/reengineering (BPR)	业务流程再设计/再造

C

calculus	微积分
capacity assignment	能力分配
capacity design	能力（产能）设计
capacity requirements planning (CPR)	能力需求规划
carbon sequestration	碳固存
cash flow	现金流
cell	制造单元
cellular layout	单元式布局
cellular manufacturing	单元制造
centralized design	集中式设计
centralized single business organization	集中式的单一企业组织

centralized system	集中式系统
change notice	变更通知单
civil engineer	土木工程师
closed-loop MRP system	闭环 MRP 系统
coaxial cable	同轴电缆
code of ethics	道德标准，职业准则
cognitive ability	认知能力
cognitive ergonomics	认知功效学
cognitive psychology	认知心理学
combinatorial optimization problem	组合优化问题
common random number	共同随机数
communication facility	通信设备
computer graphics	计算机图形学
computer integrated manufacturing (CIM)	计算机集成制造
computer integrated manufacturing system	计算机集成制造系统
computer network	计算机网络
computer numerical control (CNC)	计算机数控
computer science	计算机科学
computer simulation	计算机仿真
computer-aided design (CAD)	计算机辅助设计
computer-aided engineering (CAE)	计算机辅助工程
computer-aided manufacturing (CAM)	计算机辅助制造
computer-aided process planning (CAPP)	计算机辅助工艺规划
computer-aided systems engineering (CASE)	计算机辅助系统工程
computer-automated inspection (CAI)	计算机自动检测
computer-generated work standard	计算机生成的工作标准
computer-integrated manufacturing/services	计算机集成制造/服务
computing power	计算能力
conceptual model	概念模型
concurrent engineering	并行工程
confidence interval	置信区间
conflict resolution	冲突解决
congruential random number generator	迭代随机数生成器
consolidated facility	联合设施，公用设施
constraint	约束
constraint management	约束管理
continuous improvement (CI)	持续改进
continuous material flow	连续物料流

continuous process improvement	持续流程改进
continuous simulation model	连续仿真模型
continuous system	连续系统
contract manufacturing	契约制造
control and simulation language (CSL)	控制和仿真语言
control flow graph	控制流程图
controller	控制器
coordinate transformation	坐标变换
core memory	存储器
corporate quality culture	企业质量文化
correlation coefficient	相关系数
critical path method (CPM)	关键路线法
cross-functional analysis	交叉职能分析
cultural anthropologist	文化人类学家
current reality tree (CRT)	当前现实树
customer focus	以客户为中心
customer involvement	顾客参与
customer need	顾客需求
cyberspace security	信息空间安全

D

data collector	数据收集器
data mining	数据挖掘
data processing	数据处理
database facility	数据库设备
decentralized design	分布式设计
decentralized system	分散式系统
decision support system (DSS)	决策支持系统
decision theory	决策理论
defective part	次品
degree of unrelatedness	不相关度
delayed product differentiation	产品延迟差异化
Department of Defense (DoD)	美国国防部
dependent variable	非独立变量
design for assembly/manufacturability	面向装配/制造的设计
design for maintainability	面向维护的设计
design for reliability	面向可靠性的设计
design for reusability	面向可重复使用的设计

design of experiment (DOE)	实验设计
design priority	设计优先级
desktop	台式机
deterministic simulation model	确定型仿真模型
differential equation	微分方程
digital computer	数字计算机
direct labor cost	直接劳动力成本
direct numerical control (DNC)	直接数控
directed graph	有向图
discrete event model	离散事件模型
discrete event simulation	离散事件仿真
discrete event stochastic system (DESS)	离散事件随机系统
discrete optimization	离散优化
discrete simulation model	离散仿真模型
discrete system	离散系统
discretized simulation	离散仿真
distributed interactive simulation	分布式交互仿真
distributed layout	分布式布局
distributed numerical control (DNC II)	分布式数控
distributed system	分布式系统
distributor	分销商
divisionalized form	事业部形式
divisionalized structure	事业部式结构
drum-buffer-rope (dbr)	鼓-缓冲器-绳子
dynamic programming	动态规划
dynamic simulation model	动态仿真模型

E

economic equilibrium	经济均衡
electric relay	电子继电器
electrically-powered	电动的
electro-magnetic interference (EMI)	电磁干涉
electronic commerce	电子商务
electronic data interchange (EDI)	电子数据交换
electronic data processing (EDP)	电子数据处理
electronic delayed storage automatic computer	电子延迟储存自动计算机
electronic discrete variable automatic computer	电子离散变量自动计算机
electronic numerical integrator and calculator	电子数字集成器和计算器

employee empowerment	员工授权
employee involvement	员工参与
employee relations	员工关系
empowered employee	被授权的员工
encapsulation	封装（压缩）
end-effector	执行件
engineering economics	工程经济学
engineering management	工程管理
engineering psychology	工程心理学
engineering service	工程服务
enhanced communication	强化沟通
enterprise integration	企业集成
enterprise resource planning (ERP)	企业资源规划
entrepreneurship management	企业家管理
environmentally benign	环境友好
equipment obsolescence	设备老化
ergonomics	人因学，功效学
estimate	估算
evaporating cloud (EC)	消雾法
event	事件
event graph	事件图
events list management	事件列表管理
experimental designs (ED)	实验设计
experimental economics	实验经济学
experimental psychology	实验心理学
expert system	专家系统
exponential smoothing	指数平滑（预测方法）
extended binary-coded-decimal interchange Code (ECDIC)	扩展的十进制二元编码交换码

F

factory automation	工厂自动化
factory layout	工厂布局
failure cost	失败成本
feedback loop	反馈回路
fiber-optic cable	光纤电缆
financial management	金融/财务管理
fixed-time incrementing (FTI)	固定时间拨钟
flexible automation	柔性自动化

flexible manufacturing cell (FMC)	柔性制造单元
flexible manufacturing system (FMS)	柔性制造系统
flowchart symbol	流程图
flow-of-products-oriented layout (FPL)	面向产品流动的布局
force sensor	压力传感器
forecasting	预测
formality	形式化
formula translation (FORTRAN)	公式翻译程序语言
foundation element	基本要素
functional layout	功能式布局
fusion technology	聚变技术
future reality tree (FRT)	未来现实树

G

game	游戏
game theory	博弈论
gaming	赌博
gateway	网关
general purpose language (GPL)	通用语言
general simulation program (GSP)	通用仿真程序
generalized semi-Markov process (GSMP)	广义半马尔科夫链
general-purpose system simulator (GPSS)	通用系统仿真程序
generative CAPP	生成式计算机辅助工艺规划
genetic algorithm	基因算法
gradient-based optimization	梯度优化
group technology (GT)	成组技术

H

hard automation	刚性自动化
health informatics	卫生信息学
heterogeneous information	异构信息
hexadecimal	十六进制（的）
hierarchical control flow graph	层次（递阶）控制流程图
high level architecture (HLA)	高层体系结构
higher level language	高级计算机语言
histogram	直方图
historical data	历史数据
holding cost	库存成本

homeland security	国土安全
horizontally integrated structure	横向集成式结构
hub-and-spoke layout	轮辐式布局
human centered design	面向人类的设计
human factors	人因学，功效学
human factors engineering	人因工程
human perception	人类感知
human reliability	人类可靠性
human resource management	人力资源管理
human resource	人力资源
human-computer interaction	人机交互
hybrid organization	混合型组织
hybrid simulation	混合仿真
hydraulically-powered	液动的
hypercube queueing model	超立方排队模型

I

idiosyncratic variable	（人类的）特征变量
important factor	关键因素
incentive scheme	激励机制
independent variable	独立变量
indirect cost	间接成本
individual preference	个人偏好
industrial age/era	工业时代
industrial engineer	工业工程师
industrial engineering	工业工程
industrial psychology	工业心理学
infinite manufacturing capacity	无限制造能力，无限生产能力
information age/era	信息时代
information processing	信息处理
information system	信息系统
information technology (IT)	信息技术
inheritance	继承（遗传）
initial transient problem	初始（状态）变化问题
innovation management	创新管理
intangible cost	无形成本
integer optimization	整数优化
integrated circuit board	集成电路板

interactive expert system	交互式专家系统
interactive programming	交互式编程
interchangeable part	可互换零件
intermediate/short-term scheduling	中/长期规划，调度
internal rates of return (IRR)	内部收益率
inventory	库存
inventory allocation	存货分配
inventory control	库存控制
inventory cost	库存成本
inventory management	库存管理
inventory theory	库存论
investment analysis	投资分析
invoice	发票
irreducible cost	既约成本
iterative process	反复/迭代过程

J

jackknife sampling	刀切法抽样
Japanese management	日式管理
JIT (just-in-time)	准时制造
job design	作业设计
job enhancement	工作丰富化
job measurement	作业测量
job rotation (JR)	工作轮换，轮岗
just-in-time (JIT)	准时化

K

kaizen blitz	持续快速改进行动
kanban (KBN)	看板
keypunch	键盘打孔

L

Lagrange multiplier	拉格朗日乘数
Lagrangian relaxation	拉格朗日松弛法
laptop	便携机
large scale integration (LSI)	大型集成器
latent semantic analysis (LSA)	潜在语义分析
layout/facility design	布局/设施设计

lean manufacturing	精益制造
lean sigma	精益西格玛
level production	均衡生产
line balancing	平衡生产线
linear programming	线性规划
list processing routine	（事件）列表处理程序
local-area network (lan)	局域网
location	选址
logical relationship	逻辑关系
logistics	物流
lot sizing	批量问题

M

machine bureaucracies	机械官僚机构
machine language	机器语言
machine maintenance	机器维护
machine utilization	设备利用率
macroergonomics	宏观功效学
mainframe	主机
mainframe computer	大型计算机
mainframe host computer	大型主机
maintainability	可维护性
maintenance	维护
management-by-projects (MBP)	项目管理
management commitment	管理承诺
management information system (MIS)	管理信息系统
management science	管理科学
management service	管理服务
management support	管理层支持
manipulator	操作器
man-machine system	人机系统
manual response	手动响应
manufacturer	制造商
manufacturing automation protocol (MAP)	制造自动化协议
manufacturing line balancing	生产线平衡
manufacturing management	制造管理
manufacturing resources planning (MRP II)	制造资源规划
manufacturing system	制造系统

manufacturing/service strategy	制造/服务战略
Markov decision process	马尔可夫决策过程
mass customization	大规模订制
mass production	大规模生产
mass production of mixed models (MMP)	混合型号产品的大规模生产
master standard data (MSD)	主时间数据法
material handling	物料搬运
material requirement planning (MRP)	物料需求规划
materials management information system	物料管理信息系统
math programming	数学规划
mathematical model	数学模型
mathematical programming	数学规划
mathematical relationship	数学关系
matrix organization	矩阵式组织
Maynard operation sequence technique (MOST)	梅纳德操作排序技术
mean	均值
mechatronics	机械电子学
mega technology	巨型技术
memory	内存
message passing	消息传递
metamodeling	元模型建模
methods time measurement (MTM)	方法时间测量法
microprocessor	微处理器
microprocessor workstation	微处理器工作站
minicomputer	小型机
model	模型
modular arrangement	模块化安排法
modular layout	模块式布局
Monte Carlo model	蒙特卡罗模型
motion analysis	动作分析
motion standard times (MST)	动作标准时间法
motion study	动作研究
moving average approach	移动平均法
multichannel manufacturing	多通道制造
multi-machine manning working system (MMM)	多设备配员工作系统
multimodal	多模的
multiobjective optimization	多目标优化
musculoskeletal disorder	肌骨失调，肌骨紊乱

N

national institute of standards and technology (NIST)	美国标准技术研究院
nano technology	纳米技术
n-echelon	n 级,n 阶
negative branches	负效应枝条
net present value (NPV)	净现值
net profit	净利润
network computing	网络计算
network flow problem	网络流问题
network organization	网络型组织
network problem	网络问题
network queueing model	网络排队模型
networks of processors	处理器网络
new product development	新产品开发
nitrogen cycle	氮循环
nonconvex	非凸的
nonlinear optimization	非线性优化
nonsparse matrix	非稀疏矩阵
numerical control (NC) machine	数控机床
numerical control part programming	数控零件编程

O

objective function	目标函数,目标方程
object-oriented programming	面向对象程序设计
occupational hazard	职业危险
octal	八进制(的)
on-the-job training (OJT)	在线培训,在岗培训
open systems interconnection (OSI)	开放系统互联
operating expenses	运作费用
operating system (OS)	操作系统
operational cause	运作因素
operational research	运筹学
operations management	运作管理
operations research	运筹学
opportunity cost	机会成本
optimized production technology (OPT)	最优生产技术
order batching	批量订购

ordering cost	订购成本
organic structure	有机结构
organs transplant	器官移植
organization structure	组织结构
organizational behavior (OB)	组织行为学
organizational theory	组织理论
original equipment manufacturer (OEM)	原始设备制造商
output analysis	输出分析
outsourcing	外包
overhead	企业一般管理费

P

parallel processor	并行处理器
performance improvement engineering	绩效改善工程
performance measure	绩效测量
peripheral capability	外设（外部设备）能力
perishability	易逝性
personal computer (PC)	个人电脑
personnel selection	职员选择
physical/iconic model	物理模型
physiological arousal	生理干扰
plan-do-check-act (PDCA)	PDCA 循环
planning and scheduling	规划和调度
plastic injection-molding machine	塑料注塑机
pneumatically-powered	气动的
point-of-use manufacture	使用点制造
point-to-point (PTP) robot	点到点机器人
Poka Yoke or automatic stopping device	自动停线设施
polynomial algorithm	多项式算法
portable machine	便携式机器
POS data	销售点数据
pre-determined motion times system (PMTS)	预定动作时间系统
pre-determined time standards (PTS)	预定时间标准法
prerequisite tree (PrT)	必备树
prevention cost	预防成本
price fluctuation	价格浮动
primitives	基本构图要素
printed-circuit board	印刷电路板

probability theory	概率论
process	流程
process design	工艺设计
process design and re-engineering	流程设计和再造
process flow chart	工序流程图
process layout	工艺式布局
process management	流程管理
process modeling	过程建模
processor	处理器
product concept statement	产品概念陈述
product definition	产品定义
product feature and function	产品特征和功能
product layout	产品式布局
product life cycle	产品生命周期
product portfolio	产品汇总表
product strategy	产品策略
product/service design	产品/服务设计
production flow analysis	生产流程分析
production lead time	生产提前期
production planning	生产规划
production scheduling and control	生产调度和控制
professional bureaucracies	专业官僚机构
profile estimation	轮廓评估
program evaluation and review technique (PERT)	计划评审技术
programmable logic controller (PLC)	可编程逻辑控制器
project audit	项目审计
project justification	项目论证
project management	项目管理
project planning	项目规划
project priority	项目优先级
projected resource requirement	资源需求预估
project-specific element	项目特有要素
protocol	协议
prototyping	原型
punched card	穿孔卡片

Q

quality control	质量控制

quality control circles (QCC)	质量控制圈
quality cost	质量成本
quality function deployment	质量功能展开
quality improvement engineering	质量改善工程
quality management	质量管理
quality movement	质量运动
quality policy	质量政策
quantile estimation	分位数估算
quantitative management	定量化管理
queuing network	排队网络
quick set-up (QSU)	快速启动

R

random number generator (RNG)	随机数生成器
random number stream	随机数流
random variate generator (RVG)	随机变量生成器
ranking and selection (R&S)	排序和选择
rapid prototyping	快速原型
rate of return	收益率
rating or leveling factor	评比因子
rational	理性的
real cost	实际成本
real-time interaction	实时交互
reconfigurability	可重组性，可重塑性
regenerative process technique	再生流程技术
rehabilitation robotics	康复机器人技术
reliability	可靠性
research and development (R&D)	研究与开发，研发
research and development management	研发管理
resource constraint	资源限制
response	响应，反应
response surface	响应表面
retailer	零售商
return-on-investment (ROI)	投资收益率
risk analysis	风险分析
robotics programming	机器人编程
routing and dispatching	路径规划和调度

S

scalable machine	可扩展的机器
scheduling	调度
scientific management	科学管理
semiconductor memory	半导体存储器
sensitivity analysis	灵敏度分析
sensor	传感器
service intangibility	服务的无形性
service/product design	服务/产品设计
setup cost	生产准备成本
setup time	生产准备时间
shop-floor reduction (SFR)	车间缩减
shop-floor activities	车间活动
shop-floor control (SFC)	车间控制
simple moving average	简单移动平均（预测方法）
simple structure	简单结构
simplex algorithm	单纯形（算）法
simulation	仿真
simulation model	仿真模型
simulation modeling	仿真建模
simulation package	仿真软件包
simulation programming language (SPL)	仿真编程语言
simultaneity of production	生产的同时性
single-minute exchange of dies (SMED)	一分钟换模
singular value decomposition (SVD)	奇异值分解
six sigma	六西格玛
sketch	草图
software	软件
software engineering	软件工程
solar energy	太阳能
spectral analysis	光谱分析（法）
speed-accuracy trade-off (SATO)	速度和精度的平衡
stand-alone system	单机系统
standard operations (SO)	操作标准化
standardization	标准化
standardized language	标准计算机语言
standards engineer	标准工程师

star layout	星型布局
state	状态
state change	状态变化
state sequence	状态序列
state variable	状态变量
static simulation model	静态仿真模型
statistical process control (SPC)	随机过程控制
statistics	统计学
steady-state output	稳态输出
steady-state parameter estimation	稳态参数预算
steering committee	控制委员会，指导委员会
stochastic modeling	统计建模
stochastic network analysis	随机网络分析
stochastic service system	随机服务系统
stochastic simulation model	随机仿真模型
storage capacity	存储能力
storage device	存储设备
stored program	存储程序
strategic business unit (SBU)	战略业务单元
strategic information system (SIS)	战略信息系统
strategic quality management	战略质量管理
stress analysis	应力分析
Student's t-statistic	史蒂特氏 t 统计量
subject	实验参加者，实验主体
submodel	子模型
suggestions system (SS)	建议系统
supplier development	供应商开发
supplier partnership	与供应商的伙伴关系
supplier quality management	供应商质量管理
supply chain infrastructure design	供应链基础设施设计
supply chain management (SCM)	供应链管理
supply chain partner	供应链合作伙伴
support cost	辅助成本
system cost	系统成本
system/product life cycle	系统/产品生命周期
systems design and operations	系统设计和运作
systems engineering	系统工程
systems integration	系统集成

systems thinking	系统思维

T

tabu search	禁忌搜索
tactile sensor	触觉传感器
taguchi methods	田口法
tangible cost	有形成本
tangible product	实物产品
target market segment	目标市场部分
task	任务
task decomposition	任务分解
team building	团队建设
teamwork	团队合作
technical and office protocol (TOP)	技术和办公协议
technological cost	技术成本
technological innovation	技术创新，技术革新
technological risk management	技术风险管理
technology oriented society	技术导向型社会
terminal	终端
terminating output	中止状态输出
Institute for Defense Analysis (IDA)	防御分析研究所
theory of constraints (TOC)	约束理论
thinking process (TP)	思维流程
three-dimensional model	三维模型
threshold value	阈值
throughput	生产量，生产率
time flow mechanism	计时机制
time study	时间研究
time-and-motion study	时间和动作研究
time-sharing operating system (TSOS)	分时操作系统
total preventive maintenance (TPM)	全面预防性维护
total quality management (TQM),	全面质量管理
total quality service (TQS)	全面质量服务
Toyota production system (TPS)	丰田生产系统
training	培训
transistor	晶体管
transition tree (TrT)	转变树
transportation problem	运输问题

U

U.S. Army Missile Command (MICOM)	美国战术导弹指挥部
U-formed processing line (UPL)	U 形生产线
unconstrained optimization	无约束优化
underwriting	保险业
undesirable effects (UDEs)	不良效果
unit record machines (URMs)	单元记录机
urban infrastructure	城市基础设施
usability study	使用性研究

V

vacuum tube	真空管
value-added chain	增值链
value engineering	价值工程
value stream map	价值流图
valve	电子管
variable-time incrementing (VTI)	变动时间拨钟
variance	方差
variance estimation	方差估计
variance-reduction technique	方差消减技术
variant CAPP	变异式计算机辅助工艺规划
V-A-T process structure analysis	（企业的）VAT 流程结构分析
vector graphics	向（矢）量图
verbal response	口头响应
vertical integration	纵向集成
vertically integrated structure	纵向集成式结构
very large scale integration (VLSI)	超大规模集成器
virtual enterprise	虚拟企业
virtual environment	虚拟环境
virtual manufacturing/services	虚拟制造/服务
virtual memory	虚拟内存
virtual reality	虚拟现实
vision sensor	视觉传感器
visual interactive simulation (VIS)	视觉交互仿真
visual sense	视觉

W

waste-disposal facility	废物处理设施
web-based simulation	基于网络的仿真
wholesaler	批发商
wide-area network (wan)	广域网
work center	工作中心
work distribution charts/line balance chart	流水线平衡图
work organization	工作组织
work physiology	工作生理学
work sampling	工作抽样
Work Factor	工作要素法
work-in-process (wip)	在制品
work-measured labor standards	作业测量的劳动力标准
workpiece	工件
workplace rationalization	工作现场的合理化

Z

zero defects	零缺陷
zero inventory	零库存

Bibliography

[1] Adedeji B. Badiru, Herschel J. Baxi. Industrial engineering education for the 21st century[J]. Industrial Engineering, 1994, 26(7): 66-68.

[2] Gary A. Ferguson. Looking beyond the name to demonstrate real IE value[J]. Industrial Engineering, 1992, 24(12): 40-47.

[3] Ronald G. Askin. Grand challenges for industrial engineering in the 21st century [J]. IIE Annual Conference proceedings, Norcross, 2009, 1-6.

[4] Edgar Williamson. Operations research journals: An annotated core list[J]. Serials Review, 1992, 18(4): 21.

[5] Committee on the Next Decade in Operations Research (CONDOR). Operations research: The next decade[J]. Operations Research, 1988, 36(4).

[6] Royal J. Dossett. Work-measured labor standards: the state of the art[J]. Industrial Engineering, 1995, 27(4): 21-25.

[7] M. G. Helander. Forty years of IEA: some reflections on the evolution of ergonomics[J]. Ergonomics, 1997, 40(10): 952-961.

[8] Saif Benjaafar, Sunderesh S. Heragu, Shahrukh A. Irani. Next generation factory layouts: Research challenges and recent progress[J]. Interfaces, 2002, 32(6): 58–77.

[9] Sunil Chopra, William Lovejoy, Candace Yano. Five decades of operations management and the prospects ahead[J]. Management Science, 2004, 50(1): 8.

[10] Philippe F. Riel. The role of IE in engineering economics[J]. IIE Solutions, 1998, 30(4): 32-38.

[11] John V. Farr, Dennis M. Buede. Systems engineering and engineering management: Keys to the efficient development of products and services[J]. Engineering Management Journal, 2003, 15(3): 3.

[12] Gary A. Maddux, Patricia Martin, Philip A. Farrington. Paving the way for concurrent engineering[J]. Industrial Engineering, 1994, 26(9): 50-52.

[13] Anil Khurana and Stephen R. Rosentha. Integrating the fuzzy front end of new product development[M]. Sloan Management Review, 1997: 103-120.

[14] William B. Zachary, Eugene Richman. Building an operations management foundation that will last: TQM, JIT, and CIM. (total quality management, just-in-time, computer integrated manufacturing)[J]. Industrial Engineering, 1993, 25(8): 39-43.

[15] Richard E. Nance, Robert G. Sargent. Perspectives on the evolution of simulation[J]. Operations Research, 2002, 50(1): 161.

[16] Lumbidi Kupanhy. Classification of JIT techniques and their implications[J]. Industrial

Engineering, 1995, 27(2): 62-65.

[17] Denis R. Towill. Industrial engineering the Toyota Production System[J]. Journal of Management History, 2010, 16(3): 327-345.

[18] Phillip Marksberry, David Parsley. Managing the IE (industrial engineering) mindset: A quantitative investigation of Toyota's practical thinking shared among employees [J]. Journal of Industrial Engineering and Management, 2011, 4(4): 771-799.

[19] G. S. Sureshchandar, Chandrasekharan Rajendran, R.N. Anantharaman. A conceptual model for total quality management in service organizations [J]. Total Quality Management, 2001, 12(3): 343-363.

[20] A. Gunasekaran and Y. Y. Yusuf. Agile manufacturing: a taxonomy of strategic and technological imperatives[J]. International Journal of Operations Research, 2002, 40(6): 1357-1385.

[21] M. Gupta. Constraints management-recent advances and practices[J]. International Journal of Production Research, 2003, 41(4): 647-659.

[22] Rachel Croson, Karen Donohue. Experimental economics and supply-chain management[J]. Interfaces, 2002, 32(5): 74-82.

[23] Ananda Mukherji. The evolution of information systems: Their impact on organizations and structures[J]. Management Decision, 2002, 40(5/6): 497-507.

[24] Thomas H. Davenport, James E. Short. The new industrial engineering: information technology and business redesign [J]. Sloan Management Review, 1990, 31(4).

[25] Diane E. Bailey, Stephen R. Barley. Return to work: toward post-industrial engineering[J]. IIE Transactions, 2005, 37(8): 737.